P9-BJQ-293

REEL POWER

THE STRUGGLE FOR INFLUENCE AND SUCCESS IN THE NEW HOLLYWOOD

by Mark Litwak

SILMAN-JAMES PRESS
LOS ANGELES

Copyright © 1986 by The Center for Study of Responsive Law, Inc.

All rights reserved. No part of this book may be used
or reproduced in any manner whatsoever without
written permission from the publisher, except
in the case of brief quotations embodied in
critical articles and reviews.

10 9 8 7 6 5 4 3 2 1

Library of Congress Cataloging-in-Publication Data

Litwak, Mark.
Reel power : the struggle for influence and success in the new
Hollywood / Mark Litwak
p.   cm.
Originally published: New York : Morrow, c1986.
Includes bibliographical references and index.
1. Motion picture industry—United States. I. Title.
PN1993.5.U6L54   1994   384'.8'0979494—dc20   94-2909

ISBN: 1-879505-19-3

Cover design by Heidi Frieder

Printed and bound in the United States of America

Silman-James Press
distributed by
Samuel French Trade
7623 Sunset Blvd.
Hollywood, CA 90046

To my parents
Nettie and Sanford Litwak

PREFACE

In 1979 I left Albany, New York, and my position as an attorney with a citizen group associated with Ralph Nader to make movies in Hollywood. My friends were puzzled by the sudden change in career plans. My background was in law and politics. I had never studied film, drama, writing, acting, cinematography or any of the other disciplines that comprise filmmaking. I didn't know anyone in show business, rarely went to the movies and had not watched television in ten years. But moviemaking seemed like an exciting endeavor, and so, like so many others lured by its magic, I moved to Los Angeles with high hopes.

Upon my arrival I telephoned the heads of major studios and introduced myself. I told them that I had discovered some wonderful stories while working with Nader. They agreed to meet with me, and within several weeks three were bidding for my services. I accepted the best offer and signed a deal to produce television movies. I would provide the stories; the studio would supply me with an office, a secretary and a base salary four times what I had previously earned.

I was very pleased with myself. I didn't understand why

people said Hollywood was such a tough town to break into. I enjoyed my new occupation. Lots of bright, charming people wanted to have lunch with me, and they would always pick up the check. I wasn't intimidated meeting important producers and executives because by and large I didn't know who was important and who was not. I mistook one producer in jeans and sneakers for a messenger boy.

I had been told that Hollywood was a status-conscious town but nobody seemed to mind that I drove a dilapidated Chevy. People were amused by this eccentricity and admired me for being so secure that I didn't need to drive a fancy car. They thought I was making a statement. Back East they knew I was just poor.

At cocktail parties people found me fascinating to talk to. My background in politics and law was of great interest because it was so alien to the experiences of people immersed in the movie business. My listeners were curious about what the outside world was like.

It seemed I could do no wrong. Even my admission that I didn't own a television set offended no one. Everyone— including those who made the programs—agreed there was nothing worth watching anyway.

But several months later I was in for a rude shock. The president of my studio departed and his replacement abruptly informed me that the studio was no longer interested in pursuing my projects. My contract wouldn't be renewed. I was out on the street.

Of course, I immediately called other studios to see if they were still interested in me. I was disappointed to learn that they were not. I was no longer the new boy in town. I wondered if my exciting show business career was over.

Over the next five years I struggled to produce programs on my own. I produced several pilot shows that didn't go to series. I produced a music video and worked as a television news journalist. For a while I was vice-president of a communications company.

I learned that making movies and television programs is a lot more complicated than I had ever imagined. Had I known beforehand what a difficult enterprise it is, I might have been too discouraged to attempt it. Ironically, my initial ignorance helped me. Ultimately, however, it did not serve me well, because it's just about impossible to succeed in Hollywood without a thorough understanding of its ways. I learned that the most talented individuals are not necessarily the ones who succeed in the business. It isn't enough for a filmmaker to know his craft—perhaps it never was. Making a film is a complex endeavor that requires many other skills. Successful filmmakers are distinguished not only by a command of their medium but also by their political savvy. They know how to manipulate the studio system to their advantage, or at least how to negotiate the bureaucratic pitfalls they'll encounter. They must know how to assemble an attractive package of story and stars, how best to pitch it to studio executives and how to build momentum and support for their project. Independent filmmakers must be able to recruit investors and hustle free equipment and services.

Unless a filmmaker is adept at the politics of moviemaking it's unlikely he will ever get the chance to demonstrate his skill as a moviemaker. But such political skills are not taught in film school. Students are instructed how to cut film, not deals. They graduate knowing how to focus a zoom lens but often don't have the foggiest notion how to get an agent. For such practical knowledge they're on their own.

Typically, it takes many years to learn the ropes of the business. Those with connections—friends or family in the industry—have an advantage. For others it can be a grueling process of learning by trial and error. Many run out of money or become discouraged before they get the chance to demonstrate their talent.

The purpose of this book is to try to communicate the business savvy of industry veterans to all those who are interested in the inner workings of Hollywood. It is an examination of why some people in Hollywood succeed and others fail, why some movies are produced and others are not. It is an inquiry into what it takes to be a successful writer, director, actor, producer, agent or studio executive—how they do their jobs, and what concerns, satisfactions and frustrations they face. It is a look into how the industry has changed and is changing, and the economic and social causes behind those changes. This book is not just for people who aspire to careers in the industry. It's for anyone interested in understanding how the moviemaking machine works. It's for those who want to go beyond simplistic myths and examine the forces that shape the movies we see.

While a great deal has been written about the industry, most works fall into one of three categories: celebrities and gossip, film reviews and criticism, and how-to books of a craft or business/legal nature. Not many writers have examined Hollywood from a sociological perspective as a dynamic organism that is influenced by both human beings and the mechanics of filmmaking. The only book I have read with this approach is anthropologist Hortense Powdermaker's *Hollywood, the Dream Factory*, published thirty-five years ago.

That is not to detract from several recent books that have done an excellent job exploring certain incidents and aspects of the industry. Of these, David McClintick's *Indecent Exposure* (William Morrow, 1982) and Steven Bach's *Final Cut* (William Morrow, 1985) do the best job of capturing the flavor and dynamics of moviemaking today. Each thoroughly explores the ramifications of a studio imbroglio (the Begelman scandal and *Heaven's Gate* fiasco, respectively), and in so doing sheds light on the inner workings of the studios. Similarly, William Goldman's *Adventures in the Screen Trade* (Warner Books, 1983) does an admirable job of explaining how stories are constructed and gives a writer's view of Hollywood.

But little has been written that covers the breadth of the entire industry and how the many people involved in moviemaking today interact with each other and shape the finished film. Certain areas of the industry are rarely written about. For example, the roles of agents, managers, publicists, marketers and journalists are usually ignored, despite their importance.

This book is based on interviews conducted with more than two hundred industry members, many of whom spoke to me at length and with considerable candor. The vast majority of the interviews were conducted in person and were tape-recorded for accuracy. After telling my subjects my topic and the general kind of information I was interested in, I tried to be a good listener and not interrupt them. I also tried to avoid asking leading questions and to not let any preconceptions color my writing. I decided to quote my interviewees whenever possible rather than paraphrase their comments so the reader could fully capture the flavor of their remarks.

Interestingly, I found that top executives and filmmakers were the most outspoken and critical of the industry. Middle-management executives and up-and-coming filmmakers were often hesitant to make critical statements for fear that such comments would jeopardize their careers. Those who had already achieved success were more secure and thus more willing to speak their minds freely.

But almost everyone I interviewed refused to make personal criticisms unless I guaranteed them anonymity. While many would express dissatisfaction with industry practices, few would name names and point to those guilty of stupidity, incompetence or worse. Hollywood is a small community, and people are loath to antagonize those they may have to do business with someday. Everyone realizes that today's loser could become tomorrow's studio president.

Because my topic was so broad, I could not possibly cover every aspect of it. I have chosen to focus on the politics involved in moviemaking today. Historical precedents are mentioned only when needed to put modern practices in perspective. The politics of television production isn't discussed at all, because it requires an extensive examination of how the networks operate, which is sufficiently complex to merit a book of its own. Indeed, an excellent book about the forces that shape television programming has already been written: Todd Gitlin's *Inside Prime Time* (Pantheon, 1983).

I have found writing this book an invaluable learning experience. One of my motivations for doing it arose out of my realization that if I wanted to pursue a career in moviemaking I needed to know more about the industry. This book has provided me a fellowship to study the business. It has been a privilege to learn about moviemaking from some of the brightest and most talented individuals in the business. I have already put my newfound knowledge to use. I am pleased to report that I walked out of my first pitch meeting with a deal in hand to write a story for a feature film. If there is one thing I have learned in my research, it is that there are no overnight successes. Contrary to what is often portrayed in the news media, all the industry people I have interviewed struggled long and hard to achieve recognition. The one common denominator they share is tremendous tenacity. They made it because they had to.

MARK LITWAK
February 1986

Mr. Litwak welcomes comments from readers. He can be contacted at: Law Offices of Mark Litwak, P.O. Box 3226, Santa Monica, CA 90408, (310) 450-4500, fax (310) 450-9956.

ACKNOWLEDGMENTS

This book could not have been written without the encouragement and support of Ralph Nader. A grant from his Center for the Study of Responsive Law and an advance from William Morrow enabled me to spend a full two years researching and writing this book.

I am indebted to Harvey Ginsberg, my editor at William Morrow, for his helpful suggestions, and my literary agent, Harvey Klinger, for making it happen in the first place.

I am grateful for the assistance of Glen Brunman, Judith Jecman, Jane Kagon, Nettie Litwak, Tiiu Lukk and Jon Mostow for critiquing early drafts of my work. I also thank Linda Powers for quickly and accurately transcribing my interviews.

While I am solely responsible for the contents of this book, I could not have written it without the cooperation of the more than two hundred agents, studio executives, writers, directors, producers, actors and other industry veterans who told me about their experiences in the business. They are: Jim Abrahams, Keith Addis, Susan Aguado, Robert Altman, Marvin Antonowsky, Army Archerd, Allan Arkush, Raymond Asher, Ed Asner, Jon Avnet, Ivan Axelrod, Danilo

Bach, John Badham, Lawrence Bassoff, Martin Baum, Lee Beaupre, Sheila Benson, Jay Bernstein, John Beug, Tony Bill, Nan Blitman, Dick Bowen, Barbara Boyle, Teresa Bowman, Martin Bregman, Jim Bridges, Stephanie Brody, Cary Brokaw, David Brown, Paul Cabe, Vincent Canby, Topper Carew, Wendy Carrel, Dr. Hyla Cass, Gilbert Cates, Steven Chatoff, Sandy Climan, Walter Coblenz, Jeff Corey, Peter Coyote, Christine Cuddy.

Also, Terry Danuser, Emile de Antonio, Robert De-Laurentis, Lisa Demberg, Gary Devore, I.A.L. Diamond, Barry Diller, Ralph Donnelly, Jeff Dowd, Lisa Eichhorn, Jack Epps, Jr., Moctesuma Esparza, Robert Evans, Joseph Farrell, Edward Feldman, Mike Fenton, Maggie Field, Adam Fields, Randy Finley, Richard Fischoff, Jane Fonda, Mickey Freiberg, Richard Fried, David Freeman, Dave Friedman, Clay Frohman, Teri Garr, J. Carter Gibson, Donna Gigliotti, Menahem Golan, Leonard Goldberg, Carl Gottlieb, Harry Gould, Jr., Tom Greene, Josh Greenfeld, Debra Greenfield, Leo Greenfield, Larry Gross, Aljean Harmetz, Jerome Hellman, Catherine Hicks, Colin Higgins, Thomas Hoberman, Tamar Hoffs, Lewis Horowitz, Willie Hunt, Marty Hurwitz, Joan Hyler, Richard Ingber, Susan Ingleby, Irving Ivers, Lawrence Jackson, Leo Jaffe, Henry Jaglom, Jim Jarmusch, Melinda Jason, Lamont Johnson.

Also, Jane Kagon, Merrily Kane, Jonathan Kaplan, Nick Kazan, Gregg Kilday, Gene Kirkwood, Jim Kelly, Tom Kenny, Irvin Kershner, Richard Kletter, David Knopf, Donald Kopaloff, Ron Koslow, Jonathan Krane, Kat Krone, Alan Ladd, Jr., Robert Laemmle, Candace Lake, Jeremy Larner, Lawrence Lasker, Mary Ledding, Kay Lenz, Malcolm Leo, Johnny Levin, Mike Levett, Lisa Lieberman, Charles Lippincott, Jeff Lipsky, Robert Littman, Martha Luttrell, David Madden, Michelle Manning, Pacy Markman, Lisa Mason, Lynette Mathis, Robert McKee, Bill Mechanic, Mike Medavoy, Ross Merrin, Susan Merzbach, Gary Mezzatesta, Michael Meyer, Nicholas Meyer, Chester Migden, Gregg Moscoe, Robert Mundy, A. D. Murphy, Karen Murphy, Gregory Nava, Ben Newman, Paul Newman, Timothy Ney, David Nochimson, Blaise Noto, Dale Olson, Judith Parker, Kay Parker, Richard Pearce, Gary

Persell, Carolyn Pfeiffer, Clyde Phillips, Frank Pierson, Henry Plitt, Dale Pollock, Bill Quigley, Steve Railsback.

Also Martin Ransohoff, Rick Ray, Joel Resnick, Martin Ritt, Dolores Robinson, Phil Robinson, Susan Rogers, Dr. Jack Rosenberg, Steve Rosenthal, Steve Roth, Bill Rouhana, Albert Ruddy, Alan Rudolph, Mac St. Johns, Gary Salt, Waldo Salt, Peter Saphier, Michelle Satter, Edgar Scherick, Larry Scherzer, Charles Schreger, Suzanne Schwartz, Joan Scott, Nat Segaloff, William Self, Steve Shagan, Michael Shamberg, Martin Sheen, Peter Shepherd, Ken Sherman, Stirling Silliphant, Dina Silver, Jeff Silverman, Don Simpson, Martha Smilgis, Howard Smith, Doug Stoll, Peter Stone, H. N. Swanson, Jonathan Taplin, Walter Teller, Joan Tewkesbury, Anna Thomas, Bobbi Thompson, Claire Townsend, Robert Townsend, Richard Tuggle, Larry Turman, Harry Ufland, Chris Uszler, Renee Valente, Jean Vallely, John Van Eyssen, Michael Ventura, Harold Vogel, Michael Wadleigh, Robert Walden, Gordon Weaver, Irene Webb, Hannah Weinstein, Marty Weiser, Stanley Weiser, Eric Weissmann, Thomas Wilhite, Marvin Worth, Elio Zarmati, Don Zimmerman, David Zucker and Jerry Zucker.

And my thanks to those who wish to remain anonymous.

CONTENTS

1

"WELCOME TO HOLLYWOOD"

Don Zimmerman was about to get a big break. As film editor of *Rocky III* and *Staying Alive,* he had become friendly with Sylvester Stallone. Stallone was now bringing him in as a first-time director on his next feature, a film for Twentieth Century-Fox starring Stallone and Dolly Parton, based on a script that Fox executives said was the best they had read in years.

The assignment would be an enormous career leap for Zimmerman, a man with a reputation for being both decent and talented. Zimmerman freely admitted that Sly's "push" got him the job. He considered Stallone his friend and mentor.

Twentieth Century-Fox, in turn, was pleased to have both Sylvester Stallone and Dolly Parton in one of their films. A studio executive noted that with those two stars on the poster the movie should make $20 million the first week of release—so even if the film was awful the studio should be able to make its money back before bad word of mouth could kill it.

Stallone was happy. He was getting $5 million up front and a hefty percentage of the film's profits. He would have an opportunity to sing. While he might have directed the film himself, he was wary of exposing himself to criticism again, having just been subjected to the terrible reviews of *Staying Alive,* in which he directed John Travolta. Moreover, he told associates, he didn't want the heavy preparation and postproduction burden directing would entail. By limiting himself to acting, he could do more projects, and by anointing the director, he wouldn't have to worry about conflict with a director who had ideas different from his.

Dolly Parton was looking forward to another successful film that would continue her string of hits launched by *Nine to Five,* for which she wrote the title song and earned an Oscar nomination and two Grammys. Her next film, *The Best Little Whorehouse in Texas,* was one of 1982's top grossing films, and it brought her another Grammy nomination. Although this would be only her third film, Parton would receive $3 million and a nice chunk of the profits. Her personal managers, Sandy Gallin and Ray Katz, were to be the executive producers of the film.

Screenwriter Phil Alden Robinson was delighted that his script was going to be produced. He had spent a year writing it, and it would be his first to be filmed. "Everybody in town was saying, We love this script, we think it's fabulous," Robinson recalls. "Everybody was offering me jobs." Overnight he became a hot screenwriter.

And so it seemed from everyone's point of view that the project would be both artistically and financially rewarding. But in Hollywood appearances can be deceiving. Below the surface the players were already jockeying for position as they sought control of the film.

The project had a convoluted history, as many Hollywood pictures do. New York producer Howard Smith bought the rights to the song "Rhinestone Cowboy" and made a deal with Avco Embassy to commission a script. But after Robinson completed the script, the studio decided not to proceed with the project and put it into turnaround, which is industry lingo meaning "For Sale."

Executives at both Fox and Paramount expressed interest. Paramount's interest evaporated after president Michael Eisner reviewed the project and disliked it. Fox, however, was enthusiastic enough to buy it from Embassy for about $60,000, telling Robinson that it was the best love story and the best comedy they had read in years. They loved the dialogue and talked of offering Robinson an overall deal in which he would write, direct and produce future projects.

However, when president of production Sherry Lansing departed Fox, her successor, Joe Wizan, reviewed all projects in development. Wizan felt the *Rhinestone* script should not be made unless they could get major stars for it. With a background as an agent and producer, Wizan had a reputation for favoring star casting. He and several Fox executives reviewed the list of actors who could co-star with Parton. They were concerned that they find someone who could be believable as a New York cab driver and have enough charisma that he would not be blown off the screen by the presence of Parton—who, some Fox executives thought, had done just that to Burt Reynolds in *The Best Little Whorehouse in Texas.*

When Stallone's name came up, everyone thought he would be a great choice. Stallone was considered a top box-office star with a strong public following. The powerful Creative Artists Agency (CAA), which represented both Parton and Stallone, wanted Fox to take one of its male stars if they wanted Parton. According to one insider, CAA said, " 'If you want her, you better take him,' " and "that was the end of discussions of whether anyone else could be obtained for the part."

Wizan might not have needed much encouragement to accept Stallone anyway. Obtaining two major stars for a Fox picture would be a feather in the new studio chief's cap and would impress everyone in the industry with his deal-making prowess. Since one successful deal often begets another, Wizan, by paying Stallone's price and agreeing to his choice of director, might be able to build some momentum for his studio.

Stallone's agents at CAA had been positioning him to direct the picture himself. When Stallone declined to pursue the position, it was decided to let him direct the picture in fact, even though Zimmerman would be the director of record. But Zimmerman was never let in on the secret. He thought he was the one and only director.

Stallone was tentatively set to do a film for Paramount

before beginning production on *Rhinestone* for Fox. But when that film fell through, the start date for *Rhinestone* was moved up. The original four or five months of preparatory planning were reduced to two and a half. To complicate matters further, Stallone decided that the script needed to be rewritten. When Fox bought his script they told Robinson it was their intent that he do any rewrites, if needed; but they were honest enough to say they couldn't promise this. A meeting was scheduled by the studio for Stallone and Robinson to discuss script changes. The studio wanted Stallone to supervise Robinson in the rewrite. But the morning of the meeting Robinson was disinvited. Stallone wanted to rewrite the script himself.

According to Robinson, Stallone did two drafts, one worse than the other. Stallone had, in a few short weeks, thrown out what had taken Robinson a year to write. Stallone changed the attitude of his character, making him more streetwise and less vulnerable.

Stallone's script read very much like a first draft, according to one observer. "You didn't sense a lot of work went into the choices. There had been a lot of texture in the screenplay, a lot of charm, and the characters were very well defined and they went through carefully plotted-out progressions of character change. All that was gone." The original script worked hard to keep out clichés. Stallone added them.

Fox executives agreed that the changes by and large hurt the script. With seven weeks to go before the start of principal photography, the studio said they would not make the movie on the basis of the revised script. Robinson was brought back in and asked to "restore the charm" of the original, and "put those great characters back," without changing any of the dialogue Stallone had written for himself. Robinson objected, telling Wizan that what was wrong with the script was the awful dialogue. Wizan replied: "Welcome to Hollywood."

Robinson reluctantly agreed to the studio's restrictions on the rewrite. He says he was able to solve some structural problems and tried to make sense of Stallone's changes. When he turned it in, the studio said the new script was great, and one executive vowed that Stallone was either going to do it as written or walk. When they showed the changes to Stallone he said, "Fine, fine. I just have a few changes to make." Stallone then proceeded to restore most of his changes.

The studio was not happy with Stallone's revisions. But, says one Fox executive, "a star plays a role his way no matter what the script says. . . . We paid the guy a lot of money to do what he does, and we thought that he could make it work, that he could make the part come alive." And so nobody was unduly worried because Stallone was thought right for the part.

"CAA pretty much took over [the film]," says one insider. "And one of the reasons that they were able to take over was that Twentieth at that time was run by people who weren't strong filmmakers. They had people who were not experienced in making movies. They had marketing directors, story editors and ex-agents, but they didn't have filmmakers running the place." By turning the project over to Stallone they were giving the movie to someone who had written and directed. And they knew that if things didn't turn out well, they could always lay the blame on Stallone.

With the film start date rapidly approaching, the studio had to decide who was going to produce the movie. While there were already five producers officially aboard the project, the studio felt that for various reasons none of them could actually produce it. Sandy Gallin and Ray Katz had a successful personal-management business to run and their executive-producer credits were largely recognition for bringing their client Dolly Parton into the project. Howard Smith, the New York producer who had bought the rights to the song, wanted to produce the movie, but Fox objected because he had never produced a feature by himself before. The other two producers, Bill Blake and Richard M. Spitalny, were involved by virtue of being financial partners with Smith, having shared some of the early development expenses.

To handle the logistics of producing the film, Fox brought in veteran Marvin Worth. Worth, formerly Lenny Bruce's manager and a comedy writer himself, had produced several films for Fox including *The Rose* and *Unfaithfully Yours*. It was agreed that Blake and Spitalny would get co-producer credit, while Smith and Worth would share the producer credit. Worth, who admits he has never met most of his fellow producers, refuses to divulge who actually produced the picture. "I'll never tell," he says, apparently deciding it is best to be discreet about such matters.

When the film began, production problems immediately arose. Zimmerman thought he was the director. But Stallone told him what to do, ad-libbed scenes and made changes as he saw fit. By everyone's reckoning, including Stallone's, the first few weeks were a disaster.

Worth says that, while Zimmerman was talented, it was a big film to get as a new director. "I think he felt Sly was looking over his shoulder. He was trying to guess how Sly would want him to direct it. And Sly felt a big responsibility because he had gotten him the job." Combined with a short preproduction period and script problems, there was a lot of tension, says Worth.

Tensions were exacerbated when Stallone and Zimmerman got into a dispute over the cameraman. Stallone was unhappy with the look of the movie. Zimmerman thought the cameraman was doing a wonderful job and loyally stuck by him. Stallone forced the cameraman out, and after that, says Zimmerman, their relationship quickly deteriorated.

Three weeks into production, Zimmerman was fired. His contract was settled and the production shut down while the studio sought a new director. CAA proposed that Fox hire Bob Clark, who had directed the hit film *Porky's*, which Fox had distributed. Since the new director had to be acceptable to Stallone, it didn't hurt that both were represented by CAA. Clark reportedly received $1 million to direct, plus a guaranteed fee for his next project at Fox, whether or not it was ever produced. That project is reputed to have been previously rejected by the studio.

After a shutdown of one week, production resumed. The first three weeks of filming were thrown out. Stallone continued to rewrite the script as production proceeded. Robinson says that when Clark was hired, it was with the strong understanding that no one could touch the script except Stallone. If Clark wanted any changes he had to go to Stallone.

Among other revisions, Stallone made his role larger than Parton's, a reversal of the original script, in which her character dominated. If Parton objected to the change, she never raised a fuss. By all accounts she was a joy to work with. Clark's performance as director was admirable, considering he had so little time to prepare himself and was directing the strong-willed Stallone in a script he was locked into. Zimmerman says Stallone continued to do whatever he wanted, despite Fox's hopes that the new director would be able to control him. David Madden, who was Fox vice-president of production at the time, doubts that Clark was not in control, noting that he has a strong personality. "What I think is true," says Madden, "is that Bob was perfectly comfortable with the performance Stallone was giving, as was the studio, for the most part."

As the studio screened each day's footage, there was no hint of trouble. "We felt it would come together and it would work," says Madden. "Dailies are enormously deceptive things and they don't tell you about the run of a performance. They don't tell you about the overall effect of ninety minutes."

When the $28 million *Rhinestone* opened in 1,100 theaters, audiences were small and the criticism harsh. Domestic rentals totaled only $12.2 million, notwithstanding the studio's large advertising blitz. When the script was first brought to the studio it was estimated that it would cost $10 million to make.

Both Parton's and Stallone's fans stayed away in droves. "I think the performances are disgracefully bad, it is very poorly directed, and it is an ugly film to look at," one participant said. "You cannot for the life of me tell me where that money went."

Robinson took the highly unusual step of publicly criticizing the movie, saying that the humor and intelligence of the original script had been replaced with vulgarity, caricature and farce. Disassociating himself from the picture, he sent letters to film critics explaining what had happened to his script. It was, he said, a textbook example of a studio willingly sacrificing the quality of a script for what was perceived as the marketability of star casting.

"I thought a long time before speaking out," Robinson says. "Of course the conventional wisdom is that you don't open your mouth. But I was having a hard time living with that." By going public, he says he was giving notice that he did not want his scripts ruined, and he would just as soon not work for anyone who didn't want to hire him because of his outspokenness. "In fact I have gotten a phenomenal response," he says. "Everyone from studio executives to writers to agents, dozens of people have been calling and saying it is great, and about time somebody started talking about this." Indeed, Robinson has prospered. He has been offered numerous script assignments and has had the opportunity to direct television programs.

Stallone was reported by the press to be licking his wounds from what he regarded as bitterly personal reactions to his performance in *Rhinestone*. For his next planned picture, *Beverly Hills Cop,* he told Paramount executives he wanted to make a few changes and then proceeded to rewrite the script. The executives responded by saying that they didn't want to film the script as rewritten, thank you, and good-bye. The studio went on to cast Eddie Murphy in the lead role, and the resulting film became a box-office smash.

But Stallone's career did not suffer irreparable damage. Indeed, his star is shining brighter than ever. He went on to star in the summer hit of 1985, *Rambo: First Blood Part II,* and the Christmas 1985 hit *Rocky IV.* It has been reported that he will receive an unprecedented $12 million to star in the upcoming Cannon film *Over the Top.*

Zimmerman went back to editing and for a while lost contact with Stallone. He's philosophical about what happened, saying he learned a lot from the experience. He doesn't know whether his firing will impair his chances to direct again. Interestingly, the dispute did not deter Stallone from hiring Zimmerman to edit *Rocky IV.*

In retrospect one Fox executive says the studio's miscalculation was in failing to perceive that the public is not interested in seeing Stallone sing but only wants to see him in action pictures. Moreover, Parton's Country-Western fans grew suspicious of the movie because Stallone was in it. Rather than attract the followings of both stars, as the studio hoped, the film managed to alienate both.

"I was at La Costa getting a manicure," producer Marvin Worth recalls, "when the girl, who didn't know I was in the movie business, told me that her favorite star was Stallone but she was not going to see him in *Rhinestone*. [I asked her why and she said:] 'Who wants to see him as a singing cowboy?' There it was right there, the [audience] research. And she said she loved Dolly Parton. I couldn't believe it."

"The lesson to learn is the danger of the Hollywood syndrome," Zimmerman says. "Basically the power has left the producing element and has just run out of control." The competition for stars has put them in the driver's seat. "It is pretty hard to make a movie today without stars because everybody wants to make a hundred-million-dollar movie. No one is satisfied with less. Any business or corporation in the world that would make a one hundred percent profit on a product in a year or two would be ecstatic."

Zimmerman thinks that while some of the changes Stallone made improved the script, the change in the character he played hurt the picture. If you have a vulnerable character whom people fall in love with, they'll accept just about anything, he says. But if you have a sarcastic character, that empathy is gone. "Unfortunately for actors today, people get isolated into one character or into what they feel the public wants them to portray. And [then] they try to . . . [repeat] that character in every script."

"I think the lesson for the town is that you can't let a good script be thrown away," Robinson says. From now on he intends to either direct or produce what he writes in order to protect his work.

As *Rhinestone* sank, so did the careers of several Fox executives. President Joe Wizan was dismissed after running the studio for only eighteen months. It was his second star-studded flop, the first being the ill-fated *Two of a Kind* with Olivia Newton-John and John Travolta.

Madden defends Wizan, saying he was made a scapegoat for a lot of problems not under his control. "I think these are terrible jobs because you make constant decisions every day and you know just by the laws of probability most of them are going to be wrong." Madden says that, contrary to popular belief, most of Wizan's movies did not rely heavily on star casting. He notes that *Romancing the Stone, Bachelor Party* and *Revenge of the Nerds* didn't rely on big stars and earned good profits for the studio.

"I think Joe actually took more shots and hired more young and first-time directors than most studio heads do," says Madden, explaining that because Fox was not in as strong a position as other studios (Paramount, for example, had the *Star Trek* and *Raiders of the Lost Ark* sequels to rely on), they had to take chances on less-established talent.

But Fox's star-studded movies not only bombed, they were the subject of a great deal of media attention. Perhaps even more important, there were problems with upcoming movies. *Enemy Mine* had to be stopped in the midst of production. Other pictures went so far over budget in the planning stages that they had to be scrapped. "They didn't have a blockbuster this summer [1984] and apparently don't have one for next summer [1985]," one industry observer remarked. "And now that George Lucas is not making *Star Wars* every three years they can't count on that. [Then Fox owner] Marvin Davis was concerned that there were not enough big movies coming up, and that's what scared him."

Wizan also had been criticized for his poor relationships with the creative community. "There were a lot of people who simply didn't want to do business with him," says one writer. "I don't like the guy, I don't think he has good taste, I don't think he has good judgment and I just don't like the way he deals with people." In an industry that Louis B. Mayer characterized as one in which the principal assets go home every night, personal relationships with talent are of the utmost importance.

Shortly after Wizan left Fox, chairman of the board Alan Hirschfield departed. Owner Marvin Davis then lured Paramount chairman Barry Diller to Fox to fill Hirschfield's position. Diller's defection began an industry-wide scramble among executives. When Paramount president Michael Eisner was denied Diller's job, he resigned and went to Disney, along with Warner vice-chairman Frank Wells. Paramount president of production Jeff Katzenberg then left to accompany Eisner. The mighty Paramount, with its vaunted management team renowned for its stability and box-office success, had been broken up.

At Fox, Diller named Lawrence Gordon as president and chief operating officer, which led to the resignation of vice-chairman Norman Levy. Madden left to become a vice-president of production at Paramount. Numerous lower-echelon executives at various studios played musical chairs as they followed their mentors from one studio to another.

Davis later sold Fox to Australian newspaper tycoon Rupert Murdoch. Despite the huge losses the studio suffered from moviemaking, Davis profited from real estate deals he made with Fox land. *Variety* estimates that he made a $500 million profit on the sale.

An industry-wide realignment had taken place, precipitated when *Rhinestone* bombed at the box office.

THE RISE OF CAA

More powerful than Sylvester Stallone, Steven Spielberg or Barry Diller, the most influential person in Hollywood is not a star, a director or a studio head. While his name is rarely mentioned in the news media, and he never gets a screen credit, everyone who matters in the industry knows who he is. He is assiduously courted by producers and studio heads alike because they need his cooperation in order to gain the services of the best writers, stars and directors in the industry. He is Michael Ovitz, the president of Creative Artists Agency (CAA).

Since its formation in 1975, CAA has recruited to its stable such superstar clients as Robert Redford, Sylvester Stallone, Jane Fonda, Bill Murray, Dustin Hoffman and Paul Newman—overtaking the venerable William Morris for the distinction of operating the industry's most powerful agency. The partners are invariably described, even by their competitors, as tough, hardworking, shrewd and aggressive. They have been likened to the Yankees' "Murderers' Row"—a lineup of sluggers led by Babe Ruth that demolished the opposition.

Success has given each of the five CAA partners a reputed

base salary in excess of $1 million a year, along with such perks as matching Jaguars and Ferraris (in assorted colors) with license plates reading CAA followed by each partner's initials. In their busy offices they are pampered with shoe shines and manicures as they cradle phones, negotiating deals nonstop.

While there are five equal partners in the agency, Ovitz, as president, wields the most influence. He is respected for being smart, hard-driving and passionate in pursuit of the agency's interests. Although lower-echelon employees consider him secretive and aloof, he nevertheless knows virtually everything that transpires within the agency. He insists that CAA agents follow his low-profile approach to agenting, disdaining the personal publicity-seeking that such agents as ICM's Sue Mengers are renowned for. CAA employees are forbidden to speak to the press—which may explain why so little has been written about this agency.

Ovitz's style is that of the calm professional. "He is a smooth operator," says one industry observer. "He shakes hands nicely, doesn't rile you, always wears the right kind of suit and nothing is ever out of place." But beneath the tranquil demeanor lurks an intensely ambitious man who set out to become the most powerful agent in Hollywood, and now that he has achieved his goal he shows no sign of letting up.

Each of the other CAA partners is respected in his own right. Together they comprise such a diverse collection of characters that they could be the cast of a television sitcom.

Bill Haber is the agency eccentric, having earned his reputation by cracking a riding crop on his desk, yelling at his assistants, taking violin lessons in his office and flying off to Paris, where he maintains a second home. He is admired for his unusually deep knowledge of the television business and for being a tough negotiator.

Ron Meyer is the handsome nice guy. The most personable of the partners, he is well liked, especially by women clients. He set out to represent Sylvester Stallone and now handles him along with many other powerful clients.

Rowland Perkins is the older gentleman whose good manners and behavior prove you don't have to be a bastard to be an effective agent. He is the éminence grise of the agency, whose important role in CAA's television department is often overshadowed by the more flamboyant Haber. An unassuming individual, he has a reputation for great integrity.

Martin Baum is the bombastic, fast-talking, classic old-time agent. He spews forth a constant stream of ideas and orders, and is given to emotional outbursts that terrorize his staff. He operates semiautonomously, ignoring agency rules that don't suit his needs. As an experienced producer, executive and agent he has a wealth of industry experience to draw upon, and is a godfatherlike figure to many younger agents, who come to him for assistance with their problems.

"CAA is the best," says Melinda Jason, then head of her own small agency, echoing a widely held opinion in the industry. "Ovitz is a genius and has integrity and class. He is respected around town. The dumbest thing I ever did was not accepting a job offer from him. He is the finest agent alive today."

Says a former CAA agent, "Ovitz is the best at signing clients, at far the best at keeping clients—I don't think a single client has left that he didn't want to leave—he is a terrific deal-maker and he runs the company very efficiently. His incredible drive has made CAA what it is today. When CAA began he and the other partners had no experience in the feature-film arena. They were all television agents. Ovitz had just one feature client, [writer] Robert Towne. But he put his mind to it and within two years he was one of the top feature agents. No one has ever ascended that fast."

But not everyone is a fan of the agency. A William Morris agent complains that CAA agents are notoriously aggressive. "They are like packs of wolves. They go up to clients and surround them. 'Come with us and we'll make deals,' they say. They are like hungry tigers, stealing clients away from other agencies."

CAA has been accused of cutting its rates to attract big-name clients, a form of free-enterprise competition frowned on by other agents. Although CAA denies the allegations, there is a widespread belief that the agency lured Robert Redford and Dustin Hoffman to its stable by offering them a reduced commission of 5 percent, instead of the usual 10.

If true, the upstart CAA was able to outmaneuver William Morris, which couldn't cut its commissions for some clients without alienating others. Indeed, CAA has over the years spirited away a considerable number of big stars from both William Morris and International Creative Management (ICM)—the two behemoths of the agency business. Bright-red, full-page ads regularly appear in the trade press announcing that another star has defected to CAA.

One former CAA agent trainee says, "CAA has managed to get themselves the best client list in the business. [And] they didn't do it with just a smile." Director Martin Ritt (*Norma Rae*) is convinced that the allegations of CAA fee cuts are true. "When you're Redford or Newman you don't need an agent at all. Everything is offered to you anyway. So the financing had to be better," says Ritt. But a former CAA insider who claims to have read the agency's contract with Redford, says the star pays the full 10 percent, and signed with Ovitz simply because he is the best agent in town.

Whatever fee cutting may have occurred should not detract from the more fundamental reasons underlying CAA's success. "They're younger and they're hungrier," says producer Leonard Goldberg (*WarGames*) of the partners. "They were willing to work longer hours and work harder, seven days a week. And it paid off. . . . They're like the other agencies used to be before they got really rich and wealthy. . . . ICM and William Morris got complacent because they were so used to just having the two of them share the marketplace."

Goldberg also credits the CAA partners for dealing with their own clients firmly. "They are very aggressive with their clients. In the old MCA days you never heard an actor say he doesn't want to do something. 'What does he mean he doesn't want to do it?' [the agents would respond.] I mean they would get him in an office and he would do it. Mostly because they thought it would be a good idea for him to do it. With CAA they are not afraid to lose the client. So they say, 'You should do this, goddamn it. You should do it.' "

But others accuse CAA of running roughshod over their clients' desires. "When Steve Roth was at CAA," says writer David Freeman, "he had a script he wanted to get made and the star and director he attached to it said they didn't want to do it. But he didn't take no for an answer. He sent the script around town as a package, figuring that if he could get each of these guys a million dollars to do it, who were they to say no. He could make the deal so rich that no sentient human being would be able to pass on it."

Partner Ron Meyer has been accused of not informing his clients of offers he didn't like. "A producer friend of mine who was doing a prestigious movie for *American Playhouse* wanted to make an offer to some CAA clients," says a reporter. "Ron Meyer refused to even discuss it with her because she was paying scale. She said, 'Hey, wait a second. This is just for a couple of days' work, it is a prestigious project, it is something people will talk about for years, and the actors might want to do it.' Ron Meyer wouldn't think of it."

The rise of CAA is a particular sore point with William Morris, where the original CAA partners learned the business. (Baum joined later, along with Steve Roth. Roth and original partner Michael Rosenfeld subsequently left to produce.) The partners were considered the best and brightest, and when they left Morris it was a traumatic experience for the proud agency. "It was like their sons left," says former William Morris agent Debra Greenfield. There had never been a mass defection before. William Morris never forgave the five, says former William Morris agent Johnny Levin. "For William Morris there was a sense of betrayal. Can you imagine how much bigger and richer . . . [William Morris] would be if all that income at CAA was going into their pockets?"

"The five left because they were ambitious and wanted more acknowledgment," says agent Ken Sherman. "They were second level. The Young Turks. There is a family atmosphere at William Morris, and you can't be Daddy when Dad is still around."

"They were working to make all these octogenarians rich," says a former William Morris agent. "You can't take ambitious, bright men in their early thirties and tell them, 'You won't have control for another twenty years.' "

According to Hollywood lore, the five secretly plotted their break. When a bank executive who handled the William Morris account called the agency and mentioned that the five had applied for a large loan, the agents were called on the carpet. They confessed their plans and were immediately forced out. Their abrupt departure left them unprepared— without their company cars they had only one automobile among them. But they pooled their resources, borrowed $21,000, and got a $100,000 line of credit that enabled them to set up shop in a small unfurnished office. Their wives took turns answering the phones. During its first year, the agency booked a meager $2.5 million in deals, but it didn't collect much in commissions because many of its clients were still under contract to other agencies. Nobody expected that the new agency would someday challenge William Morris for the throne.

From its humble beginning, CAA has grown into an organization of 45 agents representing about 700 clients, with estimated commissions in the tens of millions of dollars per year. Although both William Morris and ICM have considerably more agents, clients and revenue (*Variety* estimates that Morris has 150 agents, more than 2,000 clients and earns upward of $30 million annually), CAA's client list is the most star-studded, virtually every name recognizable. Few newcomers with potential are found here; the agency has skimmed the cream, limiting its representation to proven money-makers. "They've got the people that make things happen," is the way director Jim Bridges (*Urban Cowboy*), himself a CAA client, puts it.

CAA has been able to avoid the problems that plague William Morris and ICM. Morris suffers from an overgrown bureaucracy, with levels upon levels of administrative hierarchy that make the organization slow-moving and unwieldy. There are junior agents, agents, senior agents, vice-presidents, senior vice-presidents, a president and two co-chairmen. Those in the lower echelon chafe under numerous restrictions designed to ensure that they uphold the Morris tradition of what an agent should be. Agents cannot sign clients on their own or work outside those areas assigned them. A great deal of time is spent in staff meetings, where lower-echelon agents who collect information in the field report back to their supervisors.

The agency treats its employees as if they were members of an extended family. "They take care of you like children," says ex-Morris agent Debra Greenfield. "It strips you of your adulthood. They give you a car, gas, insurance and maintenance. They wash your car and if it breaks down on the road they send someone. If you want to buy a house they will make you no-interest loans. For a young person it feels like you are under parental tutelage." But some agents like the security and are happy to stay with the agency for many years. It can be a comfortable niche, for like a doting parent, Morris is tolerant of its children, and unwilling to fire someone just because his or her performance is mediocre.

"You always see William Morris agents in clusters," says one journalist. "They go to wrap parties together, they all dress the same, walk the same and sound alike. . . . They call it teamwork. . . . I was at the Synagogue for the Performing Arts once and I saw Walter Matthau with five Morris agents with him. They all go so that the client knows he is loved and protected. Matthau sneezed and four agents took out handkerchiefs and handed it to him."

While Morris is sometimes characterized within the industry as "geriatric, Jewish and gentlemanly," ICM has an entirely different reputation. Here it's every person for himself. The agency is rife with internecine battles and power struggles. There is little cooperation among agents and much more of a free-for-all atmosphere, in which agents operate on their own. "It's survival of the fittest," explains one ex-ICM agent, who says the agency's motto should be: "We eat our young."

ICM is the product of a series of mergers of smaller agencies, and as a result the agency lacks cohesion. It functions like a collection of boutiques operating under one roof, the agents in each competing against the others. It is in a constant state of turmoil, with agents departing and new ones arriving. "It's a terrible place to work," says an ex-ICMer, "because agents are always worried about their jobs and their standing within the agency. It is trial by terror."

CAA does not have the bureaucracy of William Morris

or the bickering of ICM. It has restrained its growth and carefully chosen its agents with an eye toward their ability to work well together. CAA partner Martin Baum says his agency is successful because its agents put the welfare of the agency ahead of their own interests. "The policy of this company from its inception has been that we all profit if one succeeds. . . . It has been the first time that there has been a total sublimation of the individual ego for the betterment of the group."

"There is very little politics at CAA," according to a former CAA employee. Within the group everyone gets along. . . . It really handles as a team. No one takes credit there. They are too busy."

But some don't like the communal environment of CAA. One former CAA worker likens the agents to Moonies in their single-minded determination. "They will do whatever they have to for the agency. CAA is the ultimate corporation. Everybody follows the corporate image and line."

When Rob Rothman left CAA for another agency it shocked the partners. While Rothman was able to take only six of forty-two clients he handled, the agency was aghast that one of their agents would leave utopia. Emergency meetings were called and considerable soul-searching conducted. But no others have quit CAA for other agencies (although some have left to become producers or executives), which is a remarkable feat considering the high rate of turnover among agents in the industry.

It may well be that CAA has already passed the optimal size for an agency. If it becomes as large as William Morris or ICM it will certainly lose the sense of camaraderie that can be maintained in a small, tightly knit group. Indeed, as CAA has grown larger it has become more difficult for every agent to be kept apprised of the needs and abilities of all his or her clients. Although the agency has a reputation for being well organized, it has had to evolve into a structure where agents divide up the principal responsibility for looking after clients.

"CAA is [now] no different from the others," says former CAA trainee Terry Danuser. "They are exactly what they wanted to leave." But most CAA clients disagree. "If I had gone to William Morris I would have seen one person and maybe shaken hands with several others," says writer Richard Kletter (*Never Cry Wolf*). "When I went in [to CAA], there were six agents in the room. There would have been seven but one was sick."

CAA agents do not bear much resemblance to the stereotypical Hollywood flesh peddlers portrayed in movies. There is nothing vulgar about these agents, who, like their counterparts at other top agencies, pride themselves on their culture and good taste—qualities that, when combined with warmth, sincerity and charm, enable them to establish a strong rapport with clients and studio executives alike.

Indeed, old-time agents would probably feel quite out of place at CAA, where a professional demeanor once reserved for attorneys and doctors has replaced the rambunctious spirit of the pioneer hucksters. The upgraded image is not pretense—as the business has grown more complex, it has become essential that agents be more sophisticated. Today most are college-educated, with more than a few possessing postgraduate degrees.

The transformation of these agents into the professional class is evident in their offices. CAA is located on the fourteenth floor of a modern office building set among the gleaming high-rise towers of Century City. William Morris resides in a huge glass-and-chrome complex in the center of Beverly Hills. ICM works out of a nine-story tower on the outskirts of Beverly Hills. In fact, many agents, and much of the movie industry, have long since deserted Hollywood—its low-lying buildings are too old, dilapidated and unfashionable for them.

Inside the big agencies one finds tastefully decorated offices, typically filled with plants and expensive furnishings. Everything is designed to make clients feel they are in the hands of powerful yet sensitive people. However, the veneer of good taste and culture often masks an atavistic ruthlessness. Ovitz the art collector is as tough a negotiator as any street-corner peddler when it comes to squeezing the maximum possible out of a deal. As a former CAA employee put it: "There are a lot of sleazy agents around. At least CAA agents are classy and have good taste in cars and food, if not in their way of handling things."

One practice that CAA and other big agencies have been repeatedly criticized for is the taking of packaging fees. When an agency is able to present a package of two or more elements (writer, producer, director or actor) needed to produce a television program—as CAA did with *The Golden Girls* and William Morris did with *The Cosby Show*—it may take from 6 to 10 percent of the entire budget as its fee, instead of commissioning its clients individually. Enormous fees can be derived in this manner—for every $1 million spent by a TV network, the agency earns up to $100,000. In fact, the big agencies make more money from their television packaging departments than from representing stars.

Clients seldom object to packaging because they believe the practice helps them. As part of a package they may obtain roles they wouldn't have been able to get on their own. Clients also benefit because an agency that receives a packaging fee can't also commission its clients—the agency's fee comes out of the production budget, so clients get to keep 100 percent of their salary.

But packaging may not benefit clients as much as they think. A 1985 investigation by the Screen Actors Guild found that agencies didn't put more of their clients in television shows they packaged than in those they didn't package. Daryl Anderson, the compiler of the report, said that "it almost looked as though the packagers sought to make the smallest possible commitment of their own clients" to packages. Anderson noted that for the agencies it made good business sense not to load up their packages with their clients, since including them did not increase their packaging fee and placing them elsewhere earned the agency commissions.

While clients rarely object to packaging, production companies and the networks do object, often vociferously. They assert that packaging fees are exorbitant, and that they consume money needed for production. "Packaging was designed by the agencies to get the lion's share of a successful show," Danny Arnold, producer of *Barney Miller*, told the *Los*

Angeles Times. "As far as I'm concerned, it's the most immoral concept in our business today." Other producers agree, claiming that agencies refuse access to clients unless they are given a packaging fee. "It's really a form of extortion," according to producer Mark Carliner. "What you're doing is paying tribute to a power broker."

The agencies defend packaging, noting that they often come up with the idea for the project, gather the elements needed to make it work and provide ongoing accounting services. Critics reply that the agencies often supply only one or two important elements and their accounting services are worth far less than what they charge.

Packaging has also come under attack for ethical reasons. "There is an inherent conflict of interest where you rep a producer, writer and director," says lawyer-turned-agent Nan Blitman. "In no other area of the law is this allowed." Critics charge that writers and actors are often put into a package not so much for their benefit but to help a producer or director client of the agency get a deal. "How does the actor know he is not being swept into a package because the producer is paying the agent more than the actor is?" asks personal manager Dolores Robinson.

When CAA agent Stuart Riskin was asked to convince several clients to participate in a package the agency was preparing, he confronted a moral dilemma. Riskin did not believe the project was in the best interests of his clients, yet he was expected to persuade them to join in it. Riskin refused, went on to make a better deal for his clients outside of the package, and was subsequently fired by CAA. "It took a lot of guts to buck the system," says a former CAA insider. "Not many agents do that. . . . [Clients] are sold out every day."

At least four other CAA agents who represented television writers have been discharged, or in the case of Rob Rothman, have quit. The agents were unhappy, says one of them, because "if you are a television literary agent your clients are fodder for the packaging department."

Packaging has also been denounced for sacrificing what is best for the project in order to obtain the greatest fee. "A lot of packaging is just about making a deal rather than a film. It is not 'Will these ingredients make a good film' but a 'good package,' " says agent Martha Luttrell.

Critics charge that studios and producers are often forced to take unwanted elements in a package if they want an agency's top clients. "[CAA] would say, Look, we got this project, so-and-so is the writer, we want to connect so-and-so to it," says former Paramount president of production Don Simpson. "We would get into big fights. I would say I'm not interested in so-and-so. I'm interested in the idea and the writer. We will make the choices as to who will produce it, and who will direct it."

But Paramount has been the exception in insisting on packaging projects itself. Perhaps not coincidentally, it has recently been the most financially successful studio. (Although packaging fees are not paid on feature-film deals—it is a television practice—agencies do, in effect, package feature projects in order to get work for as many of their clients as possible, each of whom is commissionable.)

Studio executives are reluctant to turn down packages because they know that they will be offered to their competitors. Furthermore, packaged projects make the executive's job easier by assembling the major elements needed for the film. Rather than expend considerable effort recruiting talent and negotiating acceptable deals with several agents, the executive merely says yes to the package.

Moreover, packaging solves the problem of how to hold some elements while others are recruited to the project. A studio will be reluctant to sign a star to a project without having a deal with a director, and vice versa. Since contracts typically include a "pay or play" clause, the studio is obliged to pay the star his full salary even if a director is not obtained and the project is dropped. Therefore, many studio executives encourage producers and agents to submit packaged projects.

Aggressive packaging is one of the principal reasons for CAA's success, says former Twentieth Century-Fox vice-president Claire Townsend, who, along with other observers, thinks the new emphasis on packaging has had widespread repercussions throughout the industry.

Smaller agencies, seeing the huge amounts of money to be made through packaging, have emulated their larger counterparts by creating packages among themselves. The approximately three hundred agencies that operate in Los Angeles are increasingly merging together to form larger agencies in order to package projects more easily.

"It's becoming tougher and tougher to be a small agency," says agent Marty Hurwitz, who thinks small agencies will continue to consolidate into larger ones. While the large agencies hold an advantage in having more clients to draw on for packaging, the increasing complexity of the business has also made it more difficult for a small agency to cover the town adequately. There is simply too much for one agent to do, says veteran agent Robert Littman. "In the old days there were just seven major studios. [Today] there is cable, pay TV, syndication, Tri-Star, Silver Screen, foreign sales companies and television."

Another reason smaller agencies are merging is to protect themselves—to forestall having their clients stolen by large agencies. A big agency can be an irresistible lure, says agent Candace Lake, explaining that clients often think they will be packaged with top directors or stars and catapulted into the stratosphere. "But a lot of the time it chews them up and spits them out," she says.

"If you're a smaller agency, the big agencies swoop down on your clients the minute they get hot," says agent Bobbi Thompson. Agent Joan Scott complains: "They poach, they steal, they lie to people in order to get them. They promise them things they can't deliver. In the big agencies, they have meetings where they say we want this guy now, you go out and get him." "Sometimes, though, the big agencies are very moral about poaching," says Lake, because they know a small agency will die if an important client leaves.

Occasionally, the big agencies will simply buy a smaller one. ICM swallowed whole Robertson/Luttrell & Associates, thereby acquiring clients James Garner, Carol Burnett, Jennifer Beals, Glenda Jackson and Waylon Jennings. ICM's parent, Josephson International Inc., has bought Chasin-Park-Citron and Ziegler Associates, which they operate alongside ICM.

The agglomeration of small agencies into large ones, whether for self-protection or to enhance revenues, has reduced the personal attention most clients receive. While the large agencies are very solicitous of their top clients, less important clients often feel neglected. Consequently, more clients are retaining personal managers to provide individual attention to their careers. There are three or four times as many actors today with personal managers than there were ten years ago, says Dolores Robinson. "You get personal service from a personal manager. Your agency may represent thirty-five other clients like you." Of course the client pays for this service—generally 15 percent, which is in addition to the 10 percent given one's agent.

Personal managers typically run small shops, operating alone or with one or two other managers. Keith Addis and Associates, for example, is comprised of two managers and three support people. The firm manages the film careers of Sting and a dozen other clients, including actors Steve Guttenberg, C. Thomas Howell, Beverly D'Angelo and screenwriter Menno Meyjes (*The Color Purple*).

Conflict between agents and personal managers is common. "CAA kills managers," says one personal manager who blames the agency for the loss of a top client. Agents generally regard personal managers as unnecessary and troublesome intruders in their dealings with a client. "Personal managers are sometimes a necessary evil. Most times they are just an evil," agent Edgar Small told a UCLA symposium, reflecting the prevalent attitude among agents. Underlying this hostility is fear that the personal manager will develop a close relationship with the client and advise him to change agents. Furthermore, agents don't like having someone looking over their shoulder to second-guess their decisions and point out errors to the client.

While many agents dislike personal managers, clients often find managers useful. "Very few clients know how to deal with their agent," says Keith Addis. "Actors are very reluctant to call their agents every day and ask what is happening, because they want to be liked and they don't want to turn anyone off." Addis and other personal managers say that when an agent and personal manager cooperate, everyone benefits. "I've never met an artist that could not get fifty percent more service from his existing representatives," Addis says. "And if all the manager does by charging fifteen percent is get fifty percent more out of the support team, it's a great deal."

Some clients have forsaken their agent and rely entirely on a personal manager. Under the California Labor Code, however, only licensed agents are permitted to procure employment for clients. While the restriction is frequently flouted—most personal managers see their most important function as obtaining work for their clients—managers run the risk of having their contracts with clients voided by the courts, thereby forfeiting all prior and future commissions. To protect himself, a personal manager may arrange for his clients to be signed with a nominal agent for a reduced fee. The agent augments his client list with people the personal manager takes primary responsibility for servicing.

But few clients forsake a large agency for a personal manager. Personal attention is nice, but managers can't collect nearly as much information as a large agency can. William Morris provides its agents with a thick stack of notes that are updated daily with the progress of every project at every studio. The notes are considered such a valuable resource that they are treated like secret documents, with extensive security precautions taken to ensure they don't fall into the hands of outsiders.

"When you work for William Morris, CAA or ICM you are in the nerve center of the film business," says agent Gregg Moscoe. "It's like working for the CIA." (Moscoe says studio executives will slip the big agencies their production reports, thereby keeping the agency informed of the studio's projects and currying its favor.) By knowing the marketplace. well, the large agencies are able to move quickly to fill a buyer's need before personal managers and smaller agencies are even aware of an opportunity.

"Agents really have the power," an ICM agent boasts. "Power has shifted from the studios to the big agencies. Studios ask us: 'What are you up to? What have you got? Why haven't we seen this?' " First thing Monday morning studio executives call agents to find out what they read over the weekend, says Claire Townsend.

"In some ways we feel that we're just about making the movie here," says William Morris agent Irene Webb. "We get the star, the material, et cetera, and the studio just provides the money." An ICM agent puts it more bluntly: "The studios are all banks. One is as good as another."

Led by CAA and the agencies that are emulating it, the industry is rapidly changing. Power has shifted from studios, producers and small agencies to the large agencies that today control the important commodities of talent and information. While CAA is not the most powerful agency of all time (that distinction probably belongs to the old MCA, which a federal judge once described as an octopus with virtual control over the business), it's the current champion. Its formula for success has been to represent only top talent, to recruit hard-working agents who can work together cooperatively and to package its clients aggressively.

3

THE NEW POWER BROKERS

As agents have become more influential they've changed the manner in which Hollywood makes movies. "The agencies are not simply powerful," says veteran producer David Brown (*Jaws*), "they do the work that used to be done by the studios." Indeed, agents conceive story ideas for movies, hire readers to review books and screenplays, attend performances to discover new talent, package projects and talent, and sometimes even arrange financing for films. The only studio function that the agencies have yet to usurp is the actual distribution of pictures to theaters.

ICM agent Sue Mengers told an American Film Institute seminar: "Right now agents have more power than the studios. Studios need the agents because the agents are the major suppliers of talent and material." According to Mengers, agents are becoming more forceful in asserting themselves. "What used to drive us crazy is that we would work very hard to help put a picture together and then the picture would be finished, there would be a preview, and we would be told that no agents were allowed. . . . And only recently has that stopped because some of us said, 'The hell with you. How dare you? We made as much of a contribution to this film as the studio did.' Slowly now the image of the agent is returning to one of much more importance, much more respect."

The transfer of power from studio executive to agent can be traced to the breakup of the studio roster system. In the days of the moguls, studios signed stars to long-term exclusive contracts. These contracts empowered the studio to assign a star to whatever production it pleased—the star had no right to be consulted on the selection of material and could be loaned like chattel to another studio (with the studio profiting on the transaction). If the star objected, the studio could suspend the actor or actress without pay and add the period of suspension to the term of his or her contract. During suspension no other studio would employ the star.

In 1945 Olivia de Havilland challenged the roster system when she sued Warner Brothers to contest her contract. She won, and thereafter studio contracts were limited to seven years, including suspensions.

A second blow to the system was struck when the antitrust division of the U.S. Department of Justice, at the urging of independent exhibitors, sued eight major studios in 1938, alleging that they were engaged in anticompetitive practices. After a protracted legal struggle, the government won a sweeping victory in 1948, forcing the studios to divest themselves of their theater operations. The case, known as the "Paramount decision," changed the face of exhibition in the United States. The majors no longer had a guaranteed outlet for their movies.

Divestiture itself might not have had much of an impact on the studio roster system had not the demand for pictures declined as television grew. Studios reduced the number of movies produced, and with fewer films to be made it was no longer economical for the studios to carry a large roster of writers, directors and stars. The industry evolved to a system of ad hoc deal-making.

In the absence of long-term contracts, studio bosses could no longer bully talent. The writer, director and star had to be persuaded to do each picture, and salaries and benefits rose accordingly. As the power of talent increased so did the influence of their agents, particularly those who could wield the collective clout of many important clients. Agents became the indispensable middlemen, controlling access to talent. Today the studios operate with the countenance of large agencies or not at all. "All the studios are competing for the same pool of talent," says Paramount vice-president David Madden, explaining that there is enormous competition for the next Redford or Stallone film, and an increasing number of production companies with financing vying for the privilege of making it. An agency that can assemble a good script and several powerful elements knows that the movie is going to get made—the only question is where, and the agent decides who gets first crack at it.

The newest studio, Tri-Star Pictures, wouldn't even exist were it not for CAA, says a former CAA insider. The agency has worked closely with the studio, providing it with some big-name packages that a new studio wouldn't ordinarily get. CAA helped launch the studio with *The Natural*, starring Robert Redford. (The fact that Tri-Star's president had been Redford's attorney also helped.) The presence of the Redford film on its slate gave the studio instant credibility, enabling it to build strong relationships within the industry and line up exhibitors for its product.

Big-agency domination is especially evident when one of them holds an auction, forcing the studios to compete against each other for a hot package. Studio executives dislike having to read a script quickly and decide whether or not to make a bid. The agency may not allow the studio time even to meet with the director to discuss how he envisions shooting the film. Nevertheless, studios continue to participate in auctions because agencies have the power to demand the game be played by their rules.

The studios have begun to respond to agent hegemony by signing talent to long-term multiple-picture contracts. "The studios are making overall deals with writers, producers and the Eddie Murphys of the world to stop agencies from leveraging them," says producer Don Simpson (*Beverly Hills Cop*). Columbia has signed a five-year, $40 million agreement with Richard Pryor for him to produce four pictures. Paramount has made a $25 million pact with Eddie Murphy for six films, and even newcomer Michael Keaton has a four-picture pact with Fox. These contracts guarantee the studio a continuing relationship with a star, but at a considerable price and without the unfettered prerogatives enjoyed by the old moguls.

But such multiple-picture contracts are unlikely to shift much power back to the studios. The problem is more fundamental. Agents have become powerful because studio executives have become weak. Executives today exercise little power over top filmmakers and stars, and their hold on their own jobs is tenuous. The old moguls could wield great authority because they owned the studios they ran. Today's executives are hired hands who can be easily dismissed.

Consequently, they are not inclined to take risks. Their primary concern is with maintaining short-term profits and making deals with proven talent for "surefire" formula pictures. The executive who agrees to produce an unconventional story with a new director or without a star risks losing his job if the project fails. After all, how can he possibly justify such a decision to his board of directors?

But if the executive accepts a big-name package comprised of a writer, director and star, even if the idea is pedestrian and the star miscast, he can righteously exclaim, "How was I to know that Burt Reynolds's next movie would flop? I got us a top director and writer, what else could I have done?" And the board of directors will understand, knowing full well that the movie business is fickle.

As agents have come to play a more dominant role in the industry, the experience and contacts they've derived from their work has prepared them to become producers and studio executives.

Agents not content to allow producers to take credit and earn millions on deals they've made have become producers themselves. They want what they perceive to be the creative and economic satisfaction of producing, says agent-turned-personal-manager Keith Addis. Agents are frustrated when they invest a tremendous amount of energy in a project and then have to walk away from it as soon as it gets going. As an agent, "no one wants to see you on the set," says Addis. "You don't get invited to dailies. You don't get to participate in what seems like the most fascinating and enjoyable part of the [moviemaking] process."

Agents often make the transition by first producing projects for their clients. While agents can't simultaneously produce and represent a client, personal managers may do so (they are not regulated by the state). Consequently, agents are increasingly becoming personal managers so they can continue to earn commissions from their clients as well as produce projects with them.

This dual role poses a potential conflict of interest, however. The personal manager–producer (p.m.-producer) often earns more money when his client participates in one of his projects rather than in an outsider's—even if an outside project might better serve the interests of the client.

Moreover, trying to handle both roles is difficult because to do each well demands a lot of attention. Whenever a p.m.-producer goes off to shoot a movie he will necessarily neglect his management duties. Consequently, some p.m.-producers become executive producers and hire line producers to work for them and handle the logistics of making their films. Other p.m-producers drop their personal-manager role after their producing careers are firmly established.

The p.m.-producer can freely draw upon his management clients to package projects, while the ordinary producer often must take a financial risk to gain access to a star or director. Some stars and directors won't read a script without a firm offer of employment, which means that a producer cannot get them committed to a project without agreeing to pay them their full fee up front—whether or not the project ever gets made.

Recognizing the advantages of being a p.m.-producer, producers are establishing management companies. Producer-director Blake Edwards has established such a company to work closely with his production company. "The personal-management company is a supplier of raw materials, scripts, ideas, people," which, when combined with a production company, comprises a new form of ad hoc studio, says Jonathan Krane, who oversees both companies.

P.m.-producers do face some unique problems, though. Their management clients may expect to get first choice of any parts in movies they produce, creating for the p.m.-producer the dilemma of choosing between the person best suited for a part or a client.

But such problems are rare because "nine times out of ten the manager will have a hot client and develop a property around the client, rather than put a client in a production he is developing independently," explains personal manager Dolores Robinson. In such a situation, the manager is using the clout of his client to leverage himself into the producer's chair—if the studio wants a star, it must accept his manager as the producer of the project. For the client, it is great protection to have his manager be his producer, says Robinson, because "Who cares about you more?"

Just as agents have become producers, they have increasingly moved into the executive suites of studios. Orion's Mike Medavoy, Columbia's Guy McElwaine, and MGM's Alan Ladd, Jr., were agents who became studio heads. Indeed, some clients complain that it's difficult for them to hold on to an agent because the studios keep recruiting them to participate in their never-ending game of executive musical chairs.

Director Martin Ritt (*Norma Rae*) recalls how his Creative Management Associates (CMA) agent, Dick Shepard, met him for breakfast one morning and told him that he had been offered a job at Warner Brothers as head of production. Ritt replied: "Dick, take the goddamn job, if that's what you want." During their meal, fellow CMA agent David Begelman dropped by and pleaded with Ritt to stay with the agency. Ritt agreed to stay on.

Six months later, Begelman called Ritt and asked to meet for lunch, at which time he told Ritt that he was leaving to go to Columbia Pictures, and Guy McElwaine would be taking his place. Midway through the meal, McElwaine showed up and asked Ritt to stay with the agency, telling him, "The one thing I am not interested in is being a goddamn executive." Ritt once again agreed to stay on.

Six months later McElwaine left the agency to replace Dick

Shepard at Warner Brothers (who had gone on to MGM). "One of the reasons agents are constantly hired as heads of studios," says agent Robert Littman, "is because the establishment, the banks and lawyers, think that agents are the people with the closest relationship with their clients." In a business that is more dependent on the strength of relationships than on ownership of hard assets, the executive who can attract important filmmakers and stars is highly valued. But Littman says agents are not always as close to their clients as studios think. The agent-turned-executive may not be able to bring his ex-clients into the studio fold.

Agents are also chosen to run studios because the businessmen on studio boards of directors are more comfortable hiring agents than members of the creative community whose motives they don't trust. Hollywood is a town divided into two camps: creative and business—each suspicious of the other. Writers, directors and actors are members of the creative community. According to the businessmen, creative types are wonderfully talented people but, like children, cannot be trusted with money. On the other hand, says the creative community, studio executives, producers and agents are businessmen who are concerned only with making money and have no taste or artistic sensibility.

Of course neither stereotype is accurate. Many businessmen can and do make artistic contributions to films, and many artists are shrewd businessmen. Nevertheless, rarely will a creative suggestion from a businessman be welcomed by a writer, director or actor; and almost never will a creative person attempt to negotiate a business deal himself.

Agents are the people best able to bridge the gap between artists and businessmen because they operate in both worlds. They regularly deal with their artist clients, as well as with studio executives. They have experience handling those crazy, creative types, yet have a thorough grounding in the business.

But the shortcoming of the agent-turned-studio-executive is that he often doesn't understand the craft of filmmaking. "I think that the failing in the present-day system is quite simply based on the fact that studio executives are by and large ex-lawyers, agents, business-oriented people, who are fantastic executives and managers who don't have a clue about telling stories," says Don Simpson. He adds that it is virtually impossible to find an executive who can handle both the business and the artistic sides of an increasingly complex business.

Agents have a tough job. They broker deals between anxious clients who are afraid they will never work again and frightened studio executives who know they are unlikely to hold on to their jobs much longer. They must nurture the sensitive egos of artists as well as battle with hard-nosed lawyers. Not many people possess the requisites that make for a successful agent.

First, an agent must have the stamina to handle a heavy workload and be able to endure the frenetic pace in which business is conducted. "It's like working in the commodities pit," says William Morris agent Joan Hyler. "It's hectic," says agent Lisa Demberg, "because you can't do your job unless you're always on the phone, always talking to someone, or socializing with someone or trying to do business, or following up on the projects you discussed."

"Great agents," says agent-turned-executive Stephanie Brody, "have enthusiasm and tireless energy. [And they must be] efficient. The agent is juggling thirty phone calls a day. He has to send out material, and follow up. You have to be extremely well organized."

Second, agents must be able to cope with the vicissitudes of the business. "In a certain sense it's like dialing for dollars," says William Morris agent Bobbi Thompson. "Each call may be the big money. You never know. It's all a roulette wheel." Some agents adopt a fatalistic attitude. Says agent Maggie Field: "When you're hot, you're hot, and when you're not, you're not."

Third, an agent must be an effective salesman. "Agents are just glorified salesmen," says a former CAA agent. "The only reason they're glorified is because they're in the entertainment business. . . . It's no different from selling *shmattes* [rags] on the street."

Many top agents are very aggressive in their pursuit of

deals—some would say ruthless. Says a former CAA agent, "In order to be an extraordinarily successful agent you can't have any qualms about lying, cheating, stealing and being totally into yourself."

Legend has it that one agent—whose identity varies with the storyteller—would submit scripts his writer did not author. The agent was supposedly having a difficult time convincing a studio to hire an inexperienced writer, so he ripped off the title page of a veteran's screenplay, inserted a new title page with his writer's name on it, and submitted it as a sample of the new writer's work.

"Agents don't play softball," says a former CAA trainee. "They go for the throat. For their jobs you have to lie. . . . I decided I didn't want to be an agent. . . . Seeing an agent trying to make a deal for a writer or director whom he knows won't complement the project . . . was very disturbing to me."

"Some agents are very honorable and straightforward," says production executive Richard Fischoff. "Others make you think you're the first person to see . . . [a screenplay] and have forty-eight hours to decide. They say Nicholson or Beatty is interested. . . . Sometimes the [star's] interest is only contingent on whether a certain director or directors are attached. Sometimes the [studio's] interest is only that a reader gave it a positive review."

"It's not that agents lie, it's that they don't tell any more than they need to," says agent Gary Salt. "If an agent told the truth all the time he would find himself in a strange place, because nobody would expect that and believe him."

Fourth, agents must be able to discern talent. They should know a good screenplay when they read one and be able to distinguish good acting from bad. They must understand what the studios consider to be commercial subject matter so as not to waste time on projects the studios will not make.

"[Of course,] this is a business where a lot of times there is no right or wrong," says a former CAA agent. "It's very subjective whether a script is good." Moreover, being blessed with great taste can be a liability if it prevents the agent from selling more mundane projects. Agents are often asked to handle material they may not personally like.

"One for me, and one for the pope, is my attitude," says a William Morris agent. "Sometimes you have to do projects that you are not crazy about but are very commercial. If you work for a big institution, you have to keep your eye on the meter. I'm a salesperson." But some agents have no qualms about handling schlock. The prevailing shibboleth at many agencies, says agent Melinda Jason, is "Don't smell'em, sell'em."

"I remember a William Morris agent who wanted me to hire one of his writers," recalls producer Tom Greene. "He said, 'I have one of the greatest clients. He is a new kid and he is fabulous. He is going [to be so successful] that . . . [his commissions] will pay for a new parking lot for this agency. That is how hot he is.'

"The agent came over with the kid. I had looked at the writer's work before they came and it was just dreadful. And I didn't know what to say. And so when they came we . . . [chatted for a while] and then the kid [excused himself and waited outside]. I said to the agent, 'Do you really think this guy is any good?' And the agent said, 'This guy is terrific.'

"I started to talk about the kid's scripts and soon realized the agent hadn't read them. So I started making things up. I said, 'Well you know the script he did on Napoleon?' And the agent responded, 'Brilliant, brilliant.'

"I said, 'You know I just don't think Napoleon should be played by a lesbian.' The agent said, 'Well . . . [the writer's] got a very interesting kind of comic style, don't you think?' I said, 'Well he is playing it as a sort of King Learian tragedy.' The agent replied, 'Ah, but Shakespeare is hot now.' This was when Zeffirelli was doing *Romeo and Juliet.*

"Then I said, 'But did he really ride a unicorn?' And the agent said, 'Well, that's the fantasy element.' And for everything I said, he had an answer.

"Finally I said, and this is absolutely true, 'To be really honest I have been bullshitting you because you've never read any of this kid's scripts.' The agent replies, 'That's not true at all. I obviously read the Napoleon thing, right?' I said, 'There is no Napoleon thing.' He says, 'Really?'

"I said, 'I've read this stuff and the kid is a rank amateur. He has turned in scripts literally with tuna fish stains on the

page, stuff written in pencil. There is no semblance of profes-
sionalism in the way it is presented. The writing is childlike.
And frankly if this is the kind of work your clients do, then
I am concerned about anyone else you might send me.'

"He said, 'Wait a minute.' He walks to the door and screams,
'Andy, you're no longer with the agency,' and slams the
door. . . . This agent is no longer with William Morris."

The ability to discover new talent would seem an important skill for an agent to have. Nevertheless, veteran agents
admit that they often misjudge talent. Agent Robert Littman
laughs as he recalls his meeting with a young Jack Nicholson:
"He wanted me to send him for interviews for *The Virginian*
and *Bonanza.* I wouldn't do it. I told him that I thought
directing was a sensible job, and that writing was an accom-
plishment, and that acting was a lifetime of rejection. I wouldn't
be a party to his lunacy. He said if you don't represent me,
I am going to go with the Morris office. . . .

"When . . . [Nicholson] won an Academy Award for *Cuckoo's Nest* he went up to accept and said: 'I want to thank that
agent who many years ago advised me not to become an
actor.' Thank God he didn't mention me by name." Littman
admits that during his career of twenty-five years he also
turned down the Beatles.

"The difficulty," says agent Rick Ray, is that "it is fairly
easy to read a script by Alvin Sargent [*Julia*], or Robert Towne
[*Chinatown*] and know that you have somebody who has quite
extraordinary talent. But it's difficult to read somebody on
a lower level and make a judgment whether they have the
commercial and creative senses to make their way through
the maze of the entertainment business."

If an agent isn't blessed with the ability to predict success
from raw talent, then he better be able to recruit proven
talent. "Part of being a successful agent is being a signer,"
says Bobbi Thompson. "If you're not a signer, you're not
going to have the big clients. . . . I will stop at nothing if there
is somebody I really want. I've driven people back and forth
to their doctor, I've called them up at home. People like to
be pursued. Almost to the point of obnoxiousness."

The competition for big-name talent is intense. "There's

a lot of client stealing," says an ICM agent who characterizes the situation as "all-out war." One way to convince a client to leave an agency is: "If you find that an agency is favoring one client over another, you let them know they aren't favored, and it will create a rift, and then you can steal them." For this reason, agencies are careful not to let their internal memos fall into the hands of outsiders.

Agents will often go to great extent to ingratiate themselves with a potential client. When he was a young agent, Robert Littman badly wanted to sign actor Christopher Plummer. Learning that Plummer liked to barhop, he devised what he thought was an appropriate strategy: "I used to go out with him . . . four nights out of every five . . . drinking, and wenching. This went on about three weeks. And I was quickly becoming his confidant and best friend." But lack of sleep and hangovers made it difficult for Littman to function during the day. Nevertheless, he felt compelled to continue the late-night carousing in order to get close to Plummer.

Finally, Littman decided to take Plummer to brunch and ask the big question. "I was going to take the bull by the horns and I was going to say, 'You know we are such good friends and you admire and respect me, and you know how passionate I am about you, it's time you became my client.' "

Littman got up early Sunday morning, having turned in early Saturday night in order to be ready. "I mean this was important. I was twenty-three years old and this was going to be my major coup. I was sober and clean and I was standing in front of a mirror dressing myself . . . and the phone rings. [A friend calls and says:] 'Listen, I know you're having brunch with Christopher and I know you plan to ask him about being a client. . . . Do yourself a favor, don't be rejected . . . he told me last night that he would never be a client of yours. He said that Bobby Littman is one of the greatest guys I ever met in my life, but he must be a terrible agent. He is out drinking and fucking every night till four in the morning.' "

Once someone is signed, a successful agent must be able to establish rapport and cope with the emotional problems that clients face. Industry analyst A. D. Murphy says that because "public taste is fickle" filmmakers and stars never know how long they're going to be around. Consequently, they function in an atmosphere of "hysterical desperation." They always ask themselves: "Is this going to be my last picture?" Out of this uncertainty about their career flows arrogance, petulance, pressure, tension and drug abuse.

"With experience as an agent you learn that appearances can be deceiving," says a William Morris agent. "The most successful actress can be a mess inside. There is a difference between the public Robert Redford and Warren Beatty and what they are really like. After a while you lose the star-struck feeling."

"I spend a tremendous amount of time . . . holding hands," says Rick Ray, explaining that the problem is invariably that the client isn't working. "Actors are insecure when not working, and insecure about losing it when they are working," says a CAA alumnus. "They sit at home and get anxious about their careers. Good agents always return calls right away to clients. [They know] it eats away at an actor sitting at home all day, and it's taken out on the agent."

Agent Joan Scott says she tries to prepare her clients for the coldness of the business so they know what to expect when they go out on auditions. She recalls one incident where an actor spent all night reading and preparing for a part only to be told upon entering the audition room: "You're not right, good-bye."

"I bolster my clients to prepare them for when they are shattered, screwed and lied to," says Melinda Jason. "One of the most important things agents do is to be there when things are not going well," says Martha Luttrell, describing her role as one similar to that of a psychologist.

Agents must not only nurture their clients but handle the delicate task of providing feedback. "When you criticize, they think you're against them," says Dolores Robinson. "I had one actor who told me that he was going to win a Tony, a Grammy, an Oscar and an Emmy this year. I said, 'How are you going to do that?' [The actor had never recorded an album.] He looked at me and said, 'You don't believe in me.' We had a horrible scene. . . . He told me his girlfriend believed in him."

After Nan Blitman lost a client, she asked him why he had left. He said, "I thought you didn't like my script." Blitman had told him it was "very good," while his new agent had described it as the best he had ever read.

Even clients whose careers are flourishing experience emotional problems. "Success is mind-fucking," says Robinson. "Instant success, particularly the kind when they get instant television success, is mind-boggling. One day nobody knows who you are, and the next day everybody in the world knows who you are. . . . People tell you 'Now don't change,' and you feel yourself changing because you have got to change. You're growing. . . . So the person never gets a realistic picture of what is going on. Even people's parents and best friends are suddenly intimidated. Here we are suddenly making twenty-five thousand dollars a week. It's intimidating right there. It's a rare case of somebody who can really keep it all together."

What frequently happens, says Robinson, is that the star starts to believe that he is as great as people are telling him. He then adopts an attitude of "I'm a star, I can treat people any way I want." Trouble soon follows.

What such clients desperately need, says Robinson, is somebody to give them honest feedback. "If your client becomes a major star, they land up in 'Yesville.' Nobody says no. Nobody says, 'You're acting like an idiot.' Nobody says, 'You are egoed out.' Nobody says, 'You ought to stop taking these drugs right away.' You have to have someone who is brave enough, and willing to risk his or her relationship with you, to tell you the truth. If not, you're a waste of time. You're just joining the rest of the people who are stroking the star."

"When you reach the point when nobody will say no to you, it is the one certain path to madness," says writer-director Frank Pierson (writer, *Dog Day Afternoon*). "Brando is a perfect example. You have to wonder what [director] Arthur Penn thought when Brando came out to play a scene [in *The Missouri Breaks*] in a dress. . . . Brando is one of the sad losses of Western civilization because he just could not find anyone around for whom he had sufficient respect who would offer him any kind of criticism that would bring out the best in him. So there was nothing to do but to begin to become progressively a caricature of himself."

Adjusting to the loss of fame is another client problem agents must deal with. Industry careers tend to rise and fall like roller-coaster cars. "Keeping an even keel when it [fame] happens is a very difficult thing," says Joan Scott. "And keeping it when the acclamation is removed is also very hard. Most of the time they think they don't want it [the attention] and they're annoyed and they run away and they hide. . . . And then suddenly nobody's snapping your picture and saying give me your autograph. . . . It's a very strange thing."

Successful agents try to keep a professional demeanor in dealing with their clients. But because of their close working relationship, they often become emotionally involved themselves. "There is a tendency to psychologically merge with the client . . . [which is] a great trap," says Joan Hyler.

Robert Littman says that after many years of representing Ken Russell, "I began to think I was really Ken Russell. Our relationship was extremely emotional and passionate. [One day] he sent me a telegram firing me as his agent. I felt like someone had stuck a knife in my belly."

"A woman client left me after I got her four movies," a William Morris agent says. "I felt terrible. What did I do wrong? How will it look? And there was a real sense of personal loss, of a friend."

But it would be unfair to leave the impression that agents always suffer their clients. Despite the difficulties, most agents enjoy dealing with their clients and admire their abilities, taking great satisfaction in their accomplishments.

"Dealing with actors is the most fun of all because they're all insane," says agent J. Carter Gibson. "They're not insurance salesman. They're creative, insane people, a constant source of joy and laughing. The actor keeps you young, hip, makes you think. They're different from other people."

INSIDE THE STUDIOS

Studio executives are the diplomats of the industry. The tyrannical mogul has been replaced by an executive who cajoles filmmakers to work for him at the same time he placates a board of directors concerned with the financial soundness of his decisions. It's a difficult job because the artistic desires of filmmakers often conflict directly with the studio's desire to maximize profits.

To complicate matters, an executive's decisions are regularly put up to referenda when the public decides whether or not they like his movies. It's a no-win proposition, explains former Disney executive Thomas Wilhite, because "studio executives get the blame if a picture bombs, and filmmakers get the praise if it succeeds."

"It's pretty frightening to be an executive today," says producer Edgar Scherick (*Mrs. Soffel*), "because you're asked to make multimillion-dollar decisions regularly, and if you do just a competent job, which is pretty much all you can expect of a human being, you're destined to fail and be fired."

Those who survive often do so because of their political savvy as much as their creative ability. They excel at bureaucratic infighting and will do whatever is expedient for their careers.

"There are certain executives," says producer Leonard Goldberg, "who've made an art out of being able to stand next to a success and duck whenever a failure is coming, regardless of their association with either. . . . I know a man who has been at four studios. He looks like every studio executive, he talks in the same jargon, he has the buzz words, and as he moves from place to place he gets a little higher each time. . . . [His success] has nothing to do with his creative judgment but just his ability to be a political animal."

"Some executives take down six-figure incomes and move from studio to studio never green-lighting a project," says writer-producer Tom Greene. "You can last a year at a studio by always turning things down. As long as you don't say yes to a project you have more of a chance [of holding on to your job] because you haven't bombed out. What happens, of course, is that [eventually] the higher-ups realize that this person hasn't produced anything and they fire him. At which point he immediately gets a deal at another studio."

Executives preoccupied with bureaucratic intrigue have less time left to devote to moviemaking concerns. "Hollywood is like Washington," says agent Robert Littman. "The system is the same as politics. As soon as somebody gets elected they start planning the campaign for the next election. And they never get around to doing what they promised. I'm not saying their intentions are not good. It is just the nature of the beast."

Leonard Goldberg says that a new head of production for a studio told him that on the first day of work he began looking for his next job. "His theory was that he wouldn't succeed and therefore they wouldn't renew his contract beyond his three years. And he was going to do whatever he could during those three years to make certain he would have his next job."

A principal responsibility of executives today is to cultivate relationships with the stars and important directors in order to recruit them to work for the studio. While talent is certainly concerned with what they will be paid for their services, money is rarely the decisive factor in deciding which studio to work for, since they all pay about the same. "What makes filmmakers devoted to studio X as opposed to studio Y," says Paramount's David Madden, "is that they feel comfortable that the person they're working with at the studio is going to treat them well, and is going to be honorable, honest and have integrity, as opposed to the schmuck at studio Y." To lure filmmakers, executives tend to be warm, friendly and solicitous.

From an executive's point of view, filmmakers and stars are a troublesome lot. They can be obstreperous, temperamental and downright hostile. They often resent the control executives try to assert over their projects.

John Ford expressed the attitude of many filmmakers toward executives when he said: "There was this obnoxious little character—I think he was the son of some big shot. He said, 'You're way behind schedule.' He'd been pestering me for days, so I tore out ten pages of script and said, 'Now we're three days ahead of schedule. Are you happy?' "

Filmmakers resent having to answer to executives who they feel have little understanding of how movies are made. "The business is totally controlled by businessmen, which I do not like," says director Martin Ritt. "It would be nice if one of the heads of the studios would be a director or writer who had done his time and is not too old to function as a head, and had this residue of knowledge. Besides being a co-worker, it would be nice if somebody like that was around, that one could go to talk to. . . . [It is] wrong that this business is totally in the hands of agents and business people."

But few successful filmmakers want to become executives, perhaps because they can earn more working on their own. Top filmmakers get large up-front fees and a piece of the action—a profit incentive most executives don't receive. "I was responsible for making other people millionaires," says former Universal executive Peter Saphier, who, like many executives, decided to become a producer instead. Furthermore, executives don't receive screen credit for their work, recognition that in Hollywood can be as coveted as money. So while filmmakers complain about businessmen running the studios, few are anxious to take their place.

"It can be particularly frustrating working with young executives," says producer Carolyn Pfeiffer (*Endangered Species*). "You get a tremendous number of notes on your material. And sometimes those notes are good, and sometimes they aren't so good. And I ask myself if these people are even qualified to impose these things . . . on senior filmmakers. I don't believe they have any real understanding of filmmaking. They come out of school, they got a degree in arts and literature, and suddenly they are a production executive telling Coppola what to do with his movie."

Even if the executive has a good understanding of filmmaking, his suggestions may be flawed. Because they are frequently overwhelmed with scripts to review, they rely on inexperienced subordinates to read for them. Filmmakers complain that readers do not competently assess their scripts.

"Readers are frustrated egocentric people who are predisposed to hate everything," says producer Tom Greene, "because they are trying to get their own scripts made and all they want is to be Sammy Glicks climbing up the ladder. I used to deal with other readers when I was one. They used to love to see how cleverly they could trash a project. And sometimes they did not even read it. They would just look at the title. . . . They thought they could bring attention to themselves from the higher echelon as to how clever they were. They would fill in the . . . [checklist] that tells you about the story, character, budget, et cetera, by closing their eyes and sticking pins wherever they landed."

Considering how much rejection studio executives must dispense, it is remarkable that they are not held in even lower esteem. Former Twentieth Century-Fox vice-president Susan Merzbach estimates that Fox executives collectively received submissions of ten thousand screenplays, books, treatments or oral pitches each year, of which anywhere between seventy and one hundred projects were put into development, and twelve movies were made. For those lucky few filmmakers to whom Fox gave the green light, the studio still had to play Scrooge by scrutinizing budgets and frequently giving them less money than they wanted.

The key to being a successful executive today is having the ability to say no and yet not so antagonize an artist that he won't return to pitch future projects. "To be a really good studio executive you should be somewhat gracious," says former Paramount president of production Don Simpson. This means that "you are compelled to lie, because people don't want to hear the truth. When you read their screenplays they want to be told they're good, and they never are [good]."

The studio executive's greatest frustration is his lack of control over filmmaking. "I think everyone's frustration is that because it is a collaborative process, it is not a process under anyone's control," says Susan Merzbach. "After you've made the selection of a director," says Orion's Mike Medavoy, "basically you're relinquishing control to somebody else's vision."

Profligate directors are the bane of studio executives. Once a project goes into production, it's very difficult to rein in an errant director. If the studio fires him, it must quickly find a replacement. Every day the production is shut down can cost the studio tens of thousands of dollars. The principal restraints on directors are their desire to maintain a reputation for being financially responsible and their aversion to incurring financial penalties against their salaries (a provision in some studio contracts).

To monitor expenditures, studios typically reserve the right to select, or at least approve of, the production auditor or production manager, who regularly reports to the studio what is being spent. Sometimes studios use budget projections to ensure the schedule keeps pace with expenses. Such projections are often inaccurate, says director Jim Bridges. "One time Michael Eisner called me and said, 'Jim, you're at twenty-two million.' Well, we had barely started. I think we were in the third or fourth week of shooting and I said, 'How can we be at twenty-two million . . . ?' And he said, 'Well our computer said that if you keep falling behind . . . you'll be at twenty-two before you finish.' " The picture was completed at its budgeted $12.5 million, Bridges wryly notes.

The relationship between studio executives and filmmakers during production is often one of "mutual paranoia," according to director Lamont Johnson (*The Execution of Private Slovik*). He says an adversary atmosphere may arise because hardworking studio executives are envious of the fun they think cast and crew members are having.

At other times a hostile relationship is the filmmaker's doing. Paramount executive Ned Tanen recalls a director with whom he had a pleasant relationship during development, who confided without rancor: "You know you're going to end up hating me because I'm going to make you into the enemy. I need an enemy to get my creative juices going, and you're the best target."

When a production is in trouble, an executive is frequently sent to visit the location. "Nobody likes to see the studio suit [representative] show up," says former MGM vice-president Willie Hunt, who recalls her experience when she went to the *Brainstorm* location after the producer became ill and the production fell five days behind schedule. The first morning after arriving, she came down from her hotel room and approached a member of the transportation crew and asked if she could get a ride to the set in the next car out. The man's response: "We are not going to have a car going." Hunt's reply: "When you do have a car going, I'll be in the dining room." His retort: "We won't be able to find you." Her reply: "I'll wait."

Hunt might never have made it to the set if she hadn't overcome the crew's hostility toward her. "I [was] not going to start . . . by throwing my weight around," Hunt recalls. "I didn't even know if I could carry it off. So I sat down next to this man, and I said, 'Excuse me, did you ever work for Warners?' " The guy looked at Hunt, replied, "Yeah," and looked back at the television. Hunt asked: "Then you must know my dad?" Without even turning his head, he responded, "I don't think I know your dad." Hunt said, "Oh, I am sure you must. His name is Bill Hunt."

There was dead silence in the room, and then three of the guys turned to her and said: "Your Dad is Bill Hunt? Oh God, I've known him for twenty years." (Hunt's dad was driver captain at Warners and had been a teamster for forty years.) "Well they couldn't do enough. One guy was going to carry me on his back. Even before I hit the location everybody knew, 'She is one of ours, she is OK. Don't worry about it.' The attitude change was like night and day."

Troublesome filmmakers and the vagaries of production make for anxious studio executives. "It's a frustrating and yet highly rewarding job," says Orion's Mike Medavoy, who has been an executive for ten years, an atypically long tenure. Medavoy says that one can only see the wear and tear of the job by viewing X rays of his stomach.

Many have forsaken the executive ordeal to become producers. The move occurs so frequently that it has come to be expected that working for a studio is a temporary stint on the way to producing. "Studios are grad schools for producers," says Susan Merzbach, explaining that all executives want to either run a studio or be a producer. If you are still at a studio after four or five years, something must be wrong, she says, for if you were any good you would have been stolen away to run another studio or become a producer in your own right. Moreover, Merzbach believes, executive turnover is beneficial for the studios because it ensures a steady flow of new blood, invigorating management with creativity and imagination.

But most industry veterans think the rate of executive turnover is excessive and detrimental to the studios. Barry Diller, widely considered one of the best studio heads, says boards of directors are stupid to fire their executives at the first blush of failure.

"When I started at Paramount," says Diller, "it was not a successful company. And I certainly in the first two years made it worse . . . we had a really terrible reputation. We were known as the last on the list of places where people [filmmakers] would go [to bring a project]. . . . If it weren't for the fact that there was somebody wise there, who had great faith, [I would have been fired]. Because everybody was saying, 'Get rid of that guy—he's a disaster.' "

Studio heads plan for their transition to the producing ranks with provisions in their contracts that entitle them to development deals at the end of their tenure. Such arrangements benefit the studio by keeping executives loyal after their departure. No embarrassing disclosures will be made by discharged executives who continue on the payroll. If the executive is leaving after a successful term in office, having him as a producer under contract will ensure continuity with the new regime. The studio can announce that although its treasured executive is no longer running the shop, he continues to be a member of the family. Stock prices will not decline precipitously.

Relationships between executives and filmmakers are forged as they develop projects together. Initially the filmmaker will present, or "pitch," a story to an executive. If the pitcher has clout, the meeting may take place over lunch with the studio head. More often, the meeting takes place in the office of a studio vice-president or development executive.

A great deal of industry folklore has grown up around how best to pitch a story. "Pitching has become a kind of science," says former Fox vice-president Claire Townsend. Filmmakers are obviously fascinated with learning why studios decide to develop some projects and not others.

"The pitch [meeting] is fraught with peril," says director Richard Pearce (*Country*). "Something has to go on. Some magic that makes people risk everything. A spark. The . . . mythology is you go in to an executive, and spin such a tale that he says, 'What do you want, kid?' and pulls out his checkbook."

There are writers, directors and producers renowned for their pitching ability who repeatedly earn large development fees and yet rarely produce anything worthwhile. On the other hand, there are other individuals who are talented filmmakers but cannot seem to articulate what it is they want to do. Fortunately, studio executives hold them to a lesser standard.

Industry wisdom states that a good pitch quickly encapsulates the essence of the story in a way that can be easily grasped by the listener. A story that can be expressed in such shorthand is called "high-concept." Susan Merzbach offers as examples: "Teenage Cycle Sluts, Eddie Murphy in butler school, and Dolly Parton teaches Sly Stallone how to be a cowboy." The common denominator of each description is that it concisely tells the listener what the movie is about. "They [studio executives] don't want to know too much," says Don Simpson. "They want to know concept. . . . They want to know what the three-liner is, because they want it to suggest the ad campaign. They want a title. . . . They don't want to hear any esoterica. And if the meeting lasts more than five minutes they're probably not going to do the project."

"A guy comes in and says this is my idea: '*Jaws* on a spaceship,' " says writer Clay Frohman (*Under Fire*). "And they say, 'Brilliant, fantastic.' Becomes *Alien*. That is *Jaws* on a spaceship, ultimately. . . . And that's it. That's all they want to hear. Their attitude is 'Don't confuse us with the details of the story.' "

In 1977 Frohman went to Warner Brothers with an idea called *Cheerleader of the New Left*, and sold it as a sixties to seventies version of *The Way We Were*—a past Warner Brothers hit. "The studio said, 'Fantastic. Great.' I happened to be talking to Mark Rosenberg, who I knew . . . [had been] in SDS. . . . I knew he was very sixties savvy, and so I told him the sixties character becomes the seventies sell-out. And they bought it in five minutes. Truly. I was astonished. I had only about two thirds of the story worked out. I didn't have an ending, and ultimately never did."

"You sort of have a high-concept crowd out there," says agent Nan Blitman. "If it takes more than thirty seconds to tell, forget it." She complains that when she tried to sell a King Charles restoration comedy she couldn't get anyone to sit still for the ten minutes it took to explain the story. But when she described the project as a "restoration *Flashdance*," she found immediate interest. Blitman says the industry has already moved beyond high-concept to embrace "the jingle," which is a story reduced to a single phrase.

Overworked executives like stories that can be condensed into slogans because they do not have the time required to evaluate more complex material. Most of all, they want a story that is easy to market. If the title and one or two lines of ad copy can draw people into the theater, the studio need not be as concerned that the movie be well made.

Some high-concept stories are more appealing to the studios than others. The ideas liked best are sufficiently original that the audience will not feel it has already seen the movie, yet similar enough to past hits to reassure executives wary of anything too far-out. Thus the frequently used shorthand: It's *Flashdance* in the country (*Footloose*), or *High Noon* in outer space (*Outland*). Derivations of recent hits are usually well received, even though by the time the movie is made the audience may groan: "Not another breakdance movie!"

Executives also favor stories with likable characters (i.e., a hero to root for), positive endings ("Give me a *Rocky* ending") and subject matter of interest to the most frequent moviegoers, teenagers. A story with a role for a star, a "star vehicle," is preferred over stories with roles that only unknowns could fill, or would want to fill. And if a star or big-name director has already expressed interest in the project it can only encourage the studio to proceed.

Of course, the credentials of the pitcher are as important as the story itself. When George Lucas or Steven Spielberg proposes a story, nobody doubts that he can make a wonderful film from it. But when less-celebrated talent pitches, greater scrutiny is given the story and the filmmaker's ability.

Consequently, how one pitches a project depends on one's rank in the Hollywood hierarchy. "An Alvin Sargent (*Julia*) deal can be made on two sentences," says writer Richard Kletter (*Never Cry Wolf*). "If I tried that, they would throw me out [of the office]. . . . If you're on a hot streak, it's no problem [getting a deal]. If not, you have to jump through hoops."

The attitude of the pitcher is also important. Director Tony Bill (*My Bodyguard*) characterizes the attitude of some of the most effective pitchers as something between that of a parent and that of a pimp. Like a parent, you are as proud of your idea as if it were your child. But if the story doesn't fall on receptive ears, you are as ruthless as a pimp trying to sell the customer something else.

It is generally regarded as a mistake, however, to come

into a pitch meeting with a shopping bag full of ideas in the hope that if you throw enough things up against the wall, something will stick. "If someone comes in and says he has fifteen ideas for movies—pick one—my lid goes down," says former Disney executive Tom Wilhite. "But if someone comes in with a vision, and they've done their homework . . . [and believe in the project], and I think this person is substantial, why not?"

The word that studio executives repeatedly mention in describing the attitude that impresses them most is "passion." "Your conviction and your passion absolutely has an effect on the studio," says Carolyn Pfeiffer. "They want a producer and a director whom they feel desperately care about the thing."

"All that matters is passion and tenacity," says personal manager Keith Addis. "Movies get made because someone, or some group of people, were passionate enough for a long enough period of time to get it done. *Breathless* was submitted over four and a half years to over one hundred and six possible financiers. The company that made it rejected it five or six times formerly. It was all passion and tenacity. Because if you look around, you know it's not about talent, necessarily. A lot of untalented people succeed, and projects without merit get made."

"Personality in this business is more important than in other businesses," says Stephanie Brody. "Personable energy is what people respond to. Enthusiasm, charm . . . if you're dynamic and personable, people want to be around you. People are drawn to live wires. You can be very successful even if you only have a modicum of intelligence and talent." Addis agrees, attributing success not so much to intuitive brilliance as to problem-solving ability with a certain amount of charisma and flair. "It is getting people excited."

Besides feeling passionate about his project, the film-maker must also be able to engender passion among at least one executive who feels strongly enough to champion the project within the studio. "I don't know how a project can get made without one," says Paramount's David Madden. "You have in that person, who is your advocate, someone who is as tough on that project as possible, to get it into the best possible shape. Once that person is convinced that it's a good movie to make, then he is doing his best to convince the group."

This advocate is essential, Madden says, because it's hard to find a consensus within a committee of six or seven studio executives. "It's much more likely that a movie gets made because two or three executives, and obviously the boss, are convinced that a movie is good." Sometimes executives trade votes in order to get their pet projects made, and those projects without someone pushing them can be lost in the shuffle.

In addition to projecting passion, there are other strategies that may be used to induce a studio to develop a project. "You always have to give . . . [an executive] the idea that if they don't take it, somebody else is going to take it soon," says producer Harry Ufland. "Everybody is very insecure, and they don't want to let anything get away. God forbid something is going to go across the street, they will do anything to prevent it." Ufland recalls one incident where an ex-associate of his sold a script to then Paramount executive Freddie Fields. "He got Freddie to believe that nobody had seen it. And Freddie paid a fortune for it. And the truth was that everybody had seen it, and passed on it. That happens all the time."

Another strategy is to present a bargain. Producer Edward S. Feldman (*Witness*) recalls that no one wanted to make *The Other Side of the Mountain* because it was a story about a skiing champion paralyzed by polio. Only after Feldman reduced his salary to nothing and persuaded prestigious director Sidney J. Furie (*Lady Sings the Blues*) to agree to make the picture for a nominal fee, did Universal give the go-ahead. Although Furie later dropped out of the project, Feldman had built up enough momentum that the studio allowed it to continue into production.

Bringing a star to the pitch meeting is often an effective device. "Stars intimidate studio heads more than producers do," explains production executive Lisa Lieberman. Executives find it difficult to say no to a star because they are loath to alienate someone they may want to recruit for other projects.

Sometimes a studio will produce a script it doesn't want in order to induce a star to do a project it does want. The Cannon Group agreed to produce the $6 million picture *Street Smart* in order to get Christopher Reeve to make *Superman IV*. "It's a classic example of a studio being backed into making a picture it has no interest in," says a participant in the project. Likewise, Columbia agreed to make *The Razor's Edge* with Bill Murray in order to get him to star in *Ghostbusters*.

One gambit not to use during a pitch, says executive Barbara Boyle, is to talk about the big box-office grosses your story is sure to make. Executives know as well as anyone that it's impossible to predict how much money a movie will make, and declarations to the contrary are considered pure malarkey.

It is acceptable, however, to talk about how much a movie will cost. Obviously, the less expense, the less financial risk to the studio. But very low budgets may strain one's credibility. When producer Dina Silver made the rounds of the studios to get financing for her picture *Old Enough*, she asked for $3 million—fearing that no studio executive would believe her $400,000 budget was realistic. After being turned down everywhere, and being told it wasn't possible to make her movie for only $3 million, she went on to produce the film independently for $400,000, and then got Orion Pictures to pick it up for distribution.

When a pitch convinces an executive to develop a story, it is important that the filmmaker consummate the deal quickly. "You often walk out of a meeting thinking you have a deal," says writer Robert Mundy (*Chattanooga Choo Choo*). "[But] if it's not done in a finite period of time, it's blown. The energy is gone. People move on to other things." The period for finalizing it, says Mundy, is about one month.

After a studio agrees to develop a story, the next task is the writing of the script. If a writer is not already attached to the project, one who is acceptable to both the producer and studio must be hired. The selection can be difficult because the material needs to be matched with a writer who has an aptitude for the type of story at hand, whether it be comedy, drama, horror or some other genre. Few writers are considered versatile enough to be able to handle everything. Moreover, top writers are in such demand that they can pick and choose among projects. "You seldom get the person you want," says former CBS Theatrical Films president Bill Self —despite fees of hundreds of thousands of dollars paid by the studio.

Before a writer is signed to the project, the studio executive and producer will meet with him to ensure he shares their conception of the movie. Once agreement is reached, the writing will begin, with the writer conferring with producer and studio executive as the script progresses. "Inevitably there are very different opinions and different visions on how something should be accomplished," says Paramount's David Madden. "What I try to do . . . if I believe very strongly about a principle in the script, [is] convince the writer that he's wrong. If I can't convince him, sometimes I'm wrong . . . I can get turned around. . . . There's a give and take." Madden says he always wants to know what the writer has in mind before he starts writing, so there are no surprises later.

Writers often resent interference in their work. Writer Mario Puzo (*The Godfather*) says: "What happens after you do a script is—taking the case of *Superman*—you have a conference with the producers. All the suggestions they make will be to incorporate scenes from a movie that has just come out and has been a big success. They'll say, 'Why don't we have ten sharks around Superman?' or 'Why don't we have Darth Vader come out with his magic sword and try and kill Superman?' It gets really tiresome to sit there and listen to that stuff. . . . The writer does what he can, but he doesn't really have much of a say. They just do anything they want. There may be seven people rewriting the script."

If the studio is not satisfied with the final draft of the script, they can, and often do, bring in a second writer to rewrite it. Sometimes the first writer has simply reached the limits of his ability, and another writer is needed to bolster aspects of the script that are weak. At other times, however, the second writer is brought in to bolster the confidence of executives, giving them insurance should the picture turn out poorly. Writer Clay Frohman explains: "I daresay that ninety-five percent of the executives out there would prefer, no matter how good the script is, to bring in Robert Towne [*Chinatown*] or Bo Goldman [*Melvin and Howard*] . . . give him five hundred thousand dollars and let him run it through his typewriter, because if Robert Towne is involved, then you can't say that we didn't do the best we could on this screenplay. You know—just name value. You're hiring a star."

When all the writing is completed—and this can take years—the studio must decide whether or not to make the movie. Although hundreds of thousands of dollars have been spent to develop the script, millions more will have to be spent to produce and market it. Consequently, studios often decide to cut their losses and not make a project. Apart from the quality of the script, there is the question of whether the project fits in well with the overall plans of the studio. The project might be dropped simply because the studio already has several films of the same genre already slated for production.

The project competes with both the studio's other scripts and scripts packaged by agents and producers that are received over the transom. Thus the writer and producer never know what they're up against. At the last moment, after several years of painstaking work, a project may be dropped by the studio after a similar story is picked up outside.

To get their projects into production, producers try to build up momentum by lining up an important director or star for it as early as possible. They will try to persuade the studio to begin paying for preproduction activities—scouting trips and the hiring of an art director. Such financial commitments get you to what producer Carolyn Pfeiffer calls the "flashing yellow" zone: "You're still not green-lighted, but if you can get them enthusiastic enough to let you keep getting closer to production, you have a much better shot at being green-lighted." The strategy is to get the studio to spend as much money as possible, under the theory that the more spent, the less likelihood there is that the studio will back out.

If the studio decides to drop the project, it goes into "turnaround," allowing its producer an opportunity to set it up at another studio, provided the new studio reimburses the old one for its development expenses. There is surprisingly little stigma attached to projects put in turnaround—studio executives realize that there are many reasons besides script quality for dropping a project. Indeed, a great many successful movies have been made from turnaround projects, including *Splash* and the all-time box-office champ, *E.T.* The latter, which has grossed more than $350 million at the domestic box office, was developed by Columbia and then picked up by Universal.

Many projects go into turnaround when there is a change of studio regime. To justify their presence, the new team of executives often discard projects developed by their predecessors. The newcomers want to put their own stamp on the studio's lineup, and having no emotional stake in projects they have inherited, they examine each one critically. Besides, if an old project is a hit, the new team will not receive full credit for it, and if it is a bomb, they will be blamed for deciding to make it.

This constant turnover is a source of frustration to writers and producers who, after expending considerable effort to get a project into development and then molding that project to the taste of studio executives, find their work thrown out—although the departing executives sometimes pick up such projects in turnaround to bring to their new studio.

Because so little of what is developed by studios is ever produced, it has been criticized as a wasteful activity. "The development process at most studios is completely antiquated," says former Disney executive Tom Wilhite. "Most of what gets made are packages by agents, or screenplays that come in from outside."

The ratio of developed to produced projects at the studios compares unfavorably with its counterpart at the networks. Agent Rick Ray estimates that while 15 percent of the scripts developed for motion pictures get made, only 15 percent of those developed for television *don't* get made. The low success rate for features leads one former studio executive to conclude that development deals are entered into mostly for public relations—to build relationships with important writers, directors and producers. "Ninety-nine percent of development deals don't do anything but develop because they aren't designed to do anything but develop," says Claire Townsend.

But many industry insiders defend development as a necessary function that is no more wasteful than the research and development divisions of nonentertainment companies —where a lot of money is risked on research that ultimately may not prove useful. By this logic, since every movie is a unique product, it is reasonable that a lot of money be spent on development.

Nevertheless, studios are cutting back on development deals. "Fewer and fewer pictures are being developed by the studios," says Orion's Mike Medavoy, because many executives feel they have been burned by spending a lot of money and getting little in return. Medavoy notes that the studio can recoup what it has spent on developing a project only when it gets made.

Concern with high development costs leads writer Robert Mundy to speculate that studios taken over by outsiders may be in for some big surprises. Coca-Cola executives may ask themselves why they are spending millions of dollars on development when most of the projects that get made are picked up outside. They may decide they might just as well get rid of development costs and a whole host of executives.

But it is unlikely that studios will eliminate development. The industry is too competitive for studios to allow others first crack at good stories. Any policy restricting development costs is likely to be scrapped the minute a hot writer, director or star approaches the studio with a story that sounds like a sure winner.

5

STUDIO BUSINESS

Once a year Warner Brothers head of production Darryl Zanuck sat down with a big sheet of paper and lists of stars and directors under contract and matched them up with stories the studio owned. His assistant Milton Sperling remembers that Zanuck would say: "OK, we want three Bette Davises, four Cagneys, four Eddie Robinsons, three Bogarts, two Errol Flynns. Who's got a good story for Bogart—anything we can put Bogart in?" Within a few days, Zanuck put together the entire production schedule for the next year.

The studio had on hand everything needed to make movies, including writers, directors, stars, crew, sound stages, costumes, scenic designers and, of course, money. Zanuck would allocate these resources with unfettered discretion, intimately involving himself in structuring the story (sometimes writing the screenplay himself), casting the picture and closely supervising every aspect of the film's creation. Uncooperative stars and directors who thought the studio should not interfere in their art were simply not tolerated. If Zanuck was not satisfied with a completed film, he would often sit down and recut it himself.

Zanuck and the other moguls who built the industry would barely recognize the movie business of today, with studio executives spending their time immersed in a myriad of legal, financial and administrative concerns. Pictures are planned one at a time, with committees of executives carefully deliberating the appeal of each project and how much revenue it can be expected to generate from domestic, foreign, cable and home-video markets. The executives most admired are not those who can write a script or edit a movie but those whose financial legerdemain can reduce a studio's risk.

The rosters of writers, stars, directors and craftsmen under long-term contract are gone. The physical plant that was once thought essential in order to be a "studio" is no longer necessary; most movies are now shot on location. Such studios as Orion and Tri-Star don't own a single sound stage.

The object nowadays is to adapt successfully to a rapidly changing business that provides many opportunities as well as risks. Cable television and home video have created important ancillary markets for films, but at the same time, escalating production and distribution expenses have increased potential losses. The only constant from the days of the moguls is the continuing mystery as to what makes a film a hit.

In some respects the movie business is inherently risky. "A film is like no other product," explains producer Robert Evans (*Chinatown*). "It only goes around once. It is like a parachute jump. If it doesn't open you are dead.

"In the car business you can close out a car that doesn't sell. But with a picture you can price it at twenty-five cents and no one will see it. I tried it once. With *Darling Lili*. It cost twenty million dollars and got good reviews. At Radio City Music Hall it did well but nowhere else. In Los Angeles we took out a full-page ad saying every adult could bring his whole family for nothing. No one came. You can't give a picture away. There is no close-out value. So it is a very dangerous business on that level."

The business can be so treacherous that a few missteps can spell disaster. Columbia flirted with bankruptcy before several blockbusters returned the studio to good health. United

Artists lost so much money on *Heaven's Gate* and other pictures it was sold by parent Transamerica Corporation. MGM virtually left the business for years to operate a casino in Las Vegas—a venture considered less risky than moviemaking.

The studios complain that rapidly increasing costs have gotten out of hand and threaten the health of the industry. Their lament was presented in a 1984 speech by then Twentieth Century-Fox chairman Alan J. Hirschfield, who complained that from 1974 to 1984 the average cost of making a film went from $2.5 million to $12 million, while marketing costs rose from $1 million to $7 million.

"What the numbers mean," said Hirschfield, "is that in 1974 for a motion picture to break even theatrically it took about seven million dollars of gross at the box office (assuming a 50/50 split with the exhibitor), which meant selling about three and a half million tickets. In 1984, to break even on that same film, we need to gross thirty-eight million dollars at the box office. It requires that we sell at least twelve million tickets at today's prices."

"Productivity is our greatest problem," according to Hirschfield. "Today, wage rates, bad as they are, might be justified if we really received an effort commensurate with the cost—we do not! We're dealing with archaic work rules. . . . The labyrinth of these rules make the cost of railroad featherbedding look like Utopia. Our everyday dealings with the guilds and unions, so vital to our mutual well-being and success, are more akin to trench warfare than normal business practice."

Another former studio executive concurs: "The IA [International Alliance of Theatrical Stage Employees] union is worse than the United Auto Workers in having rules designed to ensure mediocre work as well as getting benefits up to the sky." Moreover, the IA rules are just one set of regulations that the studios are contractually bound to. Equally complex rules have been promulgated by the Teamsters, Writers Guild, Directors Guild and Screen Actors Guild.

Of course many union rules have arisen because of abuses perpetrated by the studios. And labor's demands don't seem so unreasonable when compared with the huge salaries and

expensive perks given to stars and studio executives. Agent
Sue Mengers blames the studios for rapidly increasing costs:
"I can't say to a star client of mine that he should take less
than a rival star client. No one is forcing the studios to pay
these prices. And as long as they're dumb enough—I mean,
Gene Hackman did not want to do *Lucky Lady*. They kept
offering him more and more and more money. Well, everyone has his price.... And finally Twentieth Century-Fox
came up with so much money [$1.25 million] that it was
almost obscene for him not to do the film."

But do these escalating costs make moviemaking unprof-
itable? One former executive who doesn't think so is Don
Simpson, who says that while he was at Paramount the studio
made thirty-seven profitable movies in row. "The truth is that
with ancillary sales . . . very few pictures lose money," claims
Simpson. "Most break even. If you're making a picture for
between seven and ten [million dollars], you don't lose money.
The studio can't lose. I've been at Paramount for eleven years,
and I can only remember two pictures losing money.... We
always got our money back. [Even on] *Reds*, the budget of
which I can't reveal [reportedly more than $35 million], we
got our money back before the picture opened. Absolutely.
People don't understand how this business works. You go
out and get guarantees. . . . [The misconceptions] are all publicity shit. . . . [The studios] try to make *Time* and *Newsweek*
believe in the poor beleaguered movie business."

While Alan Hirschfield's concerns shouldn't be dismissed
lightly, his remarks need to be seen in perspective. Studio
heads are inclined to bring out the violins and plead poverty
whenever they address the Hollywood community, thus laying the groundwork for the next round of union negotiations.

Moreover, Hirschfield's pessimism arises out of his experience at Fox, whose recent track record has been dismal.
Many of its pictures have failed at the box office, including,
of course, *Rhinestone*. The studio lost $85 million in its
1983–84 fiscal year. Paramount, on the other hand, has pursued a strategy of making modestly budgeted films, often
without stars. The studio made $110.5 million in its 1983–
84 fiscal year. Clearly, the movie business is very profitable

for those who adopt the right strategy. Paramount's success did not go unnoticed by then Fox owner Marvin Davis, who, not long after Hirschfield made his speech, replaced him with Paramount chairman Barry Diller.

But there are several trends that all studios consider ominous. Hirschfield notes: "It's not an accident that theater ticket prices have risen only sixty-five percent over the past ten years, while the price of popcorn and candy has gone up five hundred to six hundred percent. Film is being used as a loss leader to attract customers to a concession stand." Although exhibitors concede that they make most of their profits from concession sales, they blame the studios, saying that they receive such a small portion of box-office revenues (often 10 percent the first week) that they have little incentive to raise ticket prices.

Hirschfield says that the studios' share of box-office receipts (after deducting exhibitors' overhead expenses and their percentage) has dropped from 50–55 percent to 40–45 percent, and that while the studios receive increasingly greater amounts of money from cable, their share of such revenues is proportionally less than what they receive from the box office. (The studios receive only 18 percent money spent on pay-programming services in the United States. But much of their cable revenues are newfound since many subscribers are not regular moviegoers. Interestingly, box-office revenues have increased as cable has spread.)

Another worry is that the money studios used to get from the television networks is drying up. Feature films are no longer considered a surefire audience draw. When *Star Wars* was aired, it was beaten out in its time period by the television miniseries *Lace*. Extensive viewing of feature films on cable television and through videocassettes has reduced their appeal when they are shown by the networks. Consequently, the networks are buying fewer feature films, paying smaller license fees for them and making more of their own movies.

"Television does a good job selling its made-for-TV movies," says producer Al Ruddy (*The Godfather*), "because they can afford to run a lot of thirty-second spots. It would cost a distributor ten million dollars [to do the same]. A lot of those movies get good ratings. Forty million people can see them. A lot of people would have gone to the theater to see the same picture."

Cable television channels HBO and Showtime also have begun to produce their own programming. They have found that their subscribers often prefer made-for-pay programming over less successful feature films. Consequently, the cable channels have become more selective in buying films from the studios. HBO has begun producing its own feature films and has joined with Columbia Pictures and CBS to form a new studio, Tri-Star Pictures.

Diminishing studio revenues from network and cable television have been offset by increasingly greater amounts of money derived from the sale of movies on videocassette. The studios quickly saw the potential of home video (unlike cable, where they allowed HBO to gain hegemony), and established their own companies to market movies on cassettes. While the studios receive gross receipts of about $1.58 per theater ticket, 18 to 20 cents per cable subscriber, and 5 cents per broadcast-television household, they get $55.00 for each $79.95 videocassette sold to the consumer (although exhibition and videocassette revenues are offset by their greater duplication and distribution costs). The retail market for videocassettes brings in an estimated $4.55 billion a year, which is more than what exhibitors take in at the box office.

Nevertheless, the studios do not share in as much home-video revenues as they would like. Eighty to 90 percent of video transactions are rentals, from which the studios receive nothing. The "first sale" legal doctrine allows retailers to buy a videocassette from a studio and then rent it out repeatedly without further compensation.

To encourage sales, Paramount has lowered the price of videocassettes from $79.95 to $39.95. The low price enabled the studio to sell more than one million copies of *Raiders of the Lost Ark*, making it an industry best seller. Other studios have followed Paramount's lead and begun to reduce prices on selected titles. Industry observers think that the prices of many videocassettes will eventually fall to the $17 to $19 range. (Those movies that the studios think consumers might buy are likely to come down in price, while pictures that few would want to buy but many might rent are likely to retain a high price tag as an indirect way for studios to share in rental revenue.)

The revenues generated by home video would be greater if not for an estimated $1 billion a year the industry loses to pirates. William Nix, the director of worldwide antipiracy for the Motion Picture Association of America, estimates that $700 million is lost to videocassette piracy, with another $300 million lost because of the theft of satellite and cable-television signals. The problem is particularly acute abroad. In many foreign countries videocassette recorders are popular, yet there are few if any legitimate distributors of cassettes. Foreign laws against piracy are often either nonexistent or difficult to enforce.

At the same time that the studios struggle with these problems, what was thought to be the ceiling on what a movie could earn has been dramatically broken. *E.T.* has grossed an unprecedented $619 million worldwide. *Star Wars* and *The Empire Strikes Back* have together grossed more than $900 million at the box office, with another $1.5 billion collected in retail sales of *Star Wars* merchandise. Revenues from certain movie sound-track albums have also skyrocketed. *Saturday Night Fever* brought in $250 million in record sales. And while the networks and cable channels may be reluctant to buy second-rate movies, they will pay handsomely for blockbusters. CBS paid $25 million to license *Star Wars* for just three showings. Thus the rise of the blockbuster film has shown that for the right film enormous profits can be made.

The success of such movies as *Star Wars* has spread blockbuster fever among the studios, encouraging them to make bigger-budget movies in the hope of producing a smash hit. "From 1965 to 1975 there was a huge transformation," says director Richard Pearce, noting that many important films of the sixties made only several hundred thousand dollars in profits. "But suddenly someone was able to do it and make two hundred million dollars. [As a result] all other films are now gauged by that." Producer Harry Ufland agrees: "I think it has become a home-run business. Everybody is looking for home runs, not realizing that if you get a lot of singles and doubles, you can do as well."

The effort to make blockbusters has increased the studios' financial risk. In an attempt to obtain the hot stars, directors and scripts, the studios have bid up the prices of these commodities. But spending a lot of money is no guarantee of success. Only a few films each year become blockbusters, and they often are the pictures nobody expected to succeed.

Consequently, studio executives have accelerated their efforts to lay off the financial risks of moviemaking. The devices used are partnership deals with investors, presale agreements with television networks and cable channels, and exhibitor guarantees. The idea is to limit risk, so if the picture bombs, the studio will still be able to break even. The few pictures that are hits will be the principal source of profits each year.

"This business is like the commodities game," Columbia Pictures chairman Francis T. Vincent, Jr., told *Fortune* magazine in 1980. "If the risk is not hedged, you face the unknown." On the $10 million movie *Stir Crazy*, for example, Columbia laid off $3 million on West German investors and sold the television rights to ABC for another $6 million.

"Every studio is about one hundred percent covered when they start a movie," says Harry Ufland, noting a major change that has occurred throughout the industry. Ufland says that even independent producers who finance their own pictures and then distribute them through studios are usually covered for 80 percent or more of the risk.

"The majors have a very low risk on an eight-million-dollar picture," says Harry Gould, Jr., chairman of the Cinema Group, a motion-picture investment company. "You figure from all cable sources you can get three to four million dollars, and you figure that a picture, unless it is a real flukey turkey . . . is going to do at least three million in domestic rentals [distributor's gross]. . . . And you're probably going to get a least a million out of home video, and at least a million on foreign [sales]." This amounts to $8 to $9 million, which leads Gould to conclude that for a $6 million picture that costs $4 million to market, the risk is quite low. When the budget increases, there is more risk, he says, "But then again if you have a thirteen-million-dollar picture with a major star in it, you get more out of foreign, cable and video, so things tend to catch up."

Nevertheless, by laying off risk on outside investors, the studio is giving away potential profits. The Cinema Group agreed to share the risk in Paramount's *Staying Alive*, with a cost of $18.5 million, in return for equity in *Star Trek III*, with *Flashdance* thrown into the package. While *Staying Alive* was not the expected blockbuster hoped for and *Star Trek III* did reasonably well, *Flashdance* was a surprise hit with a worldwide box-office gross of more than $100 million, from which the Cinema Group profited handsomely.

Most investor deals, however, have provided much more of a financial benefit to the studio than to the investors. The SLM, Delphi, and other investment deals that gather public funds for investment in movies have been criticized for being skewed too heavily in favor of the studios. "The investors are thinking of *E.T.* all the time. They are not thinking of the other stuff," says Ufland. Gould agrees, saying that the primary motivation for someone to invest in movies is still the glamour, because on a strictly financial basis, investors can do better in oil or real estate.

The presence of outside money has inflated production costs, says industry analyst A. D. Murphy. "It is a cancer on the business. Agents see the big money raised and then demand ever greater amounts for their clients. They know you have fifty million in outside money. The outer bounds of financial limits are broken."

Investor money has also been flowing into the hands of independent producers. Such money, together with the ability to raise production funds through foreign and ancillary market presales, has provided producers with an increasing number of ways to finance their films; no longer are they completely dependent on the studios to green-light a picture. Producer Joseph E. Levine (*The Graduate*) sold the foreign distribution rights to the $25 million *A Bridge Too Far* for enough money to enable him to pocket a $5 million profit before production began. Similarly, new companies that represent American producers in selling foreign rights, such as the Producer's Sales Organization (PSO), are thriving.

The increase in independently financed films that studios pick up for distribution has reduced studio revenues. Because the studio risks only marketing and distribution expenses, it usually is entitled to a smaller portion of the proceeds.

Pictures picked up from outside help keep studio distribution pipelines full, thus amortizing distribution overhead among more pictures. The steady flow also enhances studio clout in negotiating exhibition contracts and collecting from exhibitors. And studios get more for their money with pickups since such films can be shot nonunion.

But independently made movies may ultimately weaken the studios. Universal president Frank Price has noted that pickups are not owned by the studio and therefore do not build up library values (which provide a cushion of revenues to help studios weather bad years). Furthermore, Price claims pickups don't make money for the studio. "They're strictly break-even properties." Some observers disagree with Price, but no one denies pickups are less profitable to the studio than pictures it owns.

The proliferation of financing sources has led to a surge in production. In 1984, 318 films began production, an increase of 28 percent over 1983, a year in which production rose 35 percent over 1982. "Hollywood is a boom town at the moment," says Don Simpson. "There's a lot of money to be made, and a lot of action. There's a lot of opportunity. . . . I have never seen it like this."

But it is not certain what share of industry revenues the major studios will receive. New technologies can depreciate the value of studio distribution arms. As more and more people see movies on cable television and home video, the need for theatrical exhibition declines. And if, as some experts predict, movies will soon be shot on high-definition videotape and then transmitted electronically to theaters, the current distribution apparatus of the studios may become superfluous.

Just as the studios have embraced outside financing to reduce financial risk, they have diversified their businesses so they are no longer completely dependent on moviemaking for profits. The studios have become major suppliers of programs to the television networks and have expanded into such related fields as camera equipment (Warners/Panavision), records (Columbia/Arista), and theme parks (Disneyland and the Universal Studios tour). Unrelated businesses have also been acquired. Fox bought (later divested) a Coca-Cola bottling plant and the Aspen Ski and Pebble Beach resorts. MGM opened the MGM Grand hotel and casino in Las Vegas.

Similarly, the financial risks of moviemaking have been diluted as studios have become parts of outside conglomerates. Gulf & Western acquired Paramount in 1966, Transamerica bought United Artists in 1968 (later sold to MGM), Kinney (renamed Warner Communications) purchased Warner Brothers in 1969, and Coca-Cola took over Columbia in 1982. The parent companies were attracted to the glamour of moviemaking and the tremendous cash flow that could be derived from hit films. The studios liked the financial backing that a larger enterprise could provide, ensuring that the studio would survive lean years.

The advocates of conglomerate acquisitions assert that moviemaking and other business enterprises can work synergistically, benefitting both. A sister publishing company can give a studio first choice of literary material; a record company can aggressively promote a movie sound-track album; a video-game company can develop programs based on movie characters; and a merchandising company can spin off products based on films, thus promoting movies while generating new revenues. But sometimes it is difficult to perceive what benefit a studio might derive from a conglomerate's other holdings. Columbia subsidiaries market spaghetti and plastic trash bags, while Gulf & Western companies finance earth-moving equipment and home loans.

Fortune magazine reports that Columbia Pictures has been able to benefit from Coca-Cola's volume discounts in purchasing advertising; the studio gets about 5 percent more network commercial time than it could have bought on its own. Furthermore, Columbia can now purchase large blocks of network time in advance, knowing that if a picture bombs it can reduce its advertising commitment for it and swap the ad time with the parent company for future spots. Coke also assists Columbia with free advertising on its soft-drink packages. On the other hand, Coke bottles have begun showing up in Columbia movies (*Murphy's Romance*). Coca-Cola undoubtedly realizes that the most effective advertising can be the presence of a product in a feature film.

Lawyer-turned-screenwriter Alan Trustman, writing in *The Atlantic Monthly*, noted several rarely mentioned ways that conglomerates can benefit from studio ownership. First, money can be siphoned off large production budgets and skimmed from distribution revenues without much chance of detection because these moneys are so difficult to audit. The siphoned funds can be used as a slush fund to make payments that the company doesn't want to appear on its books.

Second, money can be laundered from one country to another by rereleasing a picture through the studio's foreign-distribution arm and having it do "unexpectedly well." In this manner, illegal revenue can be legitimatized and money can be transferred from one country to another for tax reasons.

Third, by alternately siphoning and laundering funds, one can iron out corporate earnings so the company's bottom line shows steady growth year after year. This will impress shareholders and the financial community and keep one's stock price high. Of course, Trustman notes, this sort of hanky-panky can go on in any business; but it is particularly easy to do with movies.

Mutual benefit and corporate harmony are not always the outcome of conglomerate takeovers. There are frequent conflicts between studio executives and their masters. Don Simpson, former president of production at Paramount, says the higher salary scale for executives in the movie business is a constant source of irritation. "I mean a schleppy little vice-president in a movie studio makes three times what a chairman of the board makes in the gypsum business. . . . [Executives of other businesses] have a hard time dealing with that. I mean we drive around here in Mercedeses and Ferraris, and they're driving Volkswagens. . . . They say those [Hollywood] guys are living in these [beautiful] houses, and they have jets and all that stuff." Simpson says that when Coca-Cola bought Columbia "they were shocked to find out what the executives make over there."

Simpson notes that when Barry Diller was running Paramount, he had a greater salary and bonus than the chairman of parent Gulf & Western, an arrangement that is not unusual. Simpson asserts movie executives deserve to be paid more because they make more money for the company. "Nuts and bolts don't make that much money," he says. "We are a high-profile, high-glamour, high-income business."

But the parent companies do not always see it that way. Mike Medavoy recalls the problems that arose at United Artists when parent company Transamerica demanded that senior studio executives drive Fords. As a result of such annoyances, the five top executives resigned en masse and formed their own studio, Orion Pictures.

The conglomerates don't really understand the business, says Harry Ufland. "It is not a business that you can shove into a computer and get an answer. I think they're looking at it like other businesses with bottom lines and . . . that kind of stuff. You just can't handle this business that way."

"The people who are at the very top [of the conglomerates], by those I mean the chairmen of the boards, those people are business people," says Don Simpson. "They have to be business people. It's perfectly valid because they have to deal with hundreds of millions of dollars every day. Unfortunately, sometimes, oftentimes, if not all the time, they also say yes and no to what movies get made."

Thus the studio and its parent are frequently at odds. The parent company does not enjoy the risks of the movie business any more than the studio does.

For its part, the Hollywood community has not welcomed conglomerate ownership. Producer-director Jerry Hellman (producer of *Midnight Cowboy*) says there is a "big difference with conglomeration. No question about it. A depersonalization. You can no longer deal on a one-on-one basis with a studio. Now you're dealing with committees, which in turn have to answer to other committees. It has changed the process radically. It's more Kafkaesque."

Filmmakers complain that as the studios have become

larger businesses the nature of moviemaking has changed. "Now you read about the deals. It used to be about the movies," says Hellman. "They are all corporate types. You could pick them up and have them run any other business. They talk of product and the marketplace."

Many industry members feel larger enterprises are inherently less responsive and more bureaucratic than smaller ones. "The bigger you get the more cumbersome you become," says producer Leonard Goldberg. "If you look at any company over a period of years they always get too big and have too many people doing the same job and falling over each other. You appoint someone to a job and he has to appoint people to work for him. He builds his own little kingdom. And they tend to get further and further away from the firing line."

"For the most part there are too many executives participating in decisions," says producer Ed Feldman. "Movies can't be made by committee. It's an art form, a judgment call.

"When I got into the business there were maybe three vice-presidents [per studio]. . . . Today vice-presidents [are as common as] . . . water. It is unbelievable. . . . I think [what happens] is that people insulate themselves. You become a business of general managers like ball teams. The general managers never get fired on baseball teams, it's always the field manager. [The general manager says:] 'Oh, I made a mistake, let's hire another guy.' "

Another consequence of studio growth, says Barry Diller, is that executives today are not as well rounded as before. "At one time people who came up through this business got experience in many different areas because there were smaller stores in which to function in. . . . Today they're larger machines, they're more structured. . . . And I think that is not good in terms of a creative enterprise. You've got to know everything about everything in order to do it well."

"With very few exceptions . . . [executives] know nothing about storytelling," says writer-director Nicholas Meyer, "they know nothing about film. . . . They're not Jack Warner and Louis B. Mayer, semiliterate people who responded to tales. . . . They are taught like Benedictines to distrust the heart as deceitful above all things, and on no account to be swayed by personal opinion. They see that the W. C. Fields poster sells a lot, so they think, 'I don't give a shit about W. C. Fields, but the kids love it, so let's make a movie about W. C. Fields.' It's that kind of logic. You would not tell me a joke that you didn't think was funny on the off chance that I might like it. Nobody does that, but that's the way they make movies."

Indeed, executives increasingly make decisions based on market research, demographic trends and minimizing financial risks. It has become more of a lawyer-agent game, with less showmanship, says producer Martin Ransohoff. "Picture-making itself had a better shot under the old moguls. They were basicaly movie guys. Not conglomerate or bank-endorsed people." "There were giants in the industry. Now it is an era of midgets and conglomerates," is the way Otto Preminger described the change.

The trend of big business acquiring studios "bothers the hell out of me," says CAA partner Martin Baum, "because the great films were made by companies that were solely rooted in the film business. . . . They sank or swam based upon what they were able to do as film people. The people who own large corporations that acquire film companies don't know quite what to do with them. . . . You have to love the film business, know the film business to be good at it."

The studios used to be run by personalities, says producer Leonard Goldberg. "I'm not saying they were always right— God knows there are enough horror stories about them. But somebody stood up and said, 'I want to do this.' They don't do that anymore. It goes to studio committees. . . . Whoever heard of a committee making anything right? A committee made a camel."

Filmmakers are especially disturbed that the studios increasingly judge projects based on their marketing potential. Movies that are not sufficiently high-concept or that for some other reason the marketing division thinks will be difficult to sell are dropped.

Perhaps the new emphasis on marketing grows out of the frustration corporate management feels with its inability to predict which movies will make money. Marketing is more "scientific" than filmmaking and is a discipline that executives are familiar with from other businesses. Says Hellman, "There is something reassuring in the figures and market analysis in what is a terrifying business from their point of view. When you are gambling vast sums of money in what is an ephemeral process, it's like throwing money into the wind."

"[I]n the movie industry right now the middlemen known as 'sales' or 'distribution' are running the show," says former Fox vice-president Claire Townsend, who complains that, in the race to perfect the art of releasing blockbuster films, marketing and distribution executives have begun to dominate studio decision-making.

According to Townsend, "The beast known as 'market research' came into full being as the means for determining how best to lure the largest audience during the opening weekend, before people had a chance to hear from their friends that the picture was a turkey and its ad campaign a total lie."

And so the studios have discovered the ultimate way to lay off the risk of a bad movie—put it on the public.

WHAT'S COMMERCIAL

Considering the haphazard success of each year's movies, one might conclude the public is fickle. But studio executives refuse to accept that their business is ruled by fate. Instead they search for the secret that explains why some pictures succeed and others fail. Their dream is to discover the formula for success so one day they will be able to mass-produce hits in assembly-line fashion without any bothersome flops gumming up the works.

In the pursuit of this goal, they have formulated rules to explain what makes a hit. Experience derived from Hollywood's many years of moviemaking guides them. But the public refuses to cooperate in this noble venture. It continues to make blockbusters out of the most unlikely films and turn its nose up at seemingly surefire hits. And so the studios can count no more successes today than in earlier eras.

The inability of moviemakers to predict public taste has led screenwriter William Goldman to conclude: "No one person in the entire motion-picture field *knows* for a certainty what's going to work." In other words, "Nobody Knows Anything." Indeed, the most respected executives in the business regularly pass on scripts that become hits at other studios. It tells us something about the business, says producer Leonard Goldberg, that so many (an estimated 25 to 35 percent) of studio films come from scripts picked up in turnaround. "No other business has as its end product projects . . . [that have] been turned down by their competitors."

But rather than rely on their own judgment and taste, executives search for a formula to rely on. Rules, no matter how defective, comfort them by providing a rational framework within which to make decisions. Such principles can be used to justify decisions to boards of directors and provide ready-made excuses to filmmakers with unwanted projects. And they insulate executives from the frightening reality of how precariously they hold on to their jobs.

"Behind the lack of faith in their own judgment about doing something different from the hackneyed rules," wrote anthropologist Hortense Powdermaker in her 1950 study of the industry, "may be the fact that most of the top executives seem to be men without real understanding of what makes a good movie. When they have an unexpected success or failure, they appear unable to analyze the reasons for either, but attribute it to the public or to luck. In other businesses, successful designers of clothes, hats, jewelry and architecture launch new styles and take chances on their success. Theatre and publishing, which are taking on more and more characteristics of big business, still constantly take chances with new ideas. But the motion picture industry rarely has this courage, and its system of production discourages originality. This is not only detrimental to the artists who work in Hollywood, but also bad business practice."

"The great gamblers are dead," Steven Spielberg told the *L.A. Weekly*. "And I think that's the tragedy of Hollywood today. In the old days the Thalbergs and the Zanucks and the Mayers came out of nickelodeon vaudeville, they came out of borscht-belt theater, and they came with a great deal of showmanship and esprit de corps to a little citrus grove in California [Los Angeles]. They were brave. They were gamblers. They were high rollers.

"There is a paranoia today. People are afraid. People in high positions are unable to say 'okay' or 'not okay,' they're afraid to take the big gamble. They're looking for the odds-on-favorite. And that's very very hard when you're making movies. All motion pictures are a gamble. Anything having to do with creating something that nobody's seen before, and showing it, and counting on 10 or 20 million people, individuals, to go into the theater to make or break that film—that's a gamble. And I just think in the old days, in the golden age of Hollywood, gambling was just taken for granted. Today gambling is a no-no. And I'm sorry to see that go."

Spielberg says no one knows for sure how the public will respond to a film. "[George] Lucas was the most surprised kid on the block when *Star Wars* became a megahit. When I sat with George a few weeks before the film opened he was predicting $15 million in domestic rentals. 'Cause he thought he'd made a Walt Disney film that wouldn't have much appeal beyond very young pre-teens. And he had tapped a nerve that not only went deep but went global.

"[W]hen you actually make a movie like that," says Spielberg, "unless you are a preposterous ass, you never sit down and say, 'I have the spinal tap to end all spinal taps, this movie is going into the heart of America and never come out.' I've never felt that about any of my films. I always plan for failure, and I'm surprised by the success. I don't think any of us can . . . plan to make a movie that reaches out and makes a $100 million. I'm not trying to burst any bubbles here, I'm just telling you the truth."

There are many instances in which pictures thought to be certain failures became hits. Columbia Pictures had no faith in *Cat Ballou* (1965), says Frank Pierson, and would have dropped the project had it not signed a contract that guaranteed producer Harold Hecht be paid even if the picture wasn't made. So the studio assigned to the picture those people it had under contract whom it deemed losers. Pierson was assigned to rewrite the script because it was too expensive for the studio to fire him. Jane Fonda was chosen because her price was low. Lee Marvin, who was considered unemployable at the time, was also cast. "So they took all of us rejects," says Pierson, "and threw us into this damn thing and to everyone's astonishment it turned into this overwhelming success."

Despite the obvious shortcomings of the industry's rules, executives generally follow them—even if they don't always believe in them. Filmmakers find it difficult to interest studios in offbeat projects. Such movies must be made independently until their commercial worth has been proved.

The first principle of Hollywood moviemaking is that a successful movie must be entertaining. The theory is that people don't go to movies to be educated, enlightened or made better human beings, they go because they find it an enjoyable experience. Obviously there is some truth to this rule, as demonstrated by the many people who rush to see the latest Clint Eastwood movie compared to the few who watch educational films. As Alfred Hitchcock said, "The cinema is not a slice of life, it's a piece of cake."

The difficulty in applying this rule, however, is in determining what is entertaining. Some moviegoers enjoy the intellectual stimulation provided by *My Dinner with Andre,* while others prefer the more action-oriented approach of *Rocky.* Some people like pictures that frighten them, others like tearjerkers. Moreover, within genres it can be difficult to discern why some pictures are considered entertaining and others not. One horror picture is a hit, while another, equally gory one is a flop.

While Hollywood has not yet arrived at a precise definition of what is entertaining, it generally believes that escapist movies are more entertaining than ones that deal with serious subject matter. "Producers believe . . . movies succeed because they are diverting," says screenwriting instructor Robert McKee, "that people just want to check their brains at the doors."

But McKee believes just the opposite is true. "People go to the movies . . . to find meaning. . . . Whether they are aware of it or not people are entering into the watching ritual because life doesn't provide them with the patterns of meaning and sensation and emotional cohesion that they need. And so they go to the movies trying to figure out what it's like to fall in love, what happens when you do, what happens in war . . . and so on."

McKee contends that even with exploitation pictures, the essential ingredient for success is providing the audience with meaning. It is why movies like *Friday the 13th, Halloween* and *Alien* make a tremendous amount of money while their blood-soaked imitations fail.

"If you look at the originals you have a certain pattern," says McKee. "It goes like this: You have a group of people, perhaps in a spaceship like *Alien,* and each of them has a certain distinguishable trait. . . . Only one of them is going to survive. All the rest are going to be killed by the almost anonymous monster. The one that survives is going to have the right combination of courage, discretion, caution and smarts. The bold heroes, the foolhardy people, are going to get killed. The absolute running screaming cowards are going to get killed. The intellectuals are going to get killed. What you need is a balanced combination of brains, caution and courage. That is the one that is going to survive.

"The kids sit there and they love the action, they love the violence. . . . They say [to themselves], 'I'm cool, I'm careful, I'm courageous, tough, not foolhardy. I'm the right combination. I will survive.' [They] . . . are scared of the nuclear nightmare, the gangs on the street . . . and they need to have a positive image of what it takes to survive. [And] so my feeling is that it is no accident that a movie like *Halloween* finds an enormous audience."

Similarly, McKee thinks police stories are popular not just because of the action, but because there is a deep-seated need among the public to be reassured that justice will prevail. "Most of us . . . have a tremendous suspicion that there are lots of people out there carrying on in criminal ways and getting away with it, and we're fools for not doing it too. So we want to believe that there is justice in the world. . . . *Beverly Hills Cop* is a ritual in justice which says that in a corrupt world there is going to be a hero who is going to bring justice to the world. . . . [People] want to believe that justice prevails and crime doesn't pay."

But not many people in the industry subscribe to McKee's views. Most producers and executives operate on the theory that success is a function of sex, action, special effects and stars. Little, if any, attention is paid to a picture's meaning. Few heed the advice of legendary producer Sam Spiegel, who said: "The best motion pictures are those which reach you as entertainment, and by the time you leave have provoked thoughts. A picture that provokes no thoughts is usually not well conceived and does not entertain one anyway."

Although imparting meaning may be a prerequisite to entertaining audiences, it's not the only ingredient. If it was, we could expect that the most meaningful films would automatically be the most entertaining. They are not, because while a picture without meaning is boring, meaning alone does not make a picture entertaining.

What makes a picture entertaining defies easy categorization. Nevertheless, Hollywood has some very definite ideas about what is *not* entertaining. Documentaries, for example, are not considered entertaining. It is rare for Hollywood to produce one, even though television's *60 Minutes* is a highly rated documentary program watched by millions of viewers every week. Whether people will go to the theater to see what can be received at home for free may never be determined since the studios have long since given up on this form. (Exceptions are documentaries about pop culture, such as *Pumping Iron,* or those about rock music, like *The Last Waltz,* perhaps because such films have special appeal for young people.)

Similarly, pictures with a social message are anathema to Hollywood. "Messages are for Western Union," is an oft-repeated phrase of Sam Goldwyn. Stories that smack of proselytizing or make strong political statements are studiously avoided. The only exceptions are message pictures that are set in a suspenseful, comedic or otherwise entertaining genre. These are acceptable if the message is subordinate to a good story. The industry will make pictures like *The China Syndrome, Nine to Five,* and *Coming Home,* says Jane Fonda, because audiences can enjoy them whether or not they agree with the message, or are even aware of the message.

The industry is not so much opposed to messages per se as it is averse to unpopular messages that may reduce box-office receipts. Innocuous messages, such as those heralding Truth, Justice and the American Way, are never a problem. Indeed, they are not even considered message pictures. No studio ever rejected a World War II picture that glorified the American war effort because it had a message.

It's pictures that espouse minority views and challenge the prevailing attitudes or beliefs of the public that studios don't want to make. It has nothing to do with the message, it's simply that the studios want their product to appeal to the broadest possible audience. Thus, any story that may offend a significant segment of the moviegoing public is avoided.

That doesn't mean the studios are necessarily opposed to producing thought-provoking material. Such movies can bring prestige, win awards and provide periodic evidence to refute charges that Hollywood product is without socially redeeming value. But these stories are often handled in such a way that they won't offend audience mores. Sometimes a subject is treated in such a nonjudgmental manner that persons of diametrically opposing views can find validation of their beliefs in the same film.

The studios generally are not cognizant of a film's politics. Consequently, they will distribute conservative crowd pleasers such as *Red Dawn* and *The Green Berets*, along with liberal favorites like *Testament* and *In the Heat of the Night*. They will take on the oil industry (*The Formula*) and the establishment (*Easy Rider*). They will even poke fun at themselves if there is a profit to be made (*S.O.B.*). Their motives are purely mercenary.

Most Hollywood films do not appear to have any political point of view. Of course, what is political is in the eye of the beholder. Some viewers perceive political subtexts in what others consider to be innocuous stories. An example of such differing perceptions is offered by director Irvin Kershner (*The Empire Strikes Back*), who recalls being told by a Russian filmmaker that American films were highly political.

The Russian said, "You go see an ordinary [American] film and the telephone rings and somebody runs over and there is a telephone in the middle of the living room. And then you cut and the kid is talking on the telephone in his bedroom. In the hall you see . . . [another] telephone, and there is one in the kitchen. In Russia if you have a telephone it is in the closet so you can go in and close the door so nobody can hear you.

"Then you open a refrigerator in a film and it is stocked full of food and people are taking things out, spilling things, and grabbing food and running out. They are treating food as if it was nothing. My God that is propaganda. I'll bet that many of the people around the world are looking at that and not even seeing the picture. They are watching the food in the refrigerator. . . . You have a scene in a supermarket and the audience's eyes are bulging out. Cars are smashed up. . . . We wait five years to get a car. . . . Here you have kids driving huge cars. And we say to ourselves, 'How much gasoline does that car take to go a mile?' This is political."

While Hollywood avoids pictures with messages that may offend a significant portion of its audience, it is willing to tackle controversial subject matter if the controversy can be used to its benefit. As far back as the release of *Birth of a Nation,* it was noted that demonstrations could have a positive effect on the box office. When this film, which glamorized the Ku Klux Klan, was shown, riots erupted, generating publicity and swelling box-office receipts.

Likewise, when United Artists flouted the Production Code in 1953 by releasing *The Moon is Blue*—a movie whose dialogue included such then-risqué words as "seduce" and "virgin," a storm of controversy arose. The film was denied a Production Code seal, was condemned by the Catholic Legion of Decency, and Cardinal Spellman called on his diocese to boycott it—all of which only succeeded in boosting attendance. Apparently the public was anxious to sample the forbidden fruit.

But if a studio believes controversy will damage the commercial prospects of a film, the project is quickly jettisoned. In 1984 Paramount Pictures pulled the plug on *The Last Temptation of Christ* after protest by fundamentalist religious groups. The studio acted despite having spent $2 million in preproduction and having set a director and cast. According to producer Harry Ufland, the decision was precipitated by a theater chain owner who told the studio that he wouldn't book the film and would urge other exhibitors to follow suit. The man also owned several cable systems and threatened HBO that he would not run the film if they bought it.

As studios have been incorporated into conglomerates

they have become increasingly vulnerable to public pressure. Irate moviegoers can retaliate against Columbia Pictures by boycotting the products of its parent, the Coca-Cola Company. A small decline in its share of the multibillion-dollar soft-drink market can result in a loss greater than what the movie studio earns in a year. Consequently, conglomerate studios take care to avoid risqué material.

While Hollywood doesn't believe thought-provoking material is essential for a successful film, it does believe a film must provoke emotions. The theory is that, while ideas stimulate the intellectuals, what turns on the masses is a rousing *Rocky* ending that has them cheering in the aisles. That moviegoers respond to pictures emotionally rather than intellectually could be called the second great principle of Hollywood moviemaking.

Recent hits like *Jaws* and *Alien* are thought to have succeeded because of the visceral responses they evoked. The extent to which filmmakers go to manipulate the audience emotionally, says director Dick Pearce (*Country*), has become "kind of embarrassing. . . . There is a sense that if I create a particular kind of emotional response, the cash register will open."

Paramount vice-president David Madden says he was persuaded that the script for *Enemy Mine* would make a great movie because of the emotions it stirred in him. He first read it late one night after he returned home tired and slightly inebriated. "It was about two o'clock in the morning and I realized that I had cried four times while reading the script. And I don't cry very often. [I thought] either I'm so out of it that I've lost my judgment entirely, or this is something really bright.

"So I read it again the next morning when I was sober, and it still had the same impact on me. And I could sit and justify all the intellectual reasons that that script is a good script, but the key thing that stuck in my head is that it made me cry four times. That emotional reaction really made me believe in that piece. . . . Not because the dialogue was good, and not because the structure was intricate and clever, and all that, but because it made you feel."

But sometimes the strong emotional response engendered by a film alienates the audience. When a test audience viewed *Mike's Murder* they "went berserk," recalls director Jim Bridges (*Urban Cowboy*). "They started screaming at the screen. . . . They hated it. They booed, they hissed. Because the violence was so real. I had two black men cutting up a white boy and cutting his throat and the knife entering the heart and the blood spurting all over the wall. . . . Girls were heard crying in the lavatory after the screening, . . . saying, 'How can they expect us to go on with our lives after we've seen this film?' People said . . . the director should be lynched."

The reaction was so severe that Bridges recut the movie. But even the toned-down version was a flop. (Interestingly, horror movies that are equally brutal can be big successes, perhaps because the situations are so outrageous that they are not believable.)

Hollywood's preferred emotional response, however, is a positive one. "Today executives don't want anything with unhappy endings," says producer-turned-industry-analyst Jonathan Taplin. "You must have a hero. . . . They always ask, 'Who are you rooting for?' "

Indeed, this has probably always been the case. Historian Benjamin B. Hampton says that audiences in 1923 rejected *A Woman of Paris* because one of the lovers commits suicide. "The picture was an uncannily beautiful piece of work; [Charlie] Chaplin's direction was a masterpiece of characterization. *A Woman of Paris* won high praise from intellectuals, but the moment the lover committed suicide, Chaplin killed all chances of box-office success; . . . without a happy ending, pictures cannot hope to win wide approval, and no ending can be happy unless the final fade-out shows hero and heroine in a tight 'clinch.' The laws of the Medes and Persians are as wax in comparison with this adamantine statute of the American motion-picture audience."

Hollywood's criteria for selecting topics regularly changes because the industry believes subjects move in and out of public favor. There is some evidence to support this view. During World War I, pictures about the allies' struggle drew large audiences, capitalizing on patriotic feelings and the hatred of our enemies. When the war ended, however, the public quickly lost interest in war pictures, perhaps wanting to forget its horrors, and there was a resurgence of romance and adventure films.

In the late 1960s and early 1970s the slew of antiestablishment pictures (*The Graduate, Easy Rider, The Strawberry Statement, Joe*) can be interpreted as reflecting the interests of a generation immersed in social strife. Similarly, such 1980s hits as *Flashdance* and *Ghostbusters* conceivably mirror the attitudes of a more frivolous generation interested in dancing, fashion and having a good time.

But not too much faith should be placed in such sociological analyses, because in every era there have been many hits that ran contrary to the public mood. How can one explain, for instance, the success of such eighties hits as *On Golden Pond* and *Terms of Endearment*? It may be that there really is no such thing as public taste, that moviegoers are simply interested in well-told stories, no matter what the subject.

"At least Louis B. Mayer had a fix on America when he made *Andy Hardy*," says producer Edgar Scherick. "He shoveled that sentimental horseshit out there in carloads. But now . . . [society] is fragmented, there are different groups. . . . [Who knows what will catch] the fancy of this rather undefined, difficult to apprehend, polyglot people out there who now represent the American consensus, whatever that is."

Hollywood rarely ponders such philosophic questions anyway. Divining the public mood is unnecessary when the industry can simply look to box-office figures to learn what movies the public likes. Nevertheless, such a measure has shortcomings, for it cannot anticipate audience desires. It is as if the studios are barreling down a highway with their eyes fixed on the rearview mirror.

Such 20/20 hindsight makes the studios notorious copycats. Executives usually prefer to imitate a current hit than take a chance on something innovative. They are like "a herd of turtles," says Jane Fonda. "If one particular genre becomes successful [they all emulate it]. When *Easy Rider* . . . made a lot of money, everybody who came in with long hair and looked like Dennis Hopper and my brother got hired to do a film."

"The trends are all dictated by economics," says *New York Times* critic Vincent Canby. "The films that make money get made again and again and again." But it is questionable whether such a policy makes economic sense.

"The old adage is that *Animal House* ends up costing the industry fifty million dollars because everybody tries to clone it," says producer Al Ruddy (*The Godfather*). "Universal, after they did *Animal House*, figured that's it. . . . They did *Where the Buffalo Roam, Continental Divide, The Blues Brothers* [all of which performed poorly]. I mean that was the formula. [But] you come in [to the studio] with the next step . . . and it scares the shit out of them."

"I don't know of one major studio that has . . . [a single executive who] will make a film because it's something they like," says director Robert Altman (*M*A*S*H*).

"I'm sympathetic to these bright young men who come out of Stanford business school and come down here and try to run a picture studio," says veteran screenwriter Waldo Salt (*Serpico*). "How are they going to decide what to make, what the American psyche is, what it is going to respond to? They're not prepared for that. They don't have any reason to know anything about it.

"So they go to computers. Computers can't tell them anything. It could tell them what was popular last week. But it can't tell them what is going to be the new trend. In fact that will have to come out of some accident. All of a sudden *The Graduate* will come along, it is a totally fresh approach to material, and everyone will copy that for ten years."

Market research that asks the public what it wants to see is equally foolish, says Robert Altman. "They hire these people for the demographics and they go out to people standing in line and ask, What films would you like to see? What star would you like to see? What kind of story would you like to see? They're asking questions of these people and making their decisions based on the answers. The only flaw is that the question they're asking cannot be answered because what the public really wants to see is something they've never seen before. So they can't very well answer it. They can only say,

I want to see *Star Wars,* or I want to see *E.T.,* or I want to see *Ordinary People.*"

And so to meet these perceived desires, studios glut theaters with look-alike pictures and avoid genres in which there are no recent hits. Thus, in the early 1980s we find Westerns and G-rated movies are out while science fiction, romantic comedies and action/adventure yarns are in. Of course, this can change with the next hit. Gangster pictures were out until Paramount made *The Godfather.* Science fiction was untouchable until *Star Wars.*

While the popularity of each genre is cyclical, there has been a long-term trend toward more sexually explicit and violent films. In 1968, 32 percent of the pictures of major and minor studios were rated G. By 1984 that percentage had dropped to a mere 2 percent of the market. During the same time period R-rated films grew from 22 to 45 percent of all releases. PG films have remained fairly stable (about 40 to 50 percent), and X-rated films continue to be shunned, comprising 1 percent or less of studio product. (They comprise 5 percent of all pictures rated by the Motion Picture Association of America [MPAA].)

Because G- and X-rated films are considered box-office poison, studios will frequently recut a picture to avoid either rating. G pictures bear the stigma of family entertainment, a genre that studios believe the precocious youngsters of today disdain. In recent years only Disney has consistently produced such fare—with little success—and now even they have embraced more-adult subject matter through their Touchstone label. X films are avoided because of the difficulty in distributing them. Many theater owners won't exhibit them and many newspapers won't accept advertising for them. *Last Tango in Paris* was the most recent major X-rated picture distributed by a major studio. For those regions where the X could not be shown, an R version was made available.

The studios' aversion to X-rated movies doesn't preclude them from displaying considerable nudity and violence in their films, for as society's mores have changed so has the definition of X. Material that used to earn an X can nowadays be safely shown as a PG or R picture. The dramatic shift in standards is evident when one examines the industry's Production Code of 1930, which prohibited such acts as "excessive and lustful kissing," "suggestive postures," and such words as "damn," "tart" and "fanny." Indeed, it's remarkable how prescient the Code was in listing the acts that seem to comprise the basis of most studio movies today.

A second trend apparent from a review of Hollywood's movies is that youth-oriented films increasingly dominate the box office, while older moviegoers tend to be ignored.

"The studio has a basic rule," says former Fox vice-president Susan Merzbach, "and that is that the major film-going audience is fourteen to twenty. Therefore you please that audience. That audience is the one that goes to a movie more than once. . . . You have certain precedents. When *Porky's* appeals to them you suddenly go out and look for a *Porky's* type of movie. That is either teenage rites of passage, teenage sex comedy or teenage adventure. And that resulted in everything from *Sixteen Candles, Risky Business,* and *Porky's II* and *III.*"

As subjects are increasingly selected to appeal to young viewers, the nature of storytelling has been modified. Executives "believe kids have an incredibly short attention span," says Jonathan Taplin. "[You] can't let it drift for a minute, or they go to get popcorn." Taplin complains that when he turned in his ninety-five-minute film *Grandview, U.S.A.,* to CBS Theatrical Films, he was told it was too long.

To attract young viewers, younger actors are being given starring roles. "The youth market wants to see people their own age on the screen," says production executive Richard Fischoff. "Burt Reynolds may be out. Liz McGovern, Sean Penn are part of the new wave . . . Dustin [Hoffman] and Meryl [Streep] are character actors, not pinups. They [kids] want to be like Diane Lane, Matt Dillon, Tom Cruise and Daryl Hannah."

Many filmmakers object to what they consider the studios' slavish pursuit of young viewers. Screenwriter Peter Stone (*The Taking of Pelham One Two Three*) laments that "a grown-up is almost entirely frozen out of going to the movies. It's all comic strip. . . . There are three breakdancing movies, three science fiction pictures. . . . Where are the pictures about people? . . . . I think MTV in a two-hour version is what we are getting. . . . It's all Dolby, it's all loud, it's all fast, all startling, all violent, all prurient. Sexy is one thing, prurient is another. There is nothing wrong with adult themes. But these are smarmy. These are adolescent teenage sexual fantasies."

"Every other movie is a *Rocky* rip-off," says director Jonathan Kaplan (*Heart Like a Wheel*). "He had a dream, she had a dream. It's enough already. The whole sort of pandering to the teenage market, the narcissism of showing the audience themselves, and even that audience will get tired of seeing themselves, I predict. It's just boring. How many teenagers can you see not get laid, and get laid, and come of age . . . ? Everyone is running around trying to figure out what these mindless fourteen-year-olds want to see. I'm not saying we all have to sit here and solve the problems of Western civilization. Not every picture has to be *The Killing Fields*, not every picture has to be *Ordinary People*, but for Christ's sake let's make things we can be proud of."

A 1984 study commissioned by MPAA determined the breakdown of the moviegoing audience as follows:

Age	Percentage of Audience (figures rounded)
12 to 15	13%
16 to 20	23
21 to 24	18
25 to 29	13
30 to 39	18
40 to 49	8
50 to 59	4
60 and over	3

While the study found that most moviegoers are young (85 percent under forty), it cannot be said that they are predominantly teenagers (only 36 percent are from twelve to twenty years of age). Yet the studios often act as if they were their only customers.

Moreover, even if teenagers are the most important segment of the audience, it doesn't necessarily follow that only certain kinds of movies will appeal to them. "I think when you try to make a motion picture which is deliberately skewed toward a given age bracket," says agent Rick Ray, "you run into trouble. Because, among other things, I really don't think there is homogeneity among young people, whatsoever, any more than there is with middle-aged people, or old people. All my friends don't think the same. . . . We don't all have similar taste.

"It has already been proven categorically that if you produce something that's good you will get an audience at all age levels. *On Golden Pond* is probably the best recent example of that. That sure as hell is not a youth-oriented movie. Not by eight light-years. But young people went to see it, and middle-aged people went to see it, and old people went to see it . . . and I believe with all my heart and soul that if you make a good movie or good television show, people will watch it."

While well-made pictures may attract appreciative audiences and earn profits, that is not the goal of the studios. They want blockbusters, and believe that the only way to have one is to attract teenagers. "When the film history of this last few decades is written," says screenwriter Steve Shagan (*Save the Tiger*), "I think *Star Wars* [will be considered] . . . the watershed [film] that turned the perception around that our real audience is fourteen to nineteen [because they saw the film repeatedly]. And everybody over twenty-five, let's write them off. They stay home. They watch television. Come out once in a while."

Another advantage of teen-oriented films is that they often require neither great writing nor great acting. "It's easier because you don't need Redford," says Shagan. "You need a bunch of kids, girls in tight jeans with ample breast works and some sort of thin thread of a story. . . . If you can design . . . a teenage film where they're watching somebody through a peephole . . . and there are enough car chases and enough. . . . Perils of Pauline and there's enough titillation for teenage libidos, you'll get [a studio to make it]."

"Clearly kids don't demand much," says production executive Richard Fischoff. "If it's about them, has good music, they will go. And go repeatedly." "There are two audiences," says screenwriter Richard Kletter (*Never Cry Wolf*). "A built-in one, and an earned one. A not-discerning, and a discerning [one]. . . . The audience didn't come to see slick direction in [*National Lampoon's*] *Vacation*. They came to see Chevy Chase, a sort of dumb man's humor served with a smile.

"Hollywood is interested in movies where execution in acting, writing and directing doesn't have to be perfect for a film to be successful," says Kletter. "They want the story to be so strong that it can overcome problems in execution. . . . If you get fifty percent of what is inherent in a project, it will still work. . . . They want a fuck-up-proof story, so that even if Bozo the clown directs it, it will be OK."

A movie like *The Big Chill* was considered risky because it had to be well executed to work. The studios prefer such low-brow fare as *Porky's*, *Bachelor Party* and *Hot Dog*, films that have given new meaning to H. L. Mencken's description of the movies as "entertainment for the moron majority."

If teenagers have been demonstrating that no story is too insipid for them, adults have become more selective in the movies they see. "People don't go to the movies anymore," says distribution executive Leo Greenfield. "They go to see *a* movie. . . . People will watch TV or cable or rent a tape rather than see a substandard film at the theater." MGM president Alan Ladd, Jr., says, "They know they can see the film six months after the release . . . on cassette, nine months or a year later they can get it on cable. Unless it's something they really want to see, they will just stay home."

According to the MPAA, 41 percent of the public over eighteen years of age never go to the movies, while only 21 percent are frequent moviegoers who attend at least once a month. For those age twelve to seventeen, a mere 5 percent do not ever go to the movies, while 51 percent go at least once a month. The MPAA also notes that although frequent moviegoers constitute only 24 percent of the public, they account for 84 percent of all admissions.

"It seems to me that the industry is now divided into basically two film industries," says director Allan Arkush (*Rock 'n' Roll High School*). "The one film industry that caters to the moviegoing public, which is the young people and which is looked down upon by everyone else, and has a certain amount of cynicism attached to it, but basically supports the rest of the film business. And then there's the one that gets Academy Awards, where people have a sort of snobbish attitude and they make a limited number of movies and those movies are the ones that are extremely dependent on stars. And so what you have there is a lot of powerful stars and a lot of powerful directors and they make a limited number of movies which are wonderful movies. And those are the ones that grab all the attention and some of them make money and some of them don't."

Arkush says adults have no right to complain about what movies are made since they generally don't go anyway. "I've had many people come up to me . . . and they say, 'Why don't they make movies for us anymore?' And I say, 'Because you don't go. You will only go to see *Ordinary People*. . . . Why don't you go out and see some of the more marginal movies?'. . . . The older crowd will only go to see [the best movies, while] . . . the younger crowd goes to see lots of different things."

The major studios' desertion of older moviegoers is even more apparent when one considers that they do not make many of the serious pictures they distribute. Three of the five 1984 Academy Award nominees for best picture were financed outside of Hollywood (*Amadeus* by Saul Zaentz, *The Killing Fields* by Goldcrest, *A Passage to India*, primarily by Thorn EMI). Both the 1981 Academy winner, *Chariots of Fire*, and the 1982 winner, *Gandhi*, were made with foreign financing.

Today Hollywood seems willing to tackle adult-oriented material only when major stars or directors can be obtained to ensure its success. "I think you can probably make anything," says director Nicholas Meyer (*The Day After*), "as long as you have a big enough star attached to it. Barbra Streisand said she wanted a *Yentl*. Guess what. Meryl Streep said she wanted to play Karen Silkwood. Guess what. . . . If Steven Spielberg announced plans tomorrow to film the Manhattan phone directory, he'd have people offering him the financing. And that's not an exaggeration."

7

BREAKING IN, MOVING UP, HOLDING ON

Dressed in designer clothes, they drive to work in Mercedeses and Porsches from their homes in Beverly Hills and the posh communities on Los Angeles's west side. They earn hundreds of thousands of dollars each year, spending their days screening movies, attending meetings and lunching at fine restaurants. After hours they attend glamorous parties with the rich, beautiful and famous. They are the Hollywood elite, the stars, top executives, producers, agents and filmmakers.

They seem to have a wonderful life-style. It certainly sounds more appealing than selling insurance or teaching. And so thousands of young people flock to Hollywood each year, hoping to join their ranks.

But most newcomers are woefully unprepared for the task. They don't understand how the business works, or what is required of them to succeed. They are drawn by stories of overnight success—myths perpetuated by the news media, which rarely mention the hard work, years of sacrifice, and repeated rejection that are endured before success is achieved. No stories are written of the thousands of hopefuls who depart in despair.

"It's the myth that brings the prettiest boys and girls from high schools across the country to Hollywood to become stars," says Lawrence Jackson, vice-president of the Samuel Goldwyn Company. "They end up pumping gas and making sundaes and contributing to the most incredible gene pool in the country."

"The percentage of people who make it in this business is minuscule," says Chester Migden, president of the Association of Talent Agents. He estimates the success rate at less than 1 percent. "There are thousands of young people who come here every day. They wander the city. Hollywood is a magnet. We do it in a way ourselves by creating the glamour. And it's attractive to young people. How could it be otherwise? But the reality of making it in the marketplace is very very difficult.

"The reality is that highly professional actors, writers, directors, producers, all of them across the board, people who have been in the industry, find it very difficult to get employment. . . . What is misleading, terribly misleading about Hollywood, is that there are a finite number of spots and hundreds of thousands of kids trying to break in. There is a tendency to lose perspective about the possibility of success. There are simply too many people who uselessly try. . . . No one would dream of joining the Lakers without being a number-one draft choice. But when it comes to acting, people just declare, I want to be an actor [without any training]."

"You've got to be neurotic, insane or totally obsessed to make it in this business," says producer Al Ruddy (*The Godfather*). "What other business demands that you gamble the most important thing that you have in your life, your time? When you're young, that time is crucial, because if you don't make it at a certain point, you're not going to [be able to then] work as a junior executive at General Motors. Along that way, your chances of what we call a normal life are also very difficult, because of your anxiety—worrying about whether you are going to make it. You don't have any money. There's very little opportunity to start working, so you must sustain that fantasy you have. And this is the most horrendous part of it: Even if you're willing to suffer the anxieties, even if you're willing to give up the things other people want, the chances of making it are still one in a thousand. You wouldn't play odds like that in Las Vegas, would you?"

Yet despite the odds, the movie business has not lost any of its luster over the years. Indeed, it has become a respected and prestigious calling. Veteran producer David Brown (*Jaws*) remembers: "When I went to Hollywood the idea was that you were selling out. You were going only for the money. No self-respecting journalist, actor, writer, wanted movies except to make more money than they could make in more legitimate fields. Today it is an art form. And people will kill to work in film. . . . They will do anything. And I mean anything.

"We are inundated by people who wish to get into this business. . . . It reminds me of the days when I was in the book-publishing business many years ago, when every girl who got out of Vassar, Wellesley and Smith wanted to work in a publishing house.

"The desire of young, intellectually agile and gifted people to be part of the motion-picture world is so intense that there is no use in trying to discourage anyone. Many sons and daughters of some of my good friends who could do anything they wish are working on screenplays. That is what they want to do in life. They want that life.

"It isn't the glamour. They are not looking [to meet handsome men or beautiful women]. . . . It is a magnetic feeling that the motion-picture form is so pervasive in the world . . . that they want to be in on that. . . . The passion to get into it doesn't seem to me based on money. . . . There is much more money in Silicon Valley, in retail stores, in advertising, in commercials. But people are willing to leave careers in commercials, careers in television, where they make far more money, to be in film and get a feature made."

Whether the motivation be glamour, fame, wealth or art, the movie business attracts the best and the brightest of America's youth, as well as a lot of the mediocre. But the individuals with the greatest artistic ability are not necessarily the ones who succeed. What then are the traits that make for success?

Hard work and tenacity are the two characteristics universally mentioned by industry veterans. "If someone is good and they're willing to stick around and fight the battles, they will win in the end," says production executive Debra Greenfield. "Despite how brutal it is, those with perseverance will break through."

Producer Don Simpson says, "I worked so hard that I went five years without speaking to my [best friend and former roommate]. . . . Five years I never said a word to him. All I did was my job. It takes that kind of commitment. I don't know anybody who has made it who doesn't do it that way. And you won't, in this business. Anytime I see someone come into this business who is smart and talented and has all those things and likes to go to lunch and dinner and party, I know he has failed already. He hasn't got a prayer. Because someone like me is just going to run over him."

Some Hollywood veterans say blind obsession is required because anyone who has a realistic view of the odds against him would give up. "If you analyze it enough you realize it is impossible," says producer Jerry Hellman (*Midnight Cowboy*). "And if you recognize that it's impossible then you lose the will to keep going and get something done. Survival for people like myself depends on believing that it's possible."

Besides great determination, there are several other traits that make for success. "Social skills are as important to success as filmmaking ability," says agent Rick Ray. "For some people social skills have carried them way beyond their talent." As writer Clay Frohman puts it: "You can't be a complete social retard because so much of the business is social."

The congenial have an advantage because work is often obtained as much on the basis of who you know as what you know. Producers and directors tend to hire from their coterie of industry acquaintances or those recommended by them. Job openings are rarely advertised.

Cliquishness is bred by the premium placed on working with individuals one knows and likes. Because filmmaking requires close collaboration over extended periods of time, nobody wants to be stuck with someone who is sullen, irascible or otherwise difficult to get along with. And since collaborators are so mutually dependent, those who have proved their competence and reliability will be favored over untested newcomers. The individual one has worked with may not be the most talented person in the world, but he is a known quantity. With strangers, on the other hand, one never knows what one is getting. Impressive credentials can be misleading. A writer may have received sole credit for a screenplay rewritten by others.

But if it's important to be congenial, how does one account for, as one producer describes them, all those "obnoxious, disgusting, cruel and egomaniacal" people who succeed? These people succeed in spite of their disagreeable personalities because their talent is so enormous, or their power so great, that other people are willing to submit to their abuse. Most of the offensive behavior is directed to underlings. When dealing with their peers or superiors, these people are able to undergo a remarkable transformation into charming individuals.

Those who succeed in the industry are also distinguished by their political savvy and flexibility. They understand how the town operates and know when to stand on principle and when to compromise. "The people who are successful," says producer Leonard Goldberg, "in addition to being creative, understand the system. They understand how to work within the system, they understand how to use the system, or at least how to cope with the system.

"It is a very fine line [to walk]. You have on one hand people who won't compromise at all and are very difficult to deal with. . . . They say, 'I won't compromise my integrity.' . . . And everyone at the studio is waiting for them to fail so that they can jump on them. And these people are allowed a very slight margin of error. When they make a mistake or a misstep, they are jumped all over and it is very hard for them to get back in again.

"On the other hand, those people who at least on the surface are willing to deal with the system are given a certain amount of leeway, and second and third and fourth chances. That is not different from other aspects of life and other businesses. If you are a total crazo you better be right every time."

Notwithstanding the importance of talent, hard work,

congeniality and savvy to success, luck also has a role to play. While luck will not be of much help for those who lack the other prerequisites, it often determines who gets a chance to demonstrate ability.

"Success is based on hard work and quite a bit of luck," says producer Jon Avnet (*Risky Business*). "A lot of people don't know the first thing about what they are doing, they just get lucky."

Avnet says that when he entered the industry, "I, like every other idiot, thought that things worked on fairness. Talent. I was surprised that fairness had little to do with it. Although I do believe that talent will ultimately win out, it doesn't get you started.

"I mean *Beverly Hills Cop* is a different movie with Sylvester Stallone than with Eddie Murphy. I'm not saying that Jerry [Bruckheimer] and Don [Simpson] are just lucky. They're quite good producers, in my opinion. But the coming to-gether of Eddie Murphy in that project certainly made it much more than it would have been with Sylvester Stallone. . . . Those are the kind of things that are freaky and you don't have control over when you start out."

The difficulties and uncertainties of an industry career breed certain personality characteristics. Because there is a widespread belief that luck and relationships count for more than talent, many develop a cynical attitude. The feeling of many people in the industry, says one psychologist, is that "working hard, doing good work, being loyal and paying your dues count for nothing in Hollywood. The law of supply and demand is so incredible that you find people willing to com-promise their souls to work in Hollywood. It breeds a kind of a person who is invested completely in power and money, and human considerations and concerns are secondary. I would say that this type of person is prevalent in the industry."

Such people will assiduously court those in the industry who can help them. "I was at a Filmex [film festival] screening and met this really beautiful young French girl," recalls pro-ducer Tom Greene. "We were seeing *Pinocchio* of all things, and at the end of it I had tears in my eyes. She had tears in her eyes and she turns to me and says, 'I just love a man who can cry at the movies. I work at Filmex. Would you be interested in seeing a screening tonight?'

"So I said, 'Sure,' and met her that night for the screening. Afterward she said, 'I would love to have a drink with you but I am only nineteen years old. Can we go back to your place for a drink?' So I thought, 'Oh, wow, this is wonderful.' So she came to my house and spent the night.

"The next morning there is a loud knocking at the door and I hear a guy shout, 'Marie.' She says, 'Oh, my God, it's my boyfriend.' He finally gets in the house, comes upstairs and sees her sitting there stark naked. So I, the brave person I am, run downstairs into my office.

"They are screaming at each other upstairs. Then all of a sudden it is very quiet. I'm thinking, 'Oh, my God, he has killed her.' Ten minutes later I hear footsteps coming downstairs. I grab a paper spindle on the desk to protect myself. I think I'm going to die.

"He comes into the office and sits down on the couch and stares at me. I think, 'Oh, fuck.' Nobody says anything for a long time. Then he says, 'So Marie tells me you are a producer.' I say, 'Yeah, yeah, sometimes.'

"He says, 'You know, I have this script.' I said, 'That's great!' I was so relieved. He actually sent me a script and it was terrible. That [incident] really is what this town is all about."

The desire to be in show business is so widespread that it permeates life in Los Angeles. "I was shooting a low-budget feature in [a tough downtown neighborhood]," recalls Greene, "and a car comes screeching around the corner with a cop car after it. The car crashes into a wall and two guys jump out with shotguns. The director is shouting, 'Shoot this, we can use this.' The cops get the guys to put down their guns and then begin handcuffing them. We come running over and one of the cops asks us what we are doing. We tell him we are making a movie and show him our permit.

"He says 'fine.' And with his gun still drawn, he says, 'You know I used to do a lot of acting in high school. Do you guys ever need cops for your films?' The director says, 'Oh, sure. All the time.' And while the cop is talking to us, one of these guys turns and runs away. I scream, 'Hey, the guy is going!' And the cop says, 'Let me ask you a question. How do you get into SAG [Screen Actors Guild]?' And the guy got away. Absolutely true.

"The funny thing was three years later I am auditioning actors and this cop walks in. He now had a SAG card and is taking acting classes."

There are many different ways to enter the industry and build a career. It is largely a bootstrap business without initiation rites or designated steps for promotion. Each person cuts his own path. Breakthroughs can occur at any time. It is the "most wildly democratic business," says agent Nan Blitman. "Today's receptionist is tomorrow's vice-president of production."

Academic training can help prepare one for an industry career but it by no means assures entry. The competition is so great that graduates of film, law and business schools often have to swallow their pride and begin their industry careers as secretaries or messengers.

Few formal training programs exist. CAA and William Morris operate two of the more renowned ones. Trainees work long hours in exchange for an opportunity to learn the ropes of the business. It is "unaccredited postgraduate training in masochism," says former CAA trainee Greg Moscoe. Other trainees liken the experience to basic training in the army.

The programs have been criticized for their unscholarly approach. "All it does is teach you where people live and it puts a lot of wear and tear on your car," says a studio executive who started in the CAA mailroom. "There was no learning process. In the mailroom you had college grads running foolish errands for agents." Such tasks as waxing an agent's car, chauffeuring a spouse, buying an enema, delivering a fecal sample and scoring cocaine are mentioned as some of the more bizarre assignments.

But most graduates think the experience was valuable. They "verbally abuse you every minute of every day for two years," says one graduate. "It's like hazing in a fraternity.

They tell you you are a piece of shit. [However] when agents whip you, beat you, they are teaching you how to survive in Hollywood. After I was asked to get directions to a restaurant and couldn't get through, I was yelled at for not calling up the *Los Angeles Times* food critic for directions. They teach you by yelling at you. It was the greatest experience of my life."

"In the mailroom you learn who everyone is," says CAA alumnus Ken Sherman. "You begin to learn the politics . . . you listen in on agents' phone calls. They encouraged it so you would learn how deals were made." Former CAA trainee Terry Danuser says, "You learned the language used and how to talk to people. How to negotiate. How to get what you want."

"At CAA for two years I learned more than in my four years of college and three years in the industry," says one graduate. "It was invaluable as an education." Says former William Morris trainee Johnny Levin, "It's such a business of personalities . . . I don't know how you appreciate and learn that in an academic environment."

The agencies like the training programs because they provide inexpensive labor. "It's cheaper than hiring secretaries," says Moscoe. "It's much cheaper. They pay trainees less and [the trainees] work more because they are going after the carrot, the implied promise of becoming an agent." Some participants, however, do not feel they were exploited. "I figured it would be a good learning experience," says CAA alumnus Adam Fields. "Rather than my paying a couple of thousand to go to school, they paid me a couple of thousand to learn."

But the training programs are a lot tougher than school. "It sorts out the less determined. Weeds them out," says manager-lawyer Michael Meyer, who worked in the CAA mailroom for seven weeks before quitting. "You have to really want it. It's a grueling process. You deliver mail from eight A.M. to nine or ten at night. There is no lunch break. I have never been so physically exhausted in my life." By one estimate, 60 percent of the trainees drop out.

Despite the hardships of the training programs, there is

no shortage of applicants. One graduate explains that "the only place to start is in the mailroom of the big . . . agencies. Or as an NBC page. Those are the only places you can really learn the business." William Morris has provided the start for so many executives and producers that it has been dubbed the "Harvard Graduate School of Show Business."

"Assistants are enticed by the idea of being an agent," says Danuser. "That enthusiasm lasts about six months. Then you realize your chances are very limited there. It takes about a year to quit."

"At CAA they would know right off whether you would ever be an agent," says a former trainee. "They would lead people on to think they would make it. But it never happens. When asked, they won't say no. They give an ambiguous answer. They want to keep a good secretary."

Because so many young people believe working for agencies is an excellent entrée into the business, the agencies can be selective in choosing trainees. They look for young, bright, aggressive and highly motivated individuals. Those with advanced degrees or powerful connections are favored. "A lot of the people who make it into training programs are sons of, nephews of VIPs in the industry," says Moscoe.

Like any corporation, he adds, CAA wants people who are resourceful but who will also be good soldiers and toe the company line. Nonconformists have difficulty advancing. Moscoe believes his casual attire and the pet piranha he kept on his desk (labeled "Bruce the CAA mascot") dashed his chances of becoming a CAA agent.

But some trainees do earn their agent stripes. "I think I was the fastest trainee to go from the mailroom to agent," says Johnny Levin of his twenty months as a William Morris trainee. He credits his background as an English major as the key to his success. "All of a sudden I had a reputation that if you need something read well and quickly, give it to Levin. . . . I had agents seeking me out. And when you are a little shit in the mailroom, the secret is to have someone take note of you."

One estimate is that for every fifteen trainees only one or two will become agents. But many of those who don't make the grade develop relationships during their training that help them secure jobs with producers, studios and other agencies. "Most of the people I was in the mailroom with three years ago are now making more than a hundred thousand dollars a year," says a former CAA trainee.

Moreover, even if a trainee does not graduate to immediate riches, he benefits from the friendships made within the program. A strong camaraderie is forged among those who have suffered the trials and tribulations of training. "You grow up together," says Levin, who now has an industry-wide network of close friends.

While the CAA and William Morris training programs are the best-known launching pads into the industry, there are others. The Directors Guild offers an apprenticeship program of four hundred days for those who want to become assistant directors or production managers. Participants receive a modest salary as they learn union and guild regulations and other practical production knowhow. Approximately 1,100 people take the aptitude test each year to enter the program. Fewer than 20 are usually accepted.

Many industry observers believe the best method of breaking into the business is to write one's way in. "If someone asks me what is the easiest way to break into the movie business, there is only one answer," says producer Don Simpson. "Write an original screenplay. There is no easier way. There is no quicker way, no cleaner way. There is no more certain way. You can go to all the schools you want, get all the degrees and have all the connections. Write an original screenplay that's good and you'll be a star overnight. It's automatic, it's a lock, a given."

Walter Parkes and Lawrence Lasker broke into the industry that way. Their first script, *WarGames*, became the hot new script in town, says Parkes. "It was handed agent to agent. Everyone was taking us out to lunch and was interested in what we wanted to do. Even before *WarGames* was made we were able to make a deal at Twentieth Century-Fox to write another original [script]. Then when *WarGames* came out and was a hit, on the strength of that we made a deal at

Paramount to write and produce. . . . Then Spielberg wanted us to write *Peter Pan* for him. So we did that and had a great time working with him." The twosome are now producing a picture called *Project X* for Fox.

But most of the scripts written by aspiring screenwriters do not open any doors for their authors. "I read what others send me," says screenwriter-turned-executive Gary Devore (*Back Roads*). "You would be amazed at how many people spend months burning the midnight oil writing a script and the result is absolutely horrible."

Screenwriting appears deceptively simple, but "it's a lot tougher to write for the entertainment business than most people think," says agent Rick Ray. "Every person who sits out there and says 'My God, I could do better than that.' Well, it's not so. Ninety-nine and nine tenths of them can't do better. It's a genuine skill as well as a craft, and it's not so easy to do." Ron Koslow (*Into the Night*) says it took him fifteen years to master screenwriting—which is far longer than it took him to graduate from film and law schools.

"There aren't a hell of a lot of people who can write a shootable screenplay starting from scratch," according to Frank Pierson, who says about fifty writers out of the six thousand members of the Writers Guild can do it. "The rest can hack a scene and know a few things, but that's it."

Pierson explains that "there are a lot of matters of screen grammar which require some learning from the inside out. You go to school and you can be told about these things but unless you understand what rhythm and tempo mean in terms of dramatic structure, nobody can explain it to you. Writing a good movie is like writing music. You are thinking in terms of: This scene moves swiftly and then suddenly it comes to a stop. Then you go into another kind of scene with a different feeling and tempo and rhythm to it."

A common failing of aspiring screenwriters is that they don't understand the kind of stories that interest studios. They select subject matter deemed uncommercial, construct scenarios too expensive to shoot, and neglect to write roles for existing stars.

Moreover, "Writers don't think of original ideas," says

Don Simpson. "Film school has destroyed the screenwriting process. Film schools have taught kids to think about movies, not about life. . . . They are emulating former films. And that's just exactly the wrong thing to do [although that's what producers often request]. . . . They choose the wrong ideas. They either try to be trendy or are derivative."

Veteran agent H. N. Swanson says he avoids representing novice writers because "nine times out of ten it is a rehash of something they saw or read and will get them sued for plagiarism."

Because the industry is deluged with so many bad screenplays, the problem for the gifted beginner is how to have his work recognized from the "sludge." Many producers and most executives return unsolicited manuscripts unopened, so as not to waste time and to avoid possible lawsuits from writers claiming their screenplays were plagiarized. Even if frivolous, the lawsuits are bothersome to defend.

Consequently, new screenwriters often resort to unorthodox means to call attention to their scripts. "A writer friend of mine wanted to get onto the Paramount lot," recalls producer Tom Greene, "so he decided to parachute in and get some publicity for his screenplay. Unfortunately, the wind carried him across the street and he landed in a porno lot."

A more frequent approach is to enlist intermediaries, whether they be gardeners, pool men, tennis instructors, exercise trainers, astrologers, gurus or anyone else willing to pass along a script. (Sometimes these go-betweens become producers in the process.) Other writers have tried a more direct approach, advertising in the trade papers or renting billboards.

Industry functions and seminars provide additional opportunities for access. "Anytime anyone speaks at USC or UCLA, there are sixteen guys with scripts standing around backstage," quips veteran writer I.A.L. Diamond (*The Apartment*). They think they can get that lucky break if somebody will read their script. If Mr. Lucas or Mr. Spielberg gets interested, they got it made."

With so many writers trying to break in, competition is intense. "It's a very rough racket these days," says Diamond.

"There are sixty thousand film students, of whom thirty thousand come onto the market every year." Gary Devore says, "It took me thirteen years to sell something. If I had known how tough it was, I would have become a bank robber instead."

Until a writer has an agent representing him, he will have difficulty submitting his scripts to potential buyers. "If you want to sell writing to the studios you virtually need to have an agent," says writer-director Nicholas Meyer (*The Day After*), "because there are so many trees that have been ground up into screenplays that there are scarcely enough people to read them. So the agent acts as a kind of screening house, a clearinghouse."

Agent Rick Ray agrees: "Without an agent it is awfully hard to function in this business if for no other reason than ninety-eight percent of the potential marketplace won't even look at material submitted without one. Part of that is protection from a legal point of view, but part of it is the sure and certain knowledge that the agent, who is not operating an eleemosynary institution and is there to make money, must see something in this writer or he wouldn't be wasting his time. If that is so, then maybe there is something worth pursuing."

But agents, like executives, generally won't accept unsolicited manuscripts. Moreover, they are reluctant to represent a beginning writer until he has demonstrated his marketability by selling a script—a difficult task when no one will read your work. It took writer Lawrence Kasdan (*Raiders of the Lost Ark*) six scripts and five years to get an agent.

There are, however, a few mavericks in the industry who will take a chance on new talent. Actor-director-producer Tony Bill (director, *My Bodyguard*) has assisted many newcomers, including writer David Ward (*The Sting*) and actress Jennifer Beals (*Flashdance*). After Robert DeLaurentis (no relation to Dino De Laurentiis) completed his first screenplay, he mailed it to Bill, whom he had never met. Although it was sent without the benefit of even a cover letter, Bill read it, liked it and hired DeLaurentis to write a script for him.

It's the rare individual like Bill who says: "I trust my

instincts, my taste. I don't need to know that other people agree." But many industry members are so lacking in confidence in their own ability to discern talent that they wouldn't hire a newcomer even if they liked his work.

The encouragement of veteran television writer Robert Schiller kept Gary Devore going for ten years. Schiller said Devore had written the best first script he had ever read. "Many years later," Devore says, "I thanked him and told him how much it had meant to me. He had no idea. You have to find those little things because you're not going to find big things in the beginning."

While breaking into the industry for writers is tough, for directors the task is next to impossible. Indeed, many directors only get their chance to direct after they have established themselves as top writers. Holding their script as hostage, they refuse to sell it unless the studio will let them direct.

"The way the business operates," says writer-director Colin Higgins (*Nine to Five*), "you need something to sell. You don't start out with your hand out. You go with your hand full. What you do is create a script. That was always the easiest way . . . because if you have a script and you have someone who wants to buy it then you can decide on what terms you're going to sell it."

One writer who did just that is Richard Tuggle. After being fired as editor of a health magazine, he bought a book on screenwriting and moved to Los Angeles. With only a few thousand dollars to his name, he spent six months researching and writing a screenplay about a famous escape from Alcatraz prison.

Tuggle then went to the Writers Guild and received a list of agents who would accept unsolicited manuscripts—agents Tuggle describes as "usually the worst." He also submitted his screenplay to anybody else in the business he could cajole into reading it. "You use whatever connections you have to get your work read by people in the industry," he says, "whether that be contacting a cousin's dentist or a friend's uncle."

Everyone who read Tuggle's script rejected it. They said it had poor dialogue and characters, lacked a love interest, and that the public wasn't interested in prison stories. "I soon realized that those in the business didn't know anything," he says, "because I had written a good screenplay."

He decided to bypass producers and executives and deal directly with filmmakers. He called the agent for director Don Siegel (*Dirty Harry*) and lied, saying he had met Siegel at a party and the director had expressed interest in reading his script. The agent forwarded the script to Siegel, who read it, liked it and passed it on to Clint Eastwood, who agreed to star in it. *Escape from Alcatraz* was a box-office hit.

With a credit to his name, studios offered Tuggle writing assignments. He agreed to write *Earthquake II* for Universal, but his script was abandoned when the sequel to another disaster movie performed poorly. He agreed to rewrite *Rough Cut* after a series of writers had been dismissed from the project, only to soon join them. He then wrote a screenplay about drug smuggling for Fox that was shelved. "I fell into the mishmash of Hollywood," he says of the period.

Discouraged but not defeated, Tuggle set himself a new goal: to direct. He committed himself to sit in a room and write until he had a great script. He wrote ten drafts over the course of a year. Each draft he showed to friends, asking them to critique it, knowing that if he could not get them to like it, there was little chance of selling it to a studio. "The first three [drafts] everyone hated," he says. "The next couple, people felt mixed. The last ones, people said, 'This has a chance.' "

Tuggle knew that he would have an especially difficult time persuading a studio to produce his script since he was demanding that he direct it. "Studios never want to take a chance with a first-time director," he says. "If the director is lousy and the picture shuts down, the studio can lose everything. So they would rather take a mediocre director who they know will deliver. The slight benefit from good to great is not worth the terror they feel in taking a chance on a first timer."

To make the project more palatable to a studio, he tried to recruit a star for it. When Clint Eastwood said he wanted to do it, Warner Brothers agreed to let Tuggle direct. *Tight-*

rope was a success, and Tuggle's directing career was launched. "You have to take chances before you're lucky," Tuggle says in retrospect. "Because I was willing to take the chance and risk a year working on a script, I put myself in a position where I could get lucky."

Some aspiring directors produce a short film in an attempt to persuade studios to let them direct. Production executive Susan Merzbach says a good short will convince her to hire a director. "I'll hire you as a director the moment I can see that you can direct," she says. "Show me that you're talented. All I need is proof that you can do it."

But most executives and producers are reluctant to hire someone to direct a full-length feature on the basis of a short. After making several impressive shorts at UCLA, writer-director Colin Higgins showed his work to executives and was uniformly told: "Well that's terrific. . . . You can do short films, that's what it proves." No one was willing to let him direct a feature.

However, shorts are useful for getting a student in the door to see producers and studio executives. Lawrence Bassoff used his twenty-minute comedy about an outer space–themed Bar Mitzvah as his calling card. "Everybody goes around saying they want to direct," says Bassoff, "but they have no film to show. You have to go out and shoot something so you have entrée."

But it may take many meetings to get results. "You have to be willing to push, to knock on doors and be willing to go back," says Bassoff. "It took me several years to scope this out. There was no book on it. You have to go out there and knock heads with these people. Some are nice, some are not. It's an incredible roller coaster every day. . . . It's a treasure hunt out there . . . you look under every rock. . . . You have to be tough. You have to be willing to have people tell you your ideas and your short film are no good."

After three years of showing his short to anyone who would sit still to watch it, he finally received an offer from Crown International Pictures to write and direct the low-budget film *Weekend Pass*.

Many directors start their careers with low-budget features that more experienced directors are unwilling to accept because of the meager wages and spartan working conditions. "The first film is very important," explains director Richard Pearce (*Country*), because it requires someone to trust you enough to risk a lot of money on your unproven ability to direct."

Producers Sam Arkoff and Roger Corman have launched the careers of a generation of filmmakers. Arkoff financed John Milius's first picture, *Dillinger*, and released Brian De Palma's first hit, *Sisters*. Corman gave such directors as Peter Bogdanovich (*Targets*), Francis Ford Coppola (*Dementia 13*), Joe Dante (*Hollywood Boulevard*), Ron Howard (*Grand Theft Auto*) and Martin Scorsese (*Boxcar Bertha*) their starts. While these films lack great artistry, they gave the directors an opportunity to learn their craft and graduate to better pictures.

Jonathan Kaplan (*Heart Like a Wheel*) was offered his first feature when his NYU film instructor, Martin Scorsese, recommended him to Roger Corman. When Corman telephoned him at 4 A.M. to make the offer, Kaplan thought the call was a prank, and hung up. Fortunately, Corman called back. He offered Kaplan $2,000 to rewrite, direct and co-edit *Night Call Nurses*. Kaplan jumped at the opportunity and shot the film in thirteen days. Although he felt the film was "the worst thing ever made," it did well at the box office. Corman then asked him to direct a similar story about student teachers. Kaplan's directorial career was off and running.

After *The Student Teachers* was screened, Roger's brother Gene made Kaplan an offer. Because he liked the way Kaplan had handled a black subplot in *Night Call Nurses*, Gene asked him to direct a black exploitation picture, *The Slams*. Despite his unfamiliarity with the genre and the fact that he is white, Kaplan made the film. It earned him credentials as a black exploitation director, which led to his being offered another such film, *Truck Turner*, for Sam Arkoff. That film opened to great business in Chicago.

When *Truck Turner* was released, Kaplan's treatment for a film called *White Line Fever* happened to land on the desk of Columbia executive Peter Guber. Guber read in the trade papers that Kaplan's *Truck Turner* picture had broken box-office records in Chicago, and must have figured, says Kaplan, that it was a movie about trucking, and that *White Line Fever* was going to be Kaplan's next truck movie. Of course, the first movie had nothing to do with trucks; *Truck Turner* was just the name of a character. But Columbia agreed to make the film. Out of such quirks careers are made.

Another route to the director's chair is by way of the legitimate theater. Writer-director Jim Bridges (*Urban Cowboy*) began his career by leaving Los Angeles to direct an Off-Off-Broadway play in New York. He frankly admits that he went East because "I knew I'd be reviewed, and I knew that it would say in the paper that he's a director. Then I could come back." Indeed, he was able to parlay his New York debut into directing several plays in Los Angeles. Then, armed with the reviews of his plays and a script called *The Baby Maker*, Bridges got his chance to direct a film.

But talent doesn't necessarily determine who gets a chance to direct. "It's not a matter of 'Can you?' " said the late Robert Aldrich (director, *The Longest Yard*). "It's who is going to let you. You see people who probably could be marvelous directors if somebody would say, 'You start tomorrow.' It really has so little to do with qualification and so much to do with luck that you're very reluctant to tell young people that the harder they work the more chances there are for them to get a start. It really isn't true. You see dummies get opportunities who don't deserve it. Then you see people who are entitled to a shot and they don't get it."

Increasingly, those tired of waiting for their lucky break are making their own feature films outside of Hollywood. John Sayles (*Return of the Secaucus 7*) and Susan Seidelman (*Smithereens*) directed independent low-budget films with such skill that studio offers quickly followed.

David Zucker, Jerry Zucker and Jim Abrahams took the independent route after the studios rejected their proposal for *Kentucky Fried Movie*. The studios said audiences didn't like movies comprised of sketches. But the three believed in their material, which they had honed in front of the audiences in their 140-seat improvisational theater. And so they decided to make the movie on their own.

A wealthy real estate investor offered to finance the picture if they would write a script. But after they completed a screenplay, the investor had second thoughts and decided that he didn't want to finance the picture alone. He said he would try to attract other investors if the three filmmakers would produce a ten-minute excerpt of the film, which he would finance. But when the trio presented a budget for the short to the investor, he backed out.

However, the prospect of shooting the short so excited them that they decided to pay for it themselves. The ten-minute film cost $35,000, and with it they approached the studios anew. This time they attached a young director named John Landis to the project. The studios again turned it down.

Curious as to how audiences would react to their film, they persuaded exhibitor Kim Jorgenson to show it before one of his regularly scheduled movies. When Jorgenson saw the short he "fell out of his seat laughing." He was so impressed that he offered to raise the money needed to make the full-length version. By having his fellow exhibitors screen the film before audiences in their theaters, he convinced them to put up the $650,000 budget.

Kentucky Fried Movie was a box-office success, returning domestic rentals of $7.1 million. For their next picture, the threesome decided to write a film parodying the series of *Airport* movies. They spent a year writing *Airplane!* and then submitted it to the studios. Every one rejected it. Returning to their theater-owner friends, they were surprised to be turned down. The exhibitors liked the material but thought it wiser to make a sequel to *Kentucky Fried Movie* than try something new. They suggested that the *Airplane!* material be incorporated as part of a sequel. The filmmakers declined.

The movie might never have been made had it not been for Susan Baerwald, a reader at United Artists. She loved the script and was disappointed when her studio turned it down. One night, over dinner with her friend Michael Eisner, then president of Paramount Pictures, she mentioned the *Airplane!* script. Eisner was intrigued. He immediately got up from the table and called Paramount executive Jeff Katzenberg and asked him to track down the screenplay.

Eisner and Katzenberg liked the script but wanted an experienced director to make it. Even though the project had been turned down everywhere else, the three refused to part with the project unless they could direct it. After protracted negotiations, Paramount relented with the proviso that if they were not happy with the dailies they could bring in their own director. Fortunately, the Paramount executives liked what they saw.

Airplane! was a huge hit at the box office, bringing Paramount domestic rentals of $40 million while costing a mere $3.5 million to produce. Since then the three writer-directors have been actively courted by the studios. They have gone on to make the feature *Top Secret* and the television show *Police Squad* and have numerous projects in development. "It's amazing what a difference a hit picture makes," says Jerry Zucker. Adds brother David: "The movie business is impossible to get into or out of. Once you succeed there is so much pressure put on you by executives to continue."

Jim Abrahams credits their success to single-mindedness and determination. "We've seen a lot of people with more raw talent come and go. [But] they get distracted by drugs, women, etcetera." Jerry Zucker says their success is a result of having taken control of their careers. "When we first came in, we had the attitude that some big producer would discover us. . . . Later we decided to take things in our own hands." "You have to ignore ninety percent of the advice you get," says Abrahams, who notes that they lost several years because an agent had told them sketch movies were a waste of time.

While writers and directors find it difficult to break into the industry, for actors the path is truly tortuous. At least writers and directors are able to take the initiative and demonstrate their ability by writing scripts and making their own films. But actors can't show their talent until they first persuade someone to give them a role. "As an actor you're always waiting to be invited to the party," says Tony Bill. "You have to wait for the person casting a movie to put you in the perfect part."

The barriers against beginning actors are formidable. Usually one must be a member of the Screen Actors Guild (SAG) to be considered for even the most minor parts. While low-budget productions will use nonunion crews and non-Guild writers and directors, they almost never employ non-SAG actors.

To join SAG an actor must convince a production company that is a SAG signatory to hire him. But a producer's agreement with SAG generally requires him to give hiring preference to SAG members. One exception allows the producer to hire a non-SAG actor when no SAG member is available or qualified for a part. Thus, if the role calls for an Albanian midget who speaks French and can do motorcycle stunts, the producer will have little difficulty demonstrating his need to hire a non-SAG actor. But if the part calls for someone more ordinary, the producer hires outside the Guild at the risk of incurring a financial penalty.

An actor could conceivably join SAG by establishing his own production company, have it become a guild signatory and then hire himself. But this is an expensive scheme not within the means of most actors. Admission is more typically gained by taking advantage of a provision that allows directors to upgrade extras during production. If the director adds a line to the script during production and assigns it to a nonspeaking extra, even if that line is just a shout from a crowd, the extra becomes a "day player" eligible to join SAG.

Another way to join SAG is to transfer in from its sister unions in the fields of television (AFTRA) or live theater (Equity). Persons who have been members of AFTRA or Equity for a year and performed in a principal role in at least one production under their jurisdiction are eligible to enter SAG. AFTRA is easy to join since it is open to anyone at any time. Therefore, the aspiring actor has only to enroll and obtain a speaking role in a soap opera, commercial or other taped television show in order to get into SAG.

But once an actor joins SAG his troubles are far from over. The number of persons pursuing acting careers has increased enormously. Today an actor competes against 58,000 other SAG members for parts. (There were only 8,218 SAG members as recently as 1953.) The number of roles are so limited that at any time 85 percent of SAG members are unemployed. Consequently, few members are able to support themselves from acting alone (75 percent earn less than $3,000 a year). Beginning actors usually receive SAG minimum-scale payments for their work, which in 1985 is $361 a day. Many only work a couple of days a year.

Beginning actors are always at a competitive disadvantage. Says casting director Mike Fenton, "There are too many people . . . we are more aware of." For even secondary roles, casting directors look for actors whose names on a billboard might mean something to the public, perhaps piquing its interest. "What you try to do is put together a cast with people who have some visibility," explains Fenton.

Because casting directors have so many actors to choose from, they usually will not even consider hiring one who does not have an agent. So many candidates have representation that there is little need to look further. Moreover, negotiating with actors can be exasperating. They often do not understand the fine points of deal-making and they tend to become emotionally involved in their negotiations. It's far easier to deal with someone with a professional demeanor who understands industry shorthand.

For the beginning actor, getting an agent can be an insurmountable obstacle. Explained the late Joyce Selznick, a casting director, "It takes an enormous amount of spadework to take beginning actors and go through all the beginning motions of introducing them to casting directors and getting them their start. It's very painful, it takes a long time, and it costs the agent a lot of money. So for the most part, agents don't like to fool around with unknown people. It takes so long that by the time they've made all those steps to get an actor started, he has already gone off to another agent."

Actors go about seeking representation in a variety of ways. Some wander around town dropping off resumés at agents' offices. This approach rarely works, because agents want to see an actor perform. Consequently, to gain exposure, actors will take roles for little or no pay in small theater productions. They also appear in showcases sponsored by acting schools. Here short scenes are performed before agents lured in with a free lunch.

Of course, actors sometimes employ other, more outrageous, methods. Agent Ken Sherman recalls a particularly memorable encounter with an actor and actress. The pair offered to act out a scene for him in his office, and when Sherman agreed, they stepped outside to change into their "costumes." The scene began as the actor returned in his Jockey shorts and lay down on the couch. The actress entered, removed her clothes down to sheer bra and panties, and began singing at the top of her lungs. Sherman was aghast, and worried that a VIP visiting next door might drop in to find out what all the noise was about. Needless to say, the performance did not get the pair an agent.

A more businesslike approach to breaking into the business was used by Northern California resident Peter Coyote (*E.T.*). He had his San Francisco agent arrange a series of meetings for him with casting directors in Los Angeles. After each meeting he wrote the person's name and physical description and the topics they discussed on an index card. He then began corresponding with each one. "I sent them that book or article we talked about," he recalls, "and I dated it on my file card. And every month I would go through those cards, and if I had reviews out I would send them with a little note. . . . That impressed them. And they began to talk."

A Hollywood agent heard about Coyote, flew up North to see him in a play, then signed him. "Everyone seemed to think that you couldn't do it and live out of town," says Coyote. But his domicile was an advantage because it allowed him to correspond with casting directors who probably wouldn't have returned his phone calls had he lived in Los Angeles.

No matter how an actor obtains an agent, there remains the problem of securing work. Agents can only propose their clients for parts that may be appropriate for them. Ultimately, the actor must win the role himself, often in an audition.

Auditions are not ideal settings for demonstrating acting ability. It's especially difficult to perform cold readings, where actors are handed the script on the way into the room without time to prepare. "I never really understood what anybody gets out of a cold reading," says Steve Railsback (*The Stunt Man*). "It's not acting, it's not doing the character. I know some actors who can read great, but can't act worth a damn. Other actors can't read at all, but they are great actors."

"Cold readings are very difficult to do and I'm not sure they have anything to do with acting," says personal manager Michael Meyer, "but they determine if you get the job." Consequently, learning the art of auditioning is an integral part of becoming an actor.

"The key to auditioning well," says Jane Fonda, "is learning how to both concentrate and relax at the same time. One must be able to ignore distractions and focus intently on one's performance while also being relaxed enough to let one's creative juices flow. A literal interpretation of the script is usually not impressive. What matters is . . . whether the actor brings you surprises. It is not just reading naturalistically. It is 'do they bring you any presence . . . are they aware of the subtleties.' "

Sometimes an audition is in the form of a meeting to discuss the role. Peter Coyote says the key to success here is "understanding that ninety percent of the people that you meet know absolutely nothing about the art of acting. They'll ask to see film on you, which is a big mistake [to supply] because the only film they're going to be satisfied with is film of you playing the role they have in mind. They can't extrapolate.

"So when I go in for a role I try to find those aspects of my personality that are already close to the role and emphasize those in the meeting. Or find some opportunity to tell a story in the meeting that will reveal those attributes. Because when you tell a good story you act it out. So a story is the perfect cover for acting, without saying, 'Hey, I am acting for you.' And then they think they've discovered you. They think they saw something. Because most of them have no idea of the mobility and external plasticity that an actor can have. When they want a neurotic ship captain they hire a neurotic ship captain.

"After I did *E.T.*, I got twenty offers for compassionate

scientists in science fiction movies. After I did *Cross Creek,* I got twenty offers for laconic Southern gentlemen. After I did *Timerider* I got twenty offers for psychopathic idiot cowboys. So you have to understand they don't know anything about the art except for a few of the very best."

Some actors believe it wise to stay in character in all their dealings with casting people so it appears they are the character. It can be difficult to detect the impersonations of a proficient actor. American actress Lisa Eichhorn spoke with such an authentic-sounding accent that she was able to trick veteran director John Schlesinger into hiring her for *Yanks.* Because Schlesinger was only willing to audition English actresses, Eichhorn's agent warned her that she must deceive him if she hoped to get the job.

Eichhorn passed two screen tests and was awarded the part. But she felt guilty about lying and several days later confessed she was an American. Schlesinger dismissed the revelation, saying: "Oh, I know that." Several years later he admitted that she had indeed fooled him.

It's the audacious actor who often wins the part. Although Teri Garr failed to pass the first round of auditions for the play *West Side Story,* she marched right into the finals, figuring nobody would remember she had been cut. Sure enough, she got the part.

The "chutzpah" approach helped Peter Coyote land a part in a prison picture. "I went to an open cattle call to read for a one-liner, as a leg breaker," he recalls, "and when I walked into the room it was full of guys who could have ripped my thighs off and beaten me to death. Next to these guys I was not going to convince anyone that I was a leg breaker.

"There were sides [pages of script] spread all around the room. So I looked through about fifteen sides and found this one marvelous soliloquy written for a sixty-year-old con. . . . And I worked on that soliloquy for two hours as I sat there. And then I went in for this one-line audition and I said, 'Gentlemen, I would like to audition with this speech. I know I am up for a one-liner, but you can't possibly learn anything about my work in one line. I have waited two hours, and I know you are running late, but could you give me the courtesy of hearing this speech?' And they did.

"I read the speech and they all looked at each other. And I got that part. They rewrote it for a thirty-five-year-old guy . . . that taught me a lesson. . . . 'If they don't say no, you're not asking for enough.'"

Mastering the art of auditioning is important because it's a skill needed throughout one's career. Even veterans are asked to audition. Only stars are spared the ordeal.

Actors usually solicit work for many years before they become sought-after talent. Great performances and reviews have little impact unless an actor is in a high-visibility production. Actors are only considered as good as the films they are in, said Joyce Selznick. "Unless they're in a runaway hit, whereby their exposure to the public is so tremendous that they become known overnight, they can forget it. If they're in a film that doesn't make it, even with good notices, they start their career over again. They look for the next picture that is going to do it for them."

"In every career it's one picture that shoots them up," says director Jim Bridges. Shrewd agents are less concerned with wages a beginning actor can earn than with getting that breakthrough role. A part in the next Steven Spielberg film can be a tremendous career boost and enable the actor to get top dollar next time out.

But there is little an actor can do to generate that breakthrough role. Notwithstanding all his dedication and talent, he often must wait a long time to be offered the right part. As Boris Karloff said, "You could heave a brick out of the window and hit ten actors who could play my parts. I just happened to be on the right corner at the right time."

Moreover, unless an actor has mastered his craft while awaiting his lucky break, all may be for naught. You need "a foundation of craftsmanship beneath you to be able to capitalize on luck if it should strike you," says Paul Newman. How one obtains that mastery without a regular opportunity to work is a dilemma many actors face.

Just as writers, directors and actors struggle to break into the business, so do producers. Many serve lengthy apprenticeships as production managers, agents, personal managers or studio executives. A good number of writers, directors and stars also become producers, often in a dual capacity.

And then there are the pseudoproducers, who know little about producing but wear the title. This can be anyone from unemployed hustlers to wealthy businessmen willing to finance a production. "We find appalling those people who are called producers who don't know the first thing about producing," says Producers Guild president Renée Valente. "Most of these people don't perform the function, are not capable of performing the function and don't want to perform the function," says producer Walter Coblenz (*All the President's Men*). "They just want to see their names in lights."

The Producers Guild has been unable to restrict who may be designated a producer because it does not have a union contract with the studios, which have refused to recognize the Guild on the grounds that producers are part of management. The National Labor Relations Board has agreed with this and therefore declined to intervene. Without government intercession and lacking enough clout of its own, the Guild aligned itself with the Teamsters in the hope that their muscle might force the studios to negotiate. Under threat of a strike, the studios have finally relented, agreeing to negotiate with the Guild on issues of mutual concern but still refusing to recognize it as a labor union.

Until the Producers Guild and the studios can come to terms on who may be designated a producer, such credits can be freely assigned. Because it doesn't cost the studio anything to bestow such credits, they're frequently used to reward stars, writers, agents or anyone else who has a hand in putting together a deal or needs to be placated. But the proliferation of credits has diluted their value. When a picture is loaded with "associate producers," "co-producers," "supervising producers," and "executives in charge of production," the credits become meaningless.

Today it's unusual for a picture to have just one producer. Notwithstanding the titles given to pseudoproducers, the producing function is generally split in two. The person who arranges the financing, packages the project and cuts the deals is designated the "executive producer." The supervision of the logistics of production is given to a "nuts and bolts" guy who is referred to as the "line producer," and whose screen credit reads "producer." (However, executive producers sometimes take the producer credit in order to be eligible for the Academy Award for best picture.)

In the old studio days one person would handle all the producing chores. Such individuals had a solid grounding in the intricacies of production, and made creative contributions to their films as well—often conceiving the idea, developing the story, casting the picture and supervising the editing. Nowadays studio executives and directors handle many of these tasks. Picture making has suffered as a result. Moreover, the traditional producer exercised great authority over his productions and was able to keep a tight rein on temperamental stars and profligate directors.

The traditional producer became an endangered species when studios began to deal directly with stars and directors and, in their haste to attract them, let them hire their own producers or function as producers themselves. When a producer is hired by those he ostensibly supervises, he is no longer in charge. Even when the producer does the hiring, he is often not able to exercise much control over his director and stars. In the event of a dispute, the studio will side with the star or director, the producer being the more expendable commodity.

The new species of producer who has evolved by ingratiating himself with a star or director may be reluctant to exercise authority over cast and crew in the belief that it's important for everyone to like him. Says producer Martin Bregman: "Some of the young producers are more interested in having dinner with the star than in keeping in touch with what is happening on the set."

"Unfortunately, most producers today call themselves producers but what they really do is stay in their offices and make phone calls," says Don Simpson. "That's why producers have . . . gotten a bad name. They're not filmmakers by and large. They're deal-makers. And they're not developers. They don't know anything about script. They are businessmen.

They are smart with money. The good producers are self-generators. They come up with original ideas. [The others] go to lunch. They wait for agents to give them scripts. They're packagers."

Depending on their background, individuals make the transition to producing in different ways. For the businessman who has made his fortune in another field and now wants to try producing, the key to success is surrounding himself with experienced hands and hoping he learns the business before he runs out of money. Shopping-center developer Melvin Simon financed a number of flops before he had a hit with *Porky's*. He has subsequently closed shop and left the film business.

Writers and directors who become producers need to learn deal-making and the logistical aspects of production. Agents and attorneys can help with the former, while an experienced line producer can help with the latter.

Steven Spielberg and George Lucas are two of the most successful writer-directors who have graduated to producing. Their experience as filmmakers makes them ideal supervisors and collaborators for writers and directors, and their stature in the industry allows them to exercise great control over their productions. They're the modern-day equivalent of the traditional producer. It may be that only those producers who have been successful filmmakers can amass that much authority today.

Stars have a history of using their clout to take control of their films. Back in 1919 Mary Pickford, Charlie Chaplin and Douglas Fairbanks (with D. W. Griffith) formed their own studio, United Artists. They hired others to handle most of the producing chores so they could concentrate on their acting. Today, stars like Clint Eastwood, Goldie Hawn and Robert Redford own production companies that make their pictures.

Another way to become a producer is by working one's way up the production side of the business. Walter Coblenz began as first assistant director on *Downhill Racer* for director Michael Ritchie and producer Robert Redford. He was later promoted to production manager and subsequently became the producer for Ritchie and Redford on *The Candidate*.

The advantage of this route is that the producer gains hands-on experience in all aspects of production. "Few people in the film business who . . . are producing actually know the first thing about what goes on at the set," says producer Jon Avnet (*Risky Business*). Avnet began his career as a gofer for producers Fred Weintraub and Paul Heller (*Enter the Dragon*). When he complained about how little he was being paid, Weintraub responded that Avnet should be paying them for the experience. "And now, twelve years later, [I think] he's right. I mean the experience you get is invaluable."

No matter how one first becomes a producer, it's difficult to sustain a career. Studios don't value producers as much for their skill as for their projects. Rarely will a studio suggest stories to a producer, or bring him into projects it's developing, as it does with stars and directors. When a producer is no longer able to deliver desirable packages, his career is over.

Thus the burden is always on the producer to initiate projects. He is an independent entrepreneur for whom each picture is a struggle. He must overcome the resistance of frightened studio executives to convince them to make his movies. "The average office you walk into," says producer Leonard Goldberg, "is an office where they hope they'll be able to say no. Saying yes puts themselves on the line. Not making a picture isn't a bad decision because nobody can criticize you. Making a picture sets yourself up. And since they have so little faith in their own ability, they would rather say no."

"You can't just go in and get a film made," says Martin Bregman. "You have to fight for it. It's first time out every time. A little better, but not much. It's selling. It's pounding on doors. It's hard."

Historically, women and minorities have found it especially difficult to break into many occupations in the industry. While the blatant prejudice of earlier eras is rarely seen today, barriers still remain. These obstacles are largely the residue of past discrimination.

"The fundamental problem is that we don't know people," says producer Moctesuma Esparza (*The Ballad of Gregorio Cortez*). "It's a very insular and incestuous industry, and you have to gain membership in the social circles."

"It's a schmoozing business," says producer Topper Carew (*D.C. Cab*). "The main problem that black filmmakers face stems from the fact that . . . this business is decades old and it's only in the past ten years that we've begun to see black people in the center of it."

"The town is run on cronyism," says a woman studio executive. "The men grew up together and these relationships govern the industry."

"There is still a well-known old boys' network and there is no getting around that," says MGM vice-president Mary Ledding. "It's perhaps less obvious than it used to be but it's still there. . . . It's shocking to see wonderful men, well-meaning men who, when it comes down to hiring women, will say straight-facedly, 'I would love to hire women but there is just no one with twenty years' experience.'. . . The difficulty is that they don't seem to understand that nobody is ever going to get twenty years' experience unless they start hiring them."

Notwithstanding such complaints, women and minorities have made substantial strides in the industry, and many observers believe they will continue to advance. "I think things are changing," says Carew, "because Eddie Murphy, Richard Pryor, Lou Gossett, Michael Jackson . . . are major box-office attractions and it is more and more obvious that our talent is an integral factor in this business. . . . If you got a relationship with Eddie Murphy you can talk to anybody in the world. It cuts clear across color because the bottom line is the dollar. If you can help guarantee the success of a picture, people will automatically forget about your racial characteristics."

Women have made the most dramatic progress. Says Ledding, "There are a lot of women who have moved into executive capacities, having begun as assistants or secretaries to men. You see women now having opportunities . . . in union situations. You never thought women could work in any capacity of production that involved lifting or any kind of dangerous work or Teamsters. . . . Over the last ten years those barriers have broken, in large part through legislation and activism on the part of women."

Producers Guild president Renée Valente asserts that women today have a much easier time than ever before. "In the last eight to ten years the doors have opened. . . . [They] are totally open now."

Indeed, the promotion of women to important positions has become almost commonplace. "The best thing I have seen recently for women is that we no longer have our token women," says producer Willie Hunt. "Columbia doesn't feel that they need to have a woman. Tokenism is maybe a necessary step but I'm glad we are past it."

Nevertheless, many women feel that they still have to be better than their male counterparts to get a job and that they are not permitted as many mistakes as men once they are on the job. Says Valente, "I think it behooves women to be prepared and know what they're doing before they take the job because a woman has to be twice as good as a man. . . . There is still a proving process going on."

To help each other gain the skills needed to succeed, women in the industry have organized Women in Film. The group has 1,200 members, and sponsors educational seminars and events where women can meet each other and exchange information. The organization has become something of a counterpart to the old boys' network. Blacks and Latinos have their own groups, although their efforts have been less visible than those of the women.

With the enactment of equal-opportunity laws and the end of officially sanctioned discrimination, women say that the principal remaining barrier to their progress is psychological. Hunt asserts that while women have achieved a great deal in the past twenty years, there has not been any noticeable change in men's attitudes toward women. Ledding says, for example, that when veteran producer Ray Stark spoke at a Women in Film awards ceremony, he praised an honored guest for having "the best legs of any editor he had ever seen." Women in the audience booed, objecting to his characterization of the editor as a sex object. "Ray's comments . . . are so typical of the industry," says Ledding. "The heads of studios take an avuncular attitude toward women," says production executive Susan Merzbach. "That makes them affectionate and pretty respectful but if you want more, or ask for more, or demand more or make waves, they take it in a very personal way. What's difficult for females in this industry to have is any power."

If power is defined as the authority to green-light a project, then indeed no women or minorities have it. But only the handful of men who head studios have such power, and even they serve at the pleasure of their boards of directors.

Their own psychological barriers also hold women back. "We have a self-image problem," concedes Ledding. "We never see ourselves in those positions. We don't have an internal picture of being head of the studio. We were never taught to think like that."

The lack of role models makes it difficult for women to know how to exercise whatever power they obtain. The methods used by men generally don't work well for them. Women who act tough and aggressive are likely to be considered arrogant and bitchy rather than strong.

"Being assertive doesn't work," says director Tamar Hoffs. "That gruffness is unpleasant in a woman. So you have to find a way to take charge without being too tough. . . . [But you] can't be a wimp, a baby [either]. You can't use any of your normal attention-getting techniques [e.g., crying]. You have to take advantage of what you know. I create a family situation. I take care of everybody. I become a good hostess in terms of social skills." Most women find they can achieve more with charm than by wielding a bludgeon.

Some women say they're at a natural disadvantage because they're more sensitive and less ruthless than men. "I can only do what I think is honorable and that's a handicap," says a woman former-executive. "Those who succeed are the ones who are completely self-serving, tough-minded, driven and goal-oriented to the exclusion of the feelings of others. When the men executives get in a fight they don't get hurt, they strike back. Women are particularly vulnerable because we hurt easily and we take it personally. We need to take tough pills."

But other women point out that they have some inherent advantages over men. "I think what we've got going for us is terrific," says executive Barbara Boyle. "We are natural negotiators, mediators, mothers, emotional responders. Those are terrific attributes. I would hope we're not going to do things the same way as men."

As newcomers to the corridors of power, women are often naïve about studio politics and corporate intrigue. "Women don't really understand how the game is played," says Ledding. "They think that if you work well and do good you'll be recognized and you'll be rewarded. It simply doesn't work that way. You get ahead because you make people realize you are indispensable or you are important or you are intelligent or somehow you toot your own horn and let them know and demand that they recognize your ability. We need to be more aggressive in the way we position ourselves. And also women need to take more risks. I think there's much more complacency on the part of women. They like a secure position."

Some occupations in the industry are more open to women than others. Besides the clerical and secretarial positions they have traditionally filled, many women work in the "pink ghettos" of casting, publicity and story departments. On the production crew they tend to be script supervisors, editors or work in the makeup, hair, wardrobe or art departments.

Generally, women are not found in positions where great authority over others is exercised. There are few women directors or producers. As studio executives they tend to work in development, where their nurturing skills are appreciated. "It's very difficult for a woman to be placed in the mover-and-shaker category or the connector category or the facilitator category," says Willie Hunt. "Women are regarded as developers and only as developers. I always thought, 'Gee, isn't it wonderful that I'm considered a really great developer.' But then I realized that that's all you're ever going to be allowed to do."

Few women work as electricians, grips or camera

operators—jobs traditionally considered too physically demanding for them. Women who have attempted to join these unions complain of harassment. "Every woman I've met who had something to do with the unions has been blatantly propositioned," says former studio executive Susan Rogers. "It's always, 'I can help you, if you help me.' "

Women have prospered as agents and attorneys. There are many respected women agents and a few, like Sue Mengers, have joined the elite group of packagers. Women attorneys have also made progress. Christine Cuddy says, "I don't perceive being a woman attorney as a problem. There are some women and some men who want a female attorney. It's probably more of an advantage."

The most powerful women are the stars. Cynics say they're the only ones with real influence. Since Mary Pickford, women stars have been able to more or less dictate the terms on which they are willing to work. Barbra Streisand was not only able to persuade MGM/UA to produce *Yentl*—a story thought to have limited appeal—but also convinced the studio to let her make it as a first-time director.

Most women in the industry today believe their prospects are bright. "The only thing holding us back is ourselves," says Barbara Boyle. "Women are starting to learn what they need to learn. . . . By sheer numbers we're going to end up as leaders." Says Ledding, "It's a good industry for women to be in because it's more flamboyant, you have more room for personalities, more characters. So it's probably not as bad [for women] as banking or insurance."

"You can make it work for you in this town," says personal manager Dolores Robinson, who is black. At meetings "there are always nine Jewish guys with beards, the agents, and a dozen blondes with the same nose. I stick out. People remember me."

There are several other groups subject to discrimination that deserve mention. Gays are sometimes discriminated against, says Chris Uszler, chairperson of the three-hundred-member Alliance for Gay and Lesbian Artists in the Entertainment Industry (AGLA). "I think there are a fair number of people who work in the industry who don't discriminate at all, they could care less. And there are others who still have a problem.

"This business is a strange one in that deals are made on napkins in the Polo Lounge. And so it is very relationship-oriented, very personal. . . . Being gay sometimes can really cause problems with that. Even though someone might not be openly prejudiced, the sense is that gay people are not one of the gang, not one of the guys. . . . So when they are thinking of making a promotion or hiring someone, there's something that just doesn't feel right. . . . They ask themselves, Can we trust him?"

Gay actors are particularly concerned about the public's prejudices. "The fear is that the American public doesn't want to see performers who are openly gay or lesbian," says Uszler. "To be a movie star, there is more than acting involved. There is this whole persona about you. People want to find out about your personal life, they want to know who you are dating. . . . At this point [this was before Rock Hudson's AIDS disclosure] there haven't been any openly gay or lesbian actors to speak of. And those who have sometimes had rumors go out about them have seen damage to their careers."

Interestingly, the occupations in which gays are concentrated tend to be the same ones women often fill: wardrobe, makeup, hair dressing and publicity. There are also a fair number of lesbians in editing and stuntwork. It is not clear whether these clusters reflect the preferences of gays or discrimination against them.

Through AGLA and informal networks of friends, gays have helped each other advance in the industry, sometimes to such an extent that heterosexuals complain of a "gay mafia."

Perhaps the most pervasive form of discrimination in the industry today is based on age. In Hollywood the young are worshiped and the old discarded like yesterday's fashion. "There is no industry on the face of the earth that's as youth-oriented as the entertainment industry," says agent Rick Ray.

The discrimination arises from the pervasive belief that young filmmakers and executives know best what young moviegoers want to see. "I think that is horseshit," says Ray.

"Anybody over the age of twenty-seven hasn't lost touch with civilization. But you would think so, looking at the entertainment business."

Ray complains that no one wants to hire older writers. "One man is a former Academy Award nominee, has a long list of truly terrific credits . . . and I cannot get him arrested. The primary reason is because he's a man in his late fifties. . . . And the vast majority of people who are responsible for making decisions to hire somebody are so much younger than this man that they don't know who the hell he is."

Young producers don't want to work with writers older than themselves, says veteran writer I.A.L. Diamond. "The producer doesn't necessarily want the writer of *Casablanca* working for him. They sense that maybe he knows more than they do. It threatens their authority. They would rather have a twenty-five-year-old screenwriter who they can boss around, and pretend to know a hell of a lot more than they do."

"Strangely enough there are only two ways that you can grow old gracefully in the entertainment business," says Ray. "If you achieve the very highest level . . . you can grow old and everybody will love you because you're so damn talented that they can't ignore you. Or you can become an agent. . . . Everybody else is in [increasing] trouble every year they [get older, especially after forty] . . . which is just an inordinate waste of manpower."

The most bizarre form of prejudice found in the industry is the bias against persons who have grown up in California. Producer-director Malcolm Leo says, "I grew up in Los Angeles and went to New York to get into the film business. There is a geographical prejudice if you are from L.A."

Production executive Lisa Lieberman thinks the reason so many individuals from the East Coast dominate the industry is that they have more drive. "It is persistent and aggressive traits that succeed . . . [and consequently] there are relatively few Californians in high places here." When it comes to the rough-and-tumble of moviemaking, those who have grown up in a mellow environment are not highly regarded.

DEAL-MAKING

"Today we spend eighty percent of the time making deals and twenty percent making pictures," complains veteran director Billy Wilder, echoing the frustration of many filmmakers. Indeed, it appears deal-making has replaced filmmaking as the principal activity of Hollywood. In the early days of the industry, a director, for example, might make three or four pictures a year. Today he is lucky to make one.

Granted, directors then were just hired hands brought in to supervise shooting. And, granted, filmmaking was less technologically complex (although such advances as portable camera equipment and improved film stock make filmmaking faster). And, of course, more films were produced in those pretelevision days. But none of these changes adequately accounts for the shift in emphasis from filmmaking to deal-making. That change has largely come about from the breakup of the old studio system.

"The major difficulty today," says writer-director Frank Pierson (*Dog Day Afternoon*), "is that the studio system has become so fragmented that virtually every single idea is developed as a separate enterprise of its own." Assembly-line production has been replaced with a haphazard system in which executives juggle writers, directors and stars in an attempt to create viable packages. With talent no longer under long-term contract, many individual deals need to be negotiated before the cameras can roll.

As an executive scrambles to assemble a project it becomes "burdened with all sorts of obligations of one kind or another," says Pierson. Complex problems arise. "Right away you get into a situation, [for example,] where for some reason or other the star is not financeable at a particular studio that does want the project. Then how do you divest yourself of the star?" What happens is that projects go through "innumerable cycles of people who start out with it, drop away, and each one of them takes a little piece of . . . [financial interest] with them when they go." Some projects become so burdened with commitments that they collapse under their own weight.

Deal-making has become more difficult as the industry has grown. "One of the major changes in the business," says agent Rick Ray, "is that while there used to be a small coterie of studios to which you would go [to make a picture], today we have an operative list . . . [of] hundreds of people, any one of whom can be instrumental in getting something sold or getting something off the ground. [Consequently] it's fifteen times as difficult today as it used to be. You have a widely separated industry sprawled all over the place."

Deals have become more complex as studios and producers devise new methods to finance movies. Intricate schemes that involve selling ancillary rights, obtaining foreign distribution advances, taking advantage of tax benefits and laying off risk on Wall Street investment groups have become routine. It is not unusual to have eighteen-page definitions of net profits as addenda to studio contracts.

In the old days there were no business-affairs executives, recalls producer David Brown. "We would just make the deal, acquire the material and tell the lawyers what the terms were." Today it is the lawyers who instruct the creative-affairs executives what they can or cannot do.

Virtually every step in the development and production of a film requires that a separate deal be successfully concluded. The first deal is often a "literary purchase agreement" to buy the rights to a book. It's a risky proposition for the buyer, because unless a film can be produced from the material, the rights are worthless. William Morris agent Irene Webb estimates that of the one hundred book deals she makes each year only two result in films.

To reduce financial risk, buyers prefer to "option" material rather than buy it outright. An option usually costs 10 percent of the full purchase price. It gives the buyer a period of time, typically a year or two, to put together a deal to produce the picture. If he fails to get the story into production, he loses only his option money and the owner of the material regains full rights to it. If the property goes into production, the option is exercised and the full purchase price paid.

To eliminate financial risk, producers enter into "overall development deals" with studios. The studio agrees to finance the producer's projects, in return for which the producer agrees to make all his pictures with the studio, or at least give it first opportunity at his projects. Typically the studio also provides the producer with a secretary and office on its lot and pays for his screenwriters. And the studio often will compensate the producer for his services—with payments of several hundred thousand dollars a year. Additional fees and profits are due the producer for projects that go into production.

After the rights to a property have been secured, a deal to hire a screenwriter is made. Such deals may be "step deals," which provide that at each step of the development of the script the studio has the option whether to proceed forward. The steps usually are: story treatment, first draft and second draft.

When a studio purchases a completed screenplay it is often part of a package comprised of a script and director or star. The talent may receive a "pay or play" deal, under which the studio is obliged to pay their full fee irrespective of whether a film is ultimately produced. These fees hold the talent in place while the studio rewrites the script or seeks additional elements.

The least risk from a studio point of view occurs when a completed film is bought. In such "negative pickup" deals the studio typically pays the producer an advance against his share of the picture's profits and agrees to pay for the marketing and distribution of the picture. Because the risk of production is borne by the producer, he usually receives a greater share of profits than if he had produced the picture with a studio.

Amid all the deal-making, artistic considerations are sometimes lost. The parties become so involved in negotiating that they forget what makes a good picture. Acrimonious negotiations can poison the creative atmosphere, making it difficult for the parties to work together on the film.

Even if the negotiations go smoothly, terms of the deal may place parties in antagonistic positions. "Deal-making, unfortunately, is not structured to encourage the desired behavior on buyers' and sellers' parts," says agent Marty Hurwitz. "Rather, it's for one to be guaranteed as much as possible and the other to guarantee as little as possible, because people don't trust each other. People are always sure they're going to get fucked."

Deals can distort business decisions as well as artistic ones. Pay-or-play deals can push studios to make pictures they shouldn't. With *Villa Rides*, recalls writer-director Robert Towne (*Personal Best*), the studio had to pay Yul Brynner and Robert Mitchum regardless of whether they made the movie. "So you've got, say, over a million dollars tied up in salaries between two guys, and they figure it will take maybe two million to make the movie, so they say, 'What the hell, we might as well go ahead and get something for an extra million.'

"What happens is that you pay a lot of people a lot of money to make a movie that nobody particularly wants to make. The result is something that is lacking in cohesiveness, conviction, everything else. In a situation like that you are often involved with a producer who is more interested in making money on the making of the movie than he is on the releasing of the movie."

Likewise, deals with stars may be made not for the good of the picture but for the prestige they afford studio executives. And then there are the deals made to placate stars. If Steve McQueen said he wanted to play *The Baryshnikov Story*, says writer William Goldman, studio executives would say: " 'Great, Steve baby, that's a fabulous part for you. You've always been balletic on screen. We'll develop a hundred thousand dollars' worth.' " But privately the executives would say: " 'Fucking Steve McQueen is off his rocker. He wants to play Baryshnikov. Well, we want to have a nice relationship with him. Maybe he'll do a bang-bang picture next year. Let's develop it.' "

To attract stars and big-name directors, studios pay salaries that make no economic sense. "A lot of talent in the business is being paid way too much money," says producer Walter Coblenz. "The deals made for major talent often have little relation to the economics involved and the moneys that the film is going to generate."

Similarly, overall development deals with a big-name producer may look good but not produce any results. "There are disincentives in deals at studios," explains Marty Hurwitz. "Producers who have overall studio deals can frequently get a better deal on a picture at another studio which hasn't invested anything upfront. So a producer may not be enthusiastic about making his picture at the studio where he resides and receives three hundred and fifty thousand dollars a year for a first look at his projects."

The stars of deal-making are known as "the players." They are the two-hundred or so top agents, studio executives, producers and other power brokers who wield clout by virtue of the big money or talent they represent.

Although theirs is an informal club, there is little difficulty discerning who is a member. Players' phone calls are promptly returned, maître d's can always find tables for them, the trade press regularly reports on their activities.

A player's most important asset is his reputation. It distinguishes him from the many novices, charlatans and wishful thinkers who inhabit the industry; and it gives him access to other players. "It's a town of hustlers," says Cannon studio chairman Menahem Golan. "Ninety-nine percent talk and one percent make a movie. So one has to know how to eliminate [the hustlers] in order not to waste your time."

Moreover, a deal-maker's reputation rubs off on his clients.

Screenplays submitted by players are perceived differently from those purveyed by lesser deal-makers. The auspices under which a project is submitted can define its worth as much as its intrinsic merits. Consequently, everyone is very concerned with enhancing his stature. Those who aspire to power adopt its trappings. They hope that if they look, sound and act powerful, they will become that which they emulate. It's ironic that such posturing succeeds in the image-making capital of the world. One would think people in the industry would be less susceptible to illusions.

Newcomers often seek to raise their stature by affiliating themselves with respected people and institutions. It's one reason why fledgling producers are anxious to enter into development deals with studios; they get an office on the lot and instant credibility.

More so than in most businesses, deal-making in Hollywood takes place in social settings. Discussions are held over breakfasts, lunches and dinners. Encounters at screenings or industry functions provide opportunities to mention a project casually. "There are agents who are very successful . . . [because they] are at the right dinner parties, at the right cocktail parties, are seen at Le Dome [restaurant] having drinks," says agent Bobbi Thompson. "They know how to grease the cucumber."

When Israeli Menahem Golan arrived in Hollywood, he was surprised at how informally deals were made. "Usually when an American big producer has a relationship with a star or a director, they play tennis in the morning or eat breakfast together. . . . They go to American football games and one of them pulls out a cigarette or hash and says, 'Listen, I have this idea.' And movies are made in most cases when two people in this high caliber know each other and have connections. Like somebody has Robert Redford."

"The most important deals in the movie industry," says Shirley MacLaine, "are finalized on the sun-drenched turf of golf courses or around swimming pools, where the smell of barbecue sauce is borne on gentle breezes and wafts over the stereo system of houses that people seldom leave."

Players have their own honor code for conducting business. While they generally are tough and wily bargainers, they rarely engage in outright lying or cheating. The community is simply too small for anyone to get away with fraud for long. Players have to deal with each other on a recurring basis, and therefore it does not pay to take undue advantage of one's colleagues. Thus, when a player gives his word on a deal, another player can rely on it. If there is any deception in negotiations, it is usually the failure to mention pertinent facts, a practice considered fair, there being no obligation for full disclosure.

"Considering the amount of money at stake and the amount of employment that goes on, there's far more integrity and honor in this business than probably any other venture of comparable size," says agent Gary Salt. "People are going to work every single day on nothing more than an agent's word. Contracts aren't signed until well after something is finished . . . when I say to an attorney in business affairs that we have a deal, we have a deal from that moment."

But the honor code allows a certain amount of hype and exaggeration. "We try to make people think our clients are worth more than they are," says agent Robert Littman. "We're in the business of illusions."

Other shenanigans are allowed, although sometimes they only work against the uninitiated. "High-balling" is asking for an excessive amount of money in order to position oneself favorably for compromise. If a reasonable fee for a certain writer is $100,000, then his agent's request for $200,000 leaves lots of room to negotiate. Of course, the other side can counter with a "low-ball" bid of $50,000, thus setting the stage for a protracted struggle.

High-balling and low-balling do not work well against seasoned negotiators because they understand how salaries are set. The basic rule is that everybody is entitled to a modest raise over what he last received. Since salary information is freely exchanged within the industry, the parameters within which to negotiate a deal are usually fairly narrow, although sometimes a large increase is justified. If, for example, an actor is in a blockbuster hit or wins an Academy Award, he may be able to double or triple his rate overnight.

An excessive salary request may reflect an artist's lack of

interest in a project. If he feels he can't decline a project without giving offense, he can have his agent ask for so much money that a deal can't be made. Occasionally, outrageous demands are met, in which case the artist receives a financial windfall but must suffer through the project.

Low-balling games are often played with film budgets. A low-budget estimate is used to induce a studio to green-light production. Sometimes the decision is the result of an unspoken conspiracy between the filmmaker and executives. Says director Jim Bridges: "I was in the room on *Urban Cowboy* when Robert Evans said seriously to the studio that we could make the movie for eight million. The picture started going forward and we all knew it was going to cost twelve million, but that's a ploy. The idea is if you can get the studio pregnant enough they can't pull out. It's not unusual. We did it on *China Syndrome* and everybody winked."

Another favorite gambit of deal-makers is playing hard-to-get. "People want things they can't have," explains personal manager Keith Addis. "If you have a script you really love, refuse to show it to anyone. Make them beg." Producer Ed Feldman (*Witness*) agrees: "If you keep a script hidden and won't give it to somebody, they will go crazy. The reverse psychology works well."

Creating confusion is a technique of some deal-makers. If one party does not understand what is being discussed—and is too embarrassed to ask for clarification—it is difficult for him to protect his interests. "Some people do it by being long-winded," says agent Bobbi Thompson. "Some people do it by telling anecdotes and never getting around to the point. But all of it is a specific form of confusion designed to protect their own interests."

Many deals are so complex that no additional confusion need be added. Director Henry Jaglom (*Always*) complains that attorneys take advantage of creative people who don't know how to read contracts. They remove objectionable provisions only to add them later as footnotes. "When you call it to their attention some lawyer calls you back and says, 'You've read it wrong.' Finally they see that you are very right and they say they are going to change it. And then they change it and put in another loophole . . . which negates what you agreed upon." Intimidation can be another ploy. But strong-arm tactics work only when one's opponent needs a deal so badly that he will submit to such abuse. This kind of exploitation is usually avoided because "if I use leverage and kill somebody, tomorrow he is going to kill me," says attorney Eric Weissmann. "In the old days negotiating was filled with much more histrionics. There was much more ranting and raving and screaming, barring people from the lot, and fistfights. . . . [Today] people try to reason with each other."

Even insanity can be useful, it being difficult to negotiate with the insane. "If one person is nuts then he cannot be reached logically and the other person . . . who is desperately trying to reach him is already at a disadvantage," says Weissmann, who adds that the approach works best when the party is truly insane since it's a hard thing to fake.

Bursts of irrational behavior can also be used. "There's nothing more unsettling when you are negotiating with someone and they do something completely unexpected," says Weissmann. "When I was a young lawyer . . . I was negotiating with the head of the legal department at a studio, who buzzed the secretary and told her to call the studio police and have me escorted from the place and to bar me from the lot forever. Well I decided right then that I didn't feel that strongly about the point."

A variation of these last two approaches could be called "my boss is insane." A negotiator will concede his opponent's position is reasonable but profess that he cannot agree to it because his principal is crazy. It is tough to argue with someone who agrees with you and denounces the person he represents.

Even silence can be a negotiating ploy. If it makes the other party uncomfortable, he may talk himself into compromising his position. A similar passive technique is for a negotiator never to directly propose solutions but maneuver the conversation so the other party suggests them. "If you suggest it [a solution], they often resist," says attorney Christine Cuddy. "But if you can orchestrate it so that they come up with the idea, they feel better."

Indirection is often used by executives. Instead of requesting a particular client, they describe the kind of person they want and let the agent make suggestions. This cool courtship conceals how badly the studio wants a client, a position that, if disclosed, might encourage the agent to drive a hard bargain.

The best negotiators are versatile, employing tactics appropriate to the situation. "A good negotiator has some qualities of a chameleon," says agent Maggie Field. "I don't negotiate the same with everyone . . . [you] have to be flexible to accommodate the personality of the person you are negotiating with. I find that if I'm dealing with an older gentleman I have a different approach than with a woman who is a contemporary [of mine]."

First encounters can be a time of testing. "The first time I do business with someone," says Field, "it's . . . occasionally a power struggle . . . where the screaming and yelling starts. . . . [But] the people I have been [regularly] working with, we can make a deal with a phone call. Because they know what I have and I know what they need. And either we can make the deal or we can't. And it becomes less of a personality struggle and more of a 'Can you do this? I'll shove that down my people's throat if you'll make your client agree to this.' "

The best deal-makers are not necessarily those who make the toughest demands. "If you want the best deal there ever was, you are not going to make it all the time," says Eric Weissmann. "You are going to lose it some of the time. Now . . . [intractability] is very good for your reputation because the deals you made are terrific, and the deals you blew show what a tough person you are. But it is very tough on your client because he doesn't have the string of deals that you have. You may be working on a hundred deals. He only has one. He may be a millionaire or a broken body, depending on how life breaks for him. So I personally always try to do the best I can, and not to do something just to satisfy my own ego."

Ultimately, a negotiator's strength is largely a function of how badly the other party wants to make a deal. "You can be the dumbest schmuck in the world and if you own the best screenplay or the most desirable book . . . you can make [great] deals," explains Robert Littman.

Cannon head
Menahem Golan
directing Lee Marvin
in *The Delta Force*

Rhinestone writer Phil
Alden Robinson

(Peter C. Borsari)

Jane Fonda with son Troy

Paul Newman

(Peter C. Borsari)

(© 1986 Alan Berliner)

Twentieth Century-Fox chairman
Barry Diller

CAA partners and their
mentor at William
Morris, Phil Weltman
from left to right: Ron
Meyer, Bill Haber, Phil
Weltman, Rowland
Perkins, Mike
Rosenfeld, Michael
Ovitz and Marty Baum

(© 1986 Alan Berliner)

Independent filmmakers Gregory
Nava and Anna Thomas

(Jeff Slocomb/Picture Group)

(Darryl Shiff)

Producer Martin Bregman   Personal manager Dolores Robinson

Richard Tuggle directing Clint Eastwood in *Tightrope*

Agent Rick Ray

Actor Martin Sheen

(Toris Von Wolfe)

Director John Badham

Director Robert Altman

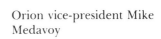

Orion vice-president Mike Medavoy

Actor-director-producer
Tony Bill

Actor Peter Coyote

Writer Jeremy Larner

(Photography by Susanne Kaspar)

Irvin Kershner directing *Return of a Man Called Horse*

Henry Jaglom directing
Dennis Hopper in *Tracks*

WRITERS

Movies originate in a writer's imagination. He creates those wonderful characters and surprising plot twists that delight audiences. He invents the witty dialogue that comes out of actors' mouths. He builds the foundation on which the entire film rests. And only after he has finished his work can the director and other craftsmen begin theirs.

Without a script, the most talented director will produce a rambling, boring, lifeless film. "It's something you can't do without," says director Irvin Kershner. "It's something that really energizes the film. It's the nucleus of a film. . . . If that film has any power it is going to come from the script. And if the film lacks that power it's because the script lacks that power—no matter how well you've done it there will be a superficiality to it."

The fundamental importance of writing to moviemaking was best expressed by legendary mogul Sam Goldwyn: "A great picture has to start with a great story. Just as water can't rise higher than its source, so a picture can't rise higher than its story. The bigger the stars, the director and producer, the harder they fall on a bad story."

Yet despite the importance of the script, little respect is given to its authors. "Screenwriters are like offensive linemen in football," says writer-director Jim Abrahams (*Airplane!*). "They do all the dirty work while the quarterback gets all the credit."

Writers complain that the industry treats them like second-class citizens. When the studios prepare invitations to premieres, says Stirling Silliphant, hardly anyone asks what writers should be invited. "No, they ask, 'What stars have we got, what producers, what directors?' "

After writer Stanley Weiser attended a sneak preview of his picture *Coast to Coast,* he walked into the theater lobby and approached a studio executive he had worked with on the movie and asked him whether he thought the audience liked the picture. The executive handed Weiser a viewer ballot card and said: "Do I know you from somewhere?" Weiser responded: "I'm the writer of the movie." The executive replied: "Oh, of course."

"Being a screenwriter is to my mind the most masochistic thing you can do," says agent Bobbi Thompson. "They all get treated like shit and they are raped right and left. It's sad to hear that even the most talented, sought-after writers are subject to the same shitty treatment and lack of respect as the newest beginner who is shafted on the money."

The lack of respect accorded the writer is evident in how freely others feel they can change his work. "Almost everyone unconsciously feels he knows as much about writing as a writer," says screenwriter Ernest Lehman (*North by Northwest*). "It would be unthinkable for a writer to tell a director how to direct or a producer how to produce or an actor how to act or a cinematographer how to light a scene. But it is not at all unthinkable for *anyone* to tell a writer how to write."

"Writing is the only art form in the world that everyone thinks they can do," says writer-producer Tom Greene. "If I commission you to do a sculpture I would never—even if I didn't like it—think of taking out a chisel and changing the nose. But everyone thinks they can write."

Writers are partially to blame for their low standing. They incur disrespect when they submit unpolished work. They may reason that since extensive changes are likely to be made anyway, it is not worth bothering to refine their script. "As a result," says screenwriting instructor Robert McKee, "they've gotten a reputation as people who don't finish their work. People look at you and say, 'Shit, we bought this . . . but look at all the work that has to be done. . . . This work wouldn't have been done if we hadn't pointed the finger.' . . . Therefore they stand around cocktail parties and say, 'It was a pretty good idea when he brought it to us, but we punched it up, we made it what it is today.' Hence the problem of gaining respect and clout in this town."

But even when a writer turns in a polished screenplay, its worth is often not appreciated. While executives and producers pay lip service to the importance of good writing, many have a hard time discerning it. "One of the secrets about screenwriting," says writer Jeremy Larner (*The Candidate*), "is that very few people can read a script. You have to be able to project a movie on the screen of your mind and hear the dialogue in counterpoint. . . . Often the most original scripts are dismissed because somebody, in effect, has not been able to read them and has never asked the writer what is happening."

"The level of competence among executives is embarrassing," says writer-director Frank Pierson. "There are very few who really have any idea what they are doing. If they knew what the hell to ask for [in a script] they wouldn't employ half the writers in the industry."

"It's all subjective judgment," says agent Rick Ray. "I guarantee you I could take an Alvin Sargent [*Ordinary People*] script, put someone else's name on it, and the response would be that the script shows a lot of talent but it needs work. On the other hand, I can put Alvin Sargent's name on a terrible script and it will be given serious consideration."

Writers are powerless to defend the integrity of their work. Once they finish a script, they become dispensable. In any dispute over the script, the writer's views are subordinate to those of stars and directors, whose cooperation remains essential to complete the picture. If the writer storms off the set and locks himself in a dressing room, nobody is likely to notice or care. Scripts can be changed without their consent, for unlike playwrights, screenwriters do not retain the copyright to their work. (Studios demand the unfettered right to modify scripts because they do not want to let a $30,000-a-day production grind to a halt because a writer doesn't want one of his words changed.)

Some directors don't even allow writers on the set. These directors are so arrogant that they believe they alone can best make last-minute script changes, or they are so insecure that they feel their authority is threatened by the presence of a writer who may disagree with them. Other directors simply do not want writers around because they feel uncomfortable changing—some would say ruining—their scripts in front of them. Whatever the reason, "the writer [on the set] is very much like a hooker who has been fucked and paid and is there by sufferance," says Stirling Silliphant. This is unfortunate because the writer is usually the person who knows the script most intimately, and thus is best able to smoothly incorporate last-minute changes.

The lack of respect accorded screenwriters is also a product of the widespread perception that the director is the primary creative force in moviemaking. This view has been lent credence by the *auteur* theory, which contends that the director is the author of a film. It is an idea first proposed by French critics and later promoted in the United States by *Village Voice* critic Andrew Sarris.

It's a theory that infuriates screenwriters. "Dig a hole in the floor and shoot up into somebody's nostrils, or shoot down through the chandelier," says veteran writer I.A.L. Diamond. "You think that is going to make a picture? Bullshit. If the words are not there, if the plot isn't there, if the characters aren't there, nothing is going to matter. I don't care how fancy you are going to shoot. . . . You can count the downfall of certain directors when they decided they could write their own scripts. . . . More directors have ruined their careers by writing their own scripts than by screwing the leading lady. And some of them have done both."

"We've created a director's cult in this country," says Silliphant. "In socialist countries . . . the writer is clearly acknowledged as the single most important element . . . witness the fact that they're always sending these poor bastards off to Siberia. . . . They realize that the writer is the cutting edge of public unrest . . . and therefore the most dangerous. That attitude is not prevalent in Hollywood, where the writer is regarded as someone you buy and replace."

"Almost anybody can do what a director does," says writer Gore Vidal. "I've worked on about fifteen movies; I've done a hundred and fifty live television plays; I've done eight plays on Broadway—I never saw a director yet who contributed anything. When I got to Cannes for *The Best Man* . . . there on this banner was the title in French: *Un film de Franklin Schaffner.* Well, I just hit the ceiling. I mean this was my play, my movie. I had helped put the thing together. I had hired Frank."

Writers complain that directors are lauded by critics for the contributions of their collaborators. "Unless you've worked on a film, it's literally impossible to know who did what," says writer-director Robert Towne. "I've read reviews . . . [where] the reviewer will assign credit for the writing to the director, or credit for the writing to the wrong writer, or credit to the actor for something the director did."

"There is absolutely no way to individuate the elements of a film," says film-critic-turned-writer-director Paul Schrader. "The people 'involved' can't separate the work of the director and the writer and the art director and the cinematographer and the actors and the producer—even the propman. You may see a wonderful bit of business in a film involving a prop and you think, 'Gee, that was clever of the writer.' It may end up that the propman was very imaginative and before the scene suggested to the director that he use this. Much of what goes as directorial skill is in fact cinematography: the laying out of shots, composition."

With so much attention focused on the director, "writing a good movie brings a writer about as much fame as riding a bicycle," said veteran screenwriter Ben Hecht. Writers think this lack of recognition unfair because directors merely interpret what they have created—as orchestra conductors interpret a composer's score. Consequently, why should writers receive less acclaim than composers? After all, Leonard Bernstein is not considered the author of a symphony written by Beethoven.

Another analogy cited by writers compares moviemaking to the construction of a building. I.A.L. Diamond says, "When a building is going up, the sidewalk superintendents see the contractor giving the orders but nobody says, 'Architecture is a contractors' medium.' But they say, 'Well, the writer just gives you the blueprint.' Well so does the architect. But the architect created the Pantheon and not the guys who schlepped the stones up there."

Nevertheless, proponents of the *auteur* theory remain unswayed. They point out that the pictures of such directors as Hawks, Ford and Hitchcock have a consistent style that does not vary with the writer.

Writing instructor Robert McKee agrees that these directors are *auteurs* of their films but contends that is because they co-wrote them even though they did not take screenwriting credit. "What Hawks and Ford and Hitchcock would do is work with the writer to get the story to work, conceiving character, conceiving conflict, conceiving the patterns and the building of the shaping of the whole understructure of the thing, and then allow the writer to go away and write the dialogue and description based on all those conferences. . . . Therefore, three quarters of the creative work was done by this writer-director team in making the story."

The *auteur* theory persists despite its many detractors (including quite a few directors) because the media finds it useful. It's difficult for reviewers to gauge each collaborator's contribution to a film. It's easier to consider the director its author and hold him responsible for everything.

Moreover, it's consistent with critics' belief in film as an art form that pictures be considered the product of a coherent vision of an artist, rather than the jumbled aggregate of many, sometimes conflicting, forces. A critic cannot discuss the meaning of a prop, for instance, if it was added on the whim of the art director or was inadvertently placed in the frame by a grip. The reviewer needs to believe that everything in a film was placed there for a purpose. Art is not supposed to be the product of serendipity, compromise or the exigencies of production.

The *auteur* theory is further bolstered because directors make better copy than writers. "When a photographer comes and takes pictures of what's going on they don't take a picture of Arthur Miller sitting in his room writing," says Directors Guild president Gilbert Cates. "They take a picture of Elia Kazan out there where there's more action."

As directors have achieved greater prominence and influence in the industry, writers have grown increasingly dissatisfied with their lot. Reasoning, "If you can't beat them join them," many have decided to become directors themselves. The exodus has depleted the available pool of experienced screenwriters. There are only two reasons to write, says screenwriter Josh Greenfeld. "First, to be a director, and second, to make money."

Similarly, many new writers entering the industry want to become directors as quickly as possible. "[Directing] is the big ego trip," says Diamond. "They see . . . [writing] as an ordeal they have to pass through on the way to directing. So they never learn their craft. . . . What they do is rip off the old pictures . . . they don't give a shit about writing. And I think the pictures reflect it. Most of them are sort of painted by the numbers. They are . . . not about anything except other pictures on the same subject."

Likewise, increasing numbers of film students aspire to direct. They lust after the power, glamour, fame and money that come from directing. They study the technical aspects of moviemaking and care little about the content of films. Says Diamond, "We've had AFI guys [students] on our set and they will talk to everybody from the makeup man to the publicist. The only person they don't talk to is the writer because they don't give a shit about writing. That's the last thing that interests them. . . . They just want to direct . . . because you become a little tin god on the set. . . . You're standing ten feet away from the coffee urn and you ask somebody to bring you a cup of coffee while you are trying to figure out how to get a Rolls-Royce into the script somehow so you can buy it back from the studio as a used car."

Script quality has also been hurt by the demise of the studio system, which, despite its shortcomings, provided an excellent environment for writing. "I think I was the last contract writer at Columbia," says Frank Pierson, "and it was really kind of nice. It was like a family there . . . [in my hall I worked alongside] Bob Altman, Bob Rafelson, Henry Jaglom, John Cassavetes, Howard Fast. Even Sidney Sheldon was there, for God's sake. And we would have lunch together and talk about mutual problems. If you ran into a script problem you would have somebody to go to and bullshit with about it. People would help each other. . . . It was fun."

Under the studio system, if a script lacked humor it would be passed on to a writer who was good with gags. Other writers would be brought in to contribute their strengths. The result was a final draft forged from the talent of many writers.

Under this collaborative approach, less of a writer's ego was invested in each script (especially since few screenplays were originals, not based on a book or play). Consequently, writers were more open to suggestions, both from other writers and from studio executives. Legend has it that the moguls made good suggestions. They had an intuitive sense of what made an interesting story and they appreciated good writing. "The executives in the days of Thalberg knew that their commodity was a script," says writer Waldo Salt. "The old guys knew about script. . . . Harry Cohn always had writers at the head of the studio. Zanuck was a writer. A great many executives came out of writing . . . [and] they hired the best writers possible."

Furthermore, writers then were salaried employees and thus in less of a rush to complete a script. They could afford to take time polishing their work. Today writers are paid piecemeal and have an incentive to churn out scripts as rapidly as possible. As they approach the completion of one screenplay they become preoccupied with getting their next assignment. They may expend as much effort attending meetings and hustling deals as writing.

Another advantage of the old studio system was the opportunity it afforded writers to see their work filmed. Few projects were shelved, so writers regularly received feedback on how their work translated to the screen. Today studios develop far more material than they intend to produce. Writers can go for years without having a script filmed. Excellent screenplays are not made because of problems packaging the project and assembling financing, unlike the old days, when scripts were developed and produced in assembly-line fashion, with the studio having on hand everything needed to make the picture.

Writers Jack Epps, Jr., and Jim Cash wrote seven unproduced screenplays between 1975 and 1985 before their first was filmed (*Top Gun*). "What was bizarre," says Epps, "was that everyone loved our scripts." Indeed, the studios paid them handsomely—up to $350,000 per screenplay—even though nothing they wrote had ever been filmed.

"Studio executives would say, 'We're going to make this movie,' " recalls Epps. "But it never happened." Attempts were made to line up the right stars and directors to no avail.

For example, they wrote a script about comic-strip character Dick Tracy for director John Landis. After completing two drafts Landis left the project and was replaced by Walter Hill. They then wrote two drafts for Hill before he was replaced by Richard Benjamin. After they had finished another two drafts, Benjamin left. The future of their script is now in limbo, the studio having let its rights to the character lapse. Those rights have been bought by Warren Beatty, who hasn't yet announced whether he is interested in the Epps/Cash script or is going to develop one of his own.

Sometimes an excellent script is not made simply because it gets caught in a power struggle. "One of the most brilliant comedies I have ever read," says Frank Pierson, "is a comedy, believe it or not, about the Black Death, written by Walter Newman. The rights to it were bought by George C. Scott, who wants to direct it. But nobody wants him to direct this particular project and he won't release it. So it will never get made."

The likelihood that nothing will come of one's labor can be demoralizing. It's difficult to write after your projects have been repeatedly shelved, says director Irvin Kershner. "I have many writer friends who . . . every time they start a project, have to . . . pump themselves up. They say, 'Ah, this time it's going to work. We're going to make it work.' But inside they know it's a gamble whether their script will ever see the light of day.

"[W]riters have to go to psychoanalysts to get rid of the problems of writing for film. I know very few who don't. . . . How would you feel writing for a year on a film, handing it in, loving it. You gave your heart to it. It gets passed around. Studio says, 'We pass.' Another studio says, 'We pass.' And finally it's on the shelf and is never done. I'll show you . . . wonderful writers with dozens of projects they struggled with that were never done. That's heartbreaking."

Writers are exploited at every turn. Ideas are plagiarized, scripts needlessly rewritten, credits stolen. They are at the mercy of producers, directors and executives, who instruct them when and how to write. Even top writers suffer in-dignities. They are used to attract a star or director to a project and then dropped.

"A writer is only a piece of bait," says Josh Greenfeld. "He is not the fish. . . . When Mario Puzo agreed to write *Superman,* that made the project viable. Then the producers got [Marlon] Brando and the whole deal fell into place. Later on they rewrote Puzo. They had [just] used him to give the project validity."

Writers without agents are the most likely to be exploited. They may pitch an idea and be turned down, only later to learn that it is being developed without them. "It's an ubiquitous phenomena," says agent Melinda Jason. "A young person comes up with an idea, or they get the rights to a story —they use their last dime to get it. [And] if they're unlucky they bring it to a slimebag, a shyster . . . and they get screwed."

"I think it clearly happens a lot," says attorney Walter Teller. "I'm not saying it's always done consciously. There is such a flurry of submissions at any production company or studio . . . [that] it's very easy for ideas to get mixed up and for someone not to really remember where they heard an idea."

It can be difficult to determine whether an idea has been stolen. "You never know what to think," says Teller, "when you go in to submit an idea to someone and they say, 'Oh, that's really a great idea but it's very similar to something we've been working on.' That may mean they've been developing a similar project for the last year, or it may mean they just like the idea and don't want to pay for it."

Sometimes what looks like theft is only coincidence. Former Writers Guild president Frank Pierson says, "All of us who have been in the business for any length of time . . . know that when you're sitting behind a desk and auditioning ideas . . . on any given day a couple of people will come in and present you with something which is essentially the same idea. It's either something that's been in the newspaper in the past few days or inspired by it. . . . Sometimes it's just something that is in the air. The creative spirit—it's not just great minds that tend to think alike."

Ideas are not legally protectable. Only after the idea has been elaborated on and put in a tangible form, such as a written story or script, can it be registered with the Copyright Office or Writers Guild. (Registration is evidence of when a story was written. In the event of a dispute the person who can prove he wrote it first will be presumed to be its author.)

Not all allegations of idea theft have merit. Blockbuster hits generate the kind of profits that provide tempting targets for frivolous lawsuits. "Every time a big movie comes out there are three housewives who claim they wrote it," says writer Clay Frohman. "Someone claimed he wrote E.T. It's preposterous. I don't believe it for a minute. . . . Steven Spielberg did not have to rip anybody off. Needless to say, he wouldn't risk it."

Idea theft typically occurs between novice writers and the less reputable producers on the fringes of the industry. Veteran writers know how to protect themselves and have lawyers and agents to guard their interests. Mainstream producers and major studios are not inclined to steal because they don't want the adverse publicity that can arise.

Veteran writers are exploited in more subtle ways. Under the pretext of meeting with them to discuss a rewrite assignment, producers will extract suggestions as to how to fix their script. Some producers may bring in a series of writers for such free consultations.

Another unethical practice is "shopping" projects. Without buying or optioning a script, a producer will submit it to studios as if it were his. If the studio is interested in it, the producer will buy the rights. Otherwise, he returns it to the writer without mentioning where it was pitched.

Shopping both defrauds a writer of money and reduces his chances of selling a script. A shopped script may be hastily packaged and pitched—as is often the case when a producer has no financial risk in a project—and thus not presented in the best possible context. The initial rejection tarnishes the property, making a subsequent sale more difficult.

Shopping is a widespread phenomenon. Frank Pierson estimates that 90 percent of the scripts submitted to studios by producers have not been optioned or bought. In many of these cases, however, the submission is with the consent of the writer, who may feel it's better to have his work shopped by a powerful producer than to sell it to a weak one, or submit it to the studio himself.

Speculative writing is another way writers are exploited. Although the Writers Guild prohibits its members from accepting employment without pay, a desperate writer will sometimes circumvent the restriction. Ostensibly he will write a screenplay for himself, but actually it is for a producer who is not obliged to pay him unless he chooses to buy it. Similarly, rewrites may be done on speculation. A producer will suggest to a writer that if he makes certain changes in his script the producer might buy it. The writer jumps through hoops to sell his project and is left penniless for his efforts.

Writers encounter other problems when they're commissioned to write a script. It's often difficult for them to collect their fee. "Beginning writers not members of the Guild are cheated every time," says writer Richard Kletter. "They don't get paid. Almost every writer I know who made a non-Guild deal got screwed."

Larry Gross (*48 HRS.*) recalls writing a script about Montgomery Clift for a dentist and his wife who fancied themselves producers. "I had never written a script for money at that point so I told my agent, 'Hey it's a free trip to New York and twenty thousand dollars.' To his credit, my agent advised me against taking it. So I got five thousand up front and wrote the script. They didn't like it and refused to pay me the rest. And that is what happens when you deal with non-signatories to the Guild."

Guild writers can also be defrauded. While the Writers Guild can punish a production company that has cheated a writer by refusing to let Guild members work for it, the producer himself can continue to hire Guild writers under the auspices of other companies. Thus an unscrupulous producer can incorporate one company after another, repeatedly swindling writers.

Although writers can sue for money owed them, legal remedies are often impractical. The amount of money in dispute may not be sufficient to justify the time and expense of a lawsuit. Moreover, writers are reluctant to sue because they don't want to gain a reputation for being litigious. "The net result," says Frank Pierson, "is that once you make a deal you have effectively surrendered all control over the property to other people. And at that point the only thing that counts is force of personality or your clout in the business—the fact that [they] . . . may want to use you again. . . . That doesn't mean that they won't go ahead and do it anyway. The phrase most often used is 'Listen, we're going to do this. We're sorry, so go ahead and sue us.' Or, 'We're going to do this anyway so . . . we'll make it up to you the next time we make a deal.' "

Besides the financial shenanigans writers are exposed to, they are also exploited by having their work rewritten without cause. "Executives consider rewriting like changing clothes," says writer Clay Frohman. "There's a joke around: 'This is a fantastic script. Who can we get to rewrite it?' "

Directors are also responsible for much rewriting. "Directors today buy projects which they have no intention of doing as such," says Frank Pierson. "They simply buy projects that will be a springboard to do something else that they have wanted to do for a long time. And then they proceed to bring in their own writers or rewrite it themselves and change it into whatever they want to do."

While rewrites may improve a script, they can also hurt it. A rewrite can "lose the basic thrust, that first bang out of the box, that first heat of energy that started the idea in the first place," says writer Joan Tewkesbury. Says Frohman, "Films that have two, three or five writers on them have a very watered-down feel."

What exasperates writers most are script revisions made for extraneous reasons. "You have all these hidden agendas on the part of the producer and his girlfriend, on the part of this actor or actress, or the director that can come into play," says Stirling Silliphant. "Let's say this director is a frustrated writer who has maybe had only one or two [of his] scripts done and they weren't very good. And he really wants to get in there to rewrite your script to show the world that he can write better than this son of a bitch. That he's going to save the script. . . . I went through this with Sam Peckinpah with a script where the problem really was that he didn't want to do my script. He was trying to knock it out so as to slip his in at the last minute."

Rewrites also generate credit problems. When several writers contribute to a script, credit must be allocated among them. This can be an exceedingly difficult task when a script has gone through numerous drafts. Although disinterested members of the Writers Guild arbitrate disputes, writers often feel they have been cheated out of a credit.

The script for *North Dallas Forty*, for example, was worked on by seven different writers. Then, says writer Jeremy Larner, the director and producer chopped up their work, restructured it and took two thirds of the writing credit for themselves. The Guild affirmed their allocation of credit.

More than professional pride is at stake in credit rulings. Credits often determine the dispensing of profits. Writers complain that when directors have scripts rewritten writers can lose all or part of their share of profits. For a blockbuster movie even a small piece of the profits can amount to millions of dollars.

The means by which writers are exploited are only limited by the imagination of producers—and in this realm they are conceded to have great creativity. Writers' interests are subordinate to those of more powerful elements, and if necessary they will be sacrificed to enable the project to proceed. Producers generally place expediency ahead of integrity. "The truth of the matter is that . . . when they [producers] have to make that choice between their bread and butter on one side, and you on the other," says Robert McKee, "it's obvious what they are going to choose."

In such situations friendships can dissolve overnight. McKee recalls getting his best friend hired as associate producer on a project only to find the friend ingratiating himself with the producer at McKee's expense. "I learned that behind my back he was saying very unpleasant things about me, was sidling up to the producer and in essence selling me down the river. And I thought why? Well it's money, it's jobs, it's careers. He is thinking I might get replaced . . . and he wants to stay on the film. So he had to sell me out."

That kind of ruthlessness is widespread, according to many writers. "[Hollywood] is as corrupt as money can make it," says Silliphant. "I don't think there is any integrity at all when it comes to making a deal in this town. I would be very surprised at anyone who wouldn't sell out his mother to get a distribution deal or a financing deal for a project. . . . There are too many producers trying to steal credit from writers, too many writers trying to get . . . a residual from the other guy. It's barracuda time."

While one would hope that those individuals with the most integrity would ultimately prosper in the industry, the dishonest ones seem to have a natural advantage. "Many of the best operators have a streak of the psychopathic," says Jeremy Larner. "They can say whatever is of most advantage to them on that particular day. They will tell a screenwriter, 'Gee, you are wonderful, just go ahead and write it,' even though they may anticipate getting his script away from the writer and giving it to another writer whom they may have already hired."

Screenwriters are a special breed. They are not really writers at all, says writer-director Paul Schrader (*American Gigolo*), but half-filmmakers.

"I can't 'be' a writer," says Schrader, "because words are not my code—words and sentences and punctuation. My code is far more elaborate. It has to deal with images, montage, cinematography, editing, sound, music. You have to think in far different terms than a writer does. My words are not up there on the screen. What is up there is a collection of talents, and if you want to get in movies you can't think like a writer."

Consequently, many novelists and playwrights fare poorly at screenwriting. "Because you're good in one field doesn't mean you will be good in another," says I.A.L. Diamond.

Movies are not good vehicles for exploring a character's thoughts and emotions because the camera can't look inside his head. Unlike the novelist, who can describe directly and in great detail exactly what a character is thinking and feeling, the screenwriter must express such interior action indirectly, suggesting it with behavior and dialogue (unless one resorts to voice-over narration, an awkward device if used repeatedly). But film does have its advantages. Each frame can instantly depict rich settings and complex actions that would take thousands of words for a novelist to describe.

Screenwriting differs from playwriting because a film can jump effortlessly from one setting to another, while a play is limited in scope to the cast, scenery and props that can fit on a stage. Thus movies are able to move around a lot and portray action sequences effectively, and plays place more emphasis on dialogue. Another difference is that films can jump from a long shot to a close-up, while plays are viewed by the audience from the same distance and perspective throughout. Actors on stage must project their lines forcefully and emphasize their gestures—acting that would seem out of place in the more realistic settings of a film.

"In the early days of talkies the best screenwriters were guys who were former newspapermen," says I.A.L. Diamond. "They were used to writing about things you could see, in this case photograph. They didn't delve deeply into what people thought or what their feelings were. . . . And they wrote graphically, and in sort of telegraphese. And that was all very good for the screen."

"Screenwriting is an artificial form of writing," says Josh Greenfeld. "Nobody would naturally write that tersely. . . . You have to write it and then cut, cut, cut. . . . Because of that there's a superficial nature." But if screenplays contain fewer words and are less suited to express complex ideas than books, they're certainly not easy to write. Indeed, distilling a story into its essential ingredients makes screen writing difficult. The digressions offered a novelist would create a rambling and unfocused film.

The most common failing of novice screenwriters is their inability to structure their stories properly. They may invent interesting dialogue and characters but their plots lack narrative drive. "Ninety-nine out of a hundred are poorly told stories," Robert McKee says of their work. "The subject matter may be interesting but the story just sucks. It doesn't start till page sixty and then doesn't go anywhere after that. It just dies at the end. Or it's so convoluted, so overstructured, the characters have proliferated . . . that it's overtold."

Writers who chase success by imitating past hits (which they are often encouraged to do by studio executives) usually produce cliché-filled stories that are predictable and boring. The audience feels it has already seen the movie. The best writing often comes from writers who draw on their own unique experiences and backgrounds. But with so many screenwriters living in Los Angeles and socializing within the industry, they risk losing their distinct flavor, producing a homogenized product.

"Writing isn't as idiosyncratic as it used to be," says truck-driver-turned-writer Gary Devore, who fights insularity by traveling around the country and talking to everyday folks. Other screenwriters try to stay fresh through research trips. "If you isolate yourself [from the world], I don't think you can write for motion pictures," says Stirling Silliphant. "I spend seventy percent of all my working time on research and conceptualizing. Writing is the easiest part of it."

A facility with words is less essential for success than the ability to conceive original stories. "There are two talents involved in screenwriting and they don't have anything to do with one another," says McKee. "The talent to write dialogue, to have an accurate cinematic eye for what you see in the world . . . is common [among screenwriters]. . . . The other talent is the talent to tell stories. That talent is rare. To conceive from scratch pure character and situations . . . has nothing to do with writing. [A story] can be put in any number of forms. Writing is just one of them." That good screenplays are rare can be attested to by studio executives and producers who continually scour the town looking for them.

One of the reasons it takes so long to master screenwriting is that writers receive so little feedback on their work. Rejection letters are brief and nondescriptive, usually saying only that the submission does not meet the needs of the buyer at the present time. Even when one is commissioned to write a script, an explanation of what a studio or producer really thinks of it may not be forthcoming.

"This is not a business set up for people to be brutally honest," says writer Robert DeLaurentis. "It's set up for a high rate of failure, after which people have to work with each other again. You turn in a script, they say it's great, it gets lost and shelved. You are confused and never get a clear answer as to why it wasn't made. Then you meet the executive at dinner and he's very friendly because he wants to work with you again. . . . You just have to figure it out and deduce why your script didn't get made. A lot of times it has nothing to do with the script."

Besides mastering his craft, a screenwriter must have a personality suited to the profession. The first prerequisite is an ego strong enough to withstand repeated rejection.

"I think if you get your feelings hurt easily it's a terrible business to be in," says Joan Tewkesbury. "You're constantly going to feel rejected . . . after the ninth script has been turned down for the ninth week in a row you say, 'Fuck, what am I doing here?' But . . . no one is really trying to do you in. They don't hate you because you didn't write it properly. They just want their problem solved. . . . So you constantly have to keep in mind that it's the script . . . they're talking about, not you. [You have] to separate your persona from the material and it's very, very difficult."

"You have to develop a really thick skin and not take it personally," says McKee. "It's just the nature of the business. . . . You have to keep your ego strong and believe that your work is valuable when everything around you seems to take delight in telling you that it isn't."

"The single most important thing is blind, stupid, tunnel-vision self-confidence," says Silliphant. "The ego of writers is worse than directors. The only difference is that directors demonstrate it dramatically and writers tend to be more introverted and sulk a lot. But we're all egomaniacs. . . . You have to believe that nobody can write better. And you have to con yourself with that thing every minute of every hour even when you're sleeping so you can get up the next day and you don't go to the typewriter and cry. You have to believe you can do it. That's the single most important element for success in a writer. That absolute blinding belief in your talent and ability."

But at the same time a screenwriter must be sufficiently humble, or at least diplomatic enough, to be able to cope with the sometimes legendary egos of directors, producers and stars. "On one hand you're their servant," says McKee. "On the other you know more than anybody [about the script]. . . . You have to bite your tongue and not get into arguments with people, because one of the important grades in this business is 'works and plays well with others.' If you become known as difficult to work with your ass is grass. . . . The best advice you can give writers is to take a lot of notes [about what they tell you to do] and then drop them in the basket on the way out. Make a show of listening and cooperating but do it your own way because ninety percent of the time they're going to forget what they told you anyway."

Because a writer often has to please a director and producer as well as studio executives, he may find himself subject to conflicting instructions—sometimes from people who have not even read the script. "A studio executive's . . . [comments] are only as good as the reader who is reading for him," says McKee. "A writer is a fool to ever make the mistake of believing that a studio executive actually reads what the writer writes." Intelligently discussing one's work with someone who is parroting what his underlings have told him can be difficult.

To protect their scripts, writers may need to stroke some

egos. Stars will frequently insist on changes in their parts that can throw an entire screenplay out of kilter. "[V]ery rarely are those changes prompted by any kind of great talent or vision," says Silliphant. "It's not like the actor is [playwright] Sam Shepard, who can come in and say this play suffers for the following reasons and fixes it. These people react to a piece of work based on their own egos and their ability to perform.

"When we were doing *The Towering Inferno* we were having a lot of trouble with Steve McQueen in terms of certain parts of the dialogue. And he . . . [wouldn't tell] me what he didn't like. He just said, 'I don't like that shit.' And I kept confronting him about it. I said, 'That's not shit, it happens to be very brilliant. Tell me what you don't like.'

"Finally he took me out in the hall and said: 'Look, I'm not an educated guy. I was a street kid. I did time. OK, I can't say certain things. . . . Certain words I can't goddamn say. I have trouble with Z's and S's . . . honestly the dialogue is OK. I just can't say it.' Well once I understood that . . . I gave him words he could pronounce."

But usually demands for script changes are for more frivolous reasons. Many writers find it difficult to accommodate the whims of stars, directors or executives by rewriting what they have labored so hard to create.

"A writer writes . . . out of some experience he has had, some emotion he feels, some anger, some rage, humor, whatever it might be," says Waldo Salt. "That's what makes a writer, that's what writing is all about. . . . That's what is going to make your creativity, your originality."

"There is a real double bind," says Ron Koslow. "To care about the work is setting yourself up for a real disappointment when your work is savaged. Yet you have to care. The men who don't are not real writers anymore. That's the real dilemma. 'Living well is the best revenge' doesn't work [here]."

"The writers who feel a lot of pride cannot survive here," says Jeremy Larner. They are better suited to writing books and plays where they can retain complete control.

Another prerequisite for a career as a screenwriter is salesmanship. "The ability to pitch is absolutely essential," says

Silliphant. "I don't care how many things you got in the trunk, if you can't sell them it doesn't mean anything. . . . Some writers simply can't tell a story. They go into a session with studios or a producer and they either reflect . . . nervousness or insecurity, or they reflect arrogance and they irritate the guy. They somehow don't understand the psychology of what has to be set up in that room.

"The new younger writers have addressed themselves to this problem. They have youth, enthusiasm, dynamism and they go in and really pitch a story. 'Like, man, listen to this, this is hot. It comes right off the street.' Zap. And the guy sits there and says, 'Yeah it sounds pretty good.' "

The best pitchers project self-confidence. "The writer has to maintain a certain sense of his power," says McKee, "and go into meetings and handle people as if 'If you don't take my screenplay, I'll take it elsewhere.' Nicely, but they have to know that. . . . When they feel that from you, it's amazing what a difference it makes.

"Recently I've been selling a lot of scripts. The difference has been mainly that I'm making so much money elsewhere that I don't need it. Consequently, when I walk into a pitch session it's like 'Guys, here is the idea, do you want it or not?' I don't care, really. They go, 'Whoosh.' And with the weakest ideas they say, 'Sit, sit, sit. We can work with this.' And I walk out of the meeting saying to myself, 'I pitched a piece of shit. They should've thrown me out.' . . . [But] they made it work. . . . They virtually wrote it in front of me.

"I now drive a Mercedes, I feel real good about myself and I know things are going to work out. I have enough money now that I don't need . . . [to take any] shit. The whole change in attitude reflected in those meetings makes them want me. And it's body language. . . . People are reading facial expressions, and the energy of people makes a tremendous amount of difference. If you can fake that as a writer, it does a hell of a lot of good.

"They're hoping you show confidence because it feeds them. It gives them a feeling of strength when they feel the writer knows what he is doing . . . they are more scared than you are. . . . They have their overhead. They have to find a good script. They're only hoping and praying that yours is good. They're desperate."

"So much of being a successful screenwriter is [establishing rapport]," says writer-producer Tom Greene. "I have sold projects where I didn't know what the project was.

"I remember one producer who had a lot of shooting trophies in his office. I made up an entire story about how I was from Belgium and my father invented the interlocking safety-trigger mechanism on shotguns. I told him all these absurd made-up tales about my trap-shooting days. And he told me every boring dull story about hunting deer and pheasant and grouse. When it was all over he says to me, 'You know you are a very, very fascinating fellow.' Even though I never pitched him a story he gave me . . . [a writing] assignment."

The final requisite for success as a screenwriter is the ability to work well on one's own. Most writers work without partners. "Writing can be very lonely," says Ron Koslow. "Basically what we do is sit alone in rooms asking ourselves questions."

A lot of self-discipline is required. "The hardest part about writing is making yourself work every day," says McKee. "I know a guy who actually chained himself to his chair and had his wife hold the key to the locks."

"The guys who really pull it off are the ones who get up in the morning and have regular hours and do the work," says Silliphant. "I don't know anyone who just waits around till he feels like writing. You never get it written. I set myself so many pages a day and I don't go to bed till I finish."

"Our discipline was greatly aided when we started using a stenographer," says Lawrence Lasker of his work with partner Walter Parkes. "We have a court reporter come in and we dictate rough drafts. The presence of another person forces you to concentrate and get it done."

Despite the hardships of screenwriting, there are some wonderful benefits. First, there are the creative satisfactions. The late Paddy Chayefsky (*Network*) said: "[T]here are many terrific moments along the way. Each scene has some. You come in tired, you sit down, you begin to boil up a little, and pretty soon things are moving ... things click and all of a sudden synapses start picking up things you had forgotten and eight, nine and ten good pages come out. ... And you write something you say is terrific, to yourself. These kind of satisfactions occur often; otherwise you couldn't keep at it."

Another satisfaction writers derive from their work is in simply being part of the movie business. They like the glamour of associating with the rich and famous and take great pride that their work is seen by millions of people.

And of course there is the money. Writers Guild minimum for a feature script is about $50,000. Top screenwriters receive $350,000 or more and additional compensation if the script is filmed.

As an anonymous screenwriter once said: "They ruin your stories. They massacre your ideas. They prostitute your art. They trample your pride. And what do you get for it? A fortune."

DIRECTORS

In the early days of talking pictures, directors were not nearly as important or powerful as they are today. Moviemaking was dominated by studio executives and producers. When a project was ready to roll, a director on the studio's payroll would be assigned to it. He was just another technician brought in to fulfill the studio's vision.

Because of its menial nature, not many people aspired to the job. Writer Gore Vidal recalls that "in the old days they used to say that the director was the brother-in-law.

"Nobody bright or ambitious wanted to be down there on the set all day. It was boring. If the director changed the script—if I had written 'medium-close shot' in the script and he decided suddenly to do a long shot—all hell would break loose upstairs in the executive dining room. . . . So imagine the laughter that went through this town when the French, who are always wrong, suddenly decided that all these hacks were truly great creators."

But the joke was on Hollywood, for the director's stature did rise, dramatically. The *auteur* theory provided intellectual justification for transforming technicians into artists. At the same time other changes in the industry gave them power. With the demise of the studio system, producers were no longer on staff. As free-lance entrepreneurs, they had to devote more time to hustling deals and had less time to attend to the creative aspects of filmmaking. Similarly, with talent no longer under long-term contract, executives had to concentrate a lot of energy on deal-making. And as the studios evolved into complex businesses, executives had to handle more administrative and business matters. Directors filled the void.

Directors also have clout because they are magnets for stars. The opportunity to work with a talented director can be decisive for a star when choosing among the many roles offered him. He knows that the quality of his appearance in a film, as well as its overall excellence, depends on the director. As a result, stars generally won't commit themselves to a part until they know who their director will be.

Today directors are involved with movies from their conception, often working with the writer on the script, then closely supervising all aspects of production and postproduction. Experienced directors are given a great deal of latitude in shooting their pictures as long as they respect the budget.

Because of the tremendous responsibility vested in them, directors are treated with great deference by executives and producers. No longer considered servants, directors today are more like ship captains, says writer-director Colin Higgins. "You're sort of steering this enormous vessel called 'making the movie' and your port of destination is making a successful film . . . you set off with a group of creative people and technicians and your job is to bring them safely to the other side of the lake."

But with greater responsibility has come greater stress. The director works in a pressure-cooker atmosphere, besieged by cast and crew members seeking advice and solace. "It's fifty questions before nine A.M. that you have to answer and do something about," says writer-director Joan Tewkesbury. "The amount of emotional wear and tear is just indescribable," says Allan Arkush. "I have sweated through an entire sports jacket, just soaked, and it's not an uncommon thing."

During production a director typically works twelve to eighteen hours a day, five to six days a week, for months on end. "It's probably the hardest job in the world," says Irvin Kershner. "It's physical and it's mental and it's a terrific strain."

Sydney Pollack (*Tootsie*) told students at AFI: "If somebody asked me what is the most important thing about directing, I would say to be in good physical shape . . . it's the most enormously grueling physical exercise you can go through, partly because there is so much emotional strain.

"It's not just a question of can you solve the artistic problem—for every moment that it takes you to solve the artistic problem, it's costing millions of dollars. And millions of dollars make people behave badly. Grown men behave like five-year-olds. They cry. They threaten you. They get hysterical. Actors, who have careers at stake and believe that you are going to destroy their careers, will get crazy at three in the morning and call you, and fight with each other, and won't come out of the trailer, and so on.

"Anybody who tells you he isn't scared to death directing a ten-million-dollar movie with major stars is a liar. . . . I don't care if you're a hundred years old, you're scared, because you've got a reputation at stake. You say, 'Jesus Christ, if this one isn't as good as the last one, then I've failed.' And there's this constant anxiety between trying to get what you want, and technical problems, and a producer who's yelling at you. In every picture there is a scene where you say, 'God, I don't know how I'm going to do this.'

"[Y]et if you ever came on a set where I'm working, you would say, 'Jeez, you're so calm, so unruffled. You never yell. You handle it so easily.' But . . . [you] don't know what's going on inside. You just get very adept in the art of hiding whatever anxiety you have."

Writer-turned-executive Gary Devore likens directing to driving a bus full of circus performers. "The director is a ringmaster, he has to organize all of it and deal with a multitude of personalities, each one eccentric because everyone in the movie industry feels they're an artist. . . . And usually people who see themselves like that aren't shy about making themselves heard."

First, the director must earn the respect of his crew. Director Jonathan Kaplan says, "A crew will sit there and watch the director to see if this guy knows what he's doing or not. They'll decide real quick. . . . If they think you know what you're doing they will kill themselves for you. If they think you're an idiot and you don't know what you're doing but you're a nice guy, they won't sabotage you but they won't rush to help you either. If they think you're not only an egomaniac and a prick but you also don't know what you are doing, then they'll drop sandbags on your head."

Second, the director must be able to draw good performances from his cast. Most actors perform best when they have an emotionally supportive relationship with a director—which can be difficult for the director to provide when he is under such intense pressure himself.

"Actors come onto a set terrified," says director John Badham. "They're in an awful position of having to stand in front of sixty or one hundred people and start doing scenes and acting, which you or I would never do. . . . You have to create . . . a very relaxed environment for that actor to function. Otherwise he's going to give you something very stiff and mechanical—something that he thinks will please everybody but not necessarily take any chances. He's not going to take any creative chances if he's going to get yelled at, shit upon or laughed at.

"Dictatorial is not necessarily the best way to do this. Sometimes it's a ploy. Sometimes it's OK to scare the shit out of somebody and yell at them if that's going to help them do it. But afterwards maybe it's a good idea to let them know you like them and it's all right."

Moreover, the director must know how to guide an actor's performance without stifling his creativity. Robert De Niro told *American Film:* "The worst thing is a director that tells someone how to do something. You know, some directors like results, and they'll tell you, 'You do this and you go over and you smile.' . . . They don't understand that you could do it another way and that it would be better for you. Not only better for you, but it would give you more confidence and more joy. And you would know that they trust you and your choice.

"Then there's the opposite, where a director is intimidated. Say, in my position, if I'm with a director and he says yes to everything. That's ridiculous. I have to have somebody I respect and who respects me and who tells me, 'No,' or 'That's OK, but try this.' You have to have a give-and-take. If it's out of balance, then it won't work."

In the event of a disagreement, the star may have more clout with the studio than the director does. A novice director with a star is like a little boy with a gorilla on a leash—its presence impresses everyone, but his control over the beast is tenuous at best.

"Stars are a pain in the ass to a director," says writer William Goldman. "They have to be coddled, they need to be stroked. Ultimately what they do is waste time, and time is the enemy of all productions. . . .

"As a general rule I would say if you corner every director in the world and say, 'This is off the record. . . . If you can make your next picture (and you have the same budget) but in one case you have a star and in one case you don't have a star . . .' there may be *one* director in the history of the world who would rather go with the star, but for the most part none of them want to."

"Very often big stars are barely trained or not very well trained," says director Elia Kazan. "They also have bad habits: They don't want to look bad, and they protect themselves; or they're not pliable anymore. They know what their act is. If I put them in a scene that's a little bit dangerous, their agents come to see me."

Another prerequisite for a director is the ability to soothe nervous studio executives and producers looking over his shoulder. Only independent filmmakers or those directors with the clout of a Steven Spielberg or George Lucas have the freedom to operate without interference.

"A director is caught between the frying pan and the fire," says director Martha Coolidge. "[O]n the one hand, you're expected to be this godlike creature running the ship—an

authority, an inspiration, somebody with all the answers. . . .
On the other hand, all the guys above you want to push you
around in some way—they all have their interests at stake,
mostly money, but also maybe a girlfriend who is an actress
or some product they want promoted in the picture."

Studio executives and producers are primarily concerned
with completing the picture on time. Delays can be expensive,
with each extra day of production frequently costing tens of
thousands of dollars. If the director falls behind, he can expect visits from anxious executives, who will scrutinize his
actions and second-guess his decisions. If he goes over budget
his fees may be subject to reduction. In extreme cases directors are fired, an increasingly likely occurrence since the
Heaven's Gate debacle in which Michael Cimino spent $36
million on a film budgeted for $7.5 million.

Even so, a director knows that no matter how competent
and prepared he may be, his control over production is frag-
ile. The shooting schedule can be disrupted for any number
of reasons: Actors blow lines, equipment fails, props break,
the weather turns bad. So many things can and do go wrong
that most directors are satisfied if they realize 75 percent of
their ideal vision. Directing is a race against time, with the
director continually confronted with difficult choices and
forced to make compromises.

Directors have evolved methods to keep their overseers
at bay. Directors Guild president Gilbert Cates says, "When
I first came to L.A. a terrific director . . . gave me this advice:
'When you start in the morning go out and shoot an insert
[a simple shot]. Just have the director of photography take
out the camera and shoot . . . because that then gets put on
the camera report as the first shot. So if your call is at seven
A.M., and you shoot the insert at seven forty-five, and then
relay the information that you got off your first shot at seven
forty-five, they'll leave you alone all morning. If you start . . .
with a complicated shot and by nine o'clock you haven't made
the shot, three guys come down to visit you to find out what
the hell is happening.' "

But while the director can sometimes take advantage of
his superiors' ignorance, many times that ignorance is a
hindrance. Working for people who don't understand film-

making can be frustrating. Irvin Kershner recalls his fights with a first-time producer: "Finally I convinced him, not that way, this way. We made the picture . . . and now in cutting he's a genius [again]. He says, 'I've seen pictures all my life. I know that's no good.' . . . [I explain to him] there is such a thing as rhythm, such a thing as not being too overt, such a thing as leading the audience in suspense, such a thing as surprise. A teaching thing goes on.

"When the picture is shown the first time to the studio, the man stands up and says, 'This is totally wrong. It's too overt.' And using the words he has learned [he criticizes it]. And the studio liked it. [But] they looked at him and said, 'Well you may have a point there. We didn't see it that way. Let's make some changes.'

"I didn't realize until later what a ploy it was. When the picture now goes out, if it's successful, he's a hero. He made certain changes. If the picture fails, it's 'See, I told you it wasn't working.'

"Now the truth is that the studio empowered him to come in and sit in on the final cut and make changes. And he just ripped the thing to shreds. . . . I came in at night, after the editors were gone. I went back into the editing room and I repaired the damage. Put things back, changed it, made it work, myself. Nobody ever knew I came in that night. Next day they looked at it and said, 'It's great.'

"Twice I have done that. . . . The editor didn't even know I was doing it. He thought something was peculiar, but it looked good. He thought maybe he had made some changes that were good. . . . You don't fight. If you fight you lose because they can throw you off."

Most directors have learned to avoid direct confrontations. "If you go in and get very arrogant with studio people," says John Badham, "the next time the subject comes up of maybe making a picture with you they're a lot less inclined to have you there. They say, 'Oh, don't use him, he's trouble. He's a pain in the ass.'

"[Of course] if the 'he' in question has had a couple of enormous hits, suddenly all bets are off, and he's much more in favor, because studio executives are whores for success. Yesterday's asshole is today's fair-haired boy. . . . Marty Brest was fired from *WarGames* . . . and was a virtual leper in Hollywood. I mean nobody would have anything to do with him. And Don Simpson at Paramount had the conviction and balls to hire him for a picture which has now turned out to be a giant hit, *Beverly Hills Cop*. Well no longer is Marty Brest a leper, he's the guy who you have to have to direct your next comedy."

For most directors their greatest problem is convincing a studio to hire them in the first place. While directors with strong track records are always in demand, only about 10 percent of Guild directors work regularly.

"It's very sad because some people [with a lot of talent] . . . say, 'I can't do the business part,' " explains Joan Tewkesbury. "I say, Then don't even entertain this [profession]. Because this isn't a business about talent . . . it's a business about putting elements together. . . . It's a game and you better learn all the stations of that game. It's like a Monopoly board."

"You have to package yourself in such a way to be inviting," says director Tamar Hoffs. "You must make compromises or you won't get anywhere. If you want their money you have to listen to what they want. And you have to make yourself that thing." If you are a beginning director that may mean directing an exploitation film or accepting an actor against your wishes.

For accomplished directors the battle is often over subject matter. The hardest thing about being a director in Hollywood, says Nicholas Meyer, is "being able to make the films you would like to make. All art is inevitably intertwined, at some point, with commerce. It's helpful to remember that the Globe Theatre was a money-making, not a subsidized, operation. But nowhere are art and commerce more inextricably linked than in that so-called art of motion pictures.

"As motion pictures become increasingly expensive . . . the more reluctant the financial component is to invest or put money into something that may be problematic . . . Your instinct as an artist to explore new territory, to stretch yourself, is in direct conflict with the entire mercantile process on the other side of the coin which says hedge your bet, find out what's a sure thing. And what that means to a person like me is that it's very hard to find a script . . . that interests me sufficiently that also interests them."

A director's attractiveness to a studio is primarily a function of the box-office success of his pictures. "So much of what goes on in Hollywood is who's hot at the moment," says director Allan Arkush. "It's very frustrating to see a director's name on a list of 'A' directors if he has done only one picture but it happened to be successful. And if you look at it, it's not necessarily attributable to the director."

The successful director is both an artist and a politician. He must not only be a talented filmmaker, but also savvy enough to enlist the support of studio executives and collaborators in his movie endeavors.

A director must know his medium. "You have to know your tools," says Robert Altman (*M*A*S*H*). "It's like a painter. If you don't know how to mix paint, if you don't know how to apply it . . . if you don't understand perspective . . . you can't paint very well. . . . In film you have to know your camera and your sound equipment, color and light and detail, and you have to know something about acting and performance."

That doesn't mean, however, that a director must be a proficient writer, cinematographer, actor and editor. A director needs to know only what he wants, what is possible, and how to get his cast and crew to create it.

"You hire a cinematographer, you hire an editor and they do a lot of what is called directing," says director Michael Wadleigh (*Wolfen*). "And you ought to get the hell out of the way. When I hire a cinematographer I don't look through the viewfinder. That's what they are supposed to do. (And I am a cinematographer myself.) That's their great creativity."

A director who refuses to delegate tasks to his collaborators will demoralize them, and by immersing himself in too many details he risks losing an overall perspective of the film. The result is often a picture that is technically brilliant in parts but boring in its entirety.

Overemphasis on the technical aspects of filmmaking is a common failing of novice directors. "They want to show the world that they are directing," says John Badham. "And their technique gets very self-conscious, depending on whatever is in vogue at the time. When zoom lenses first came in . . . boy, you weren't any good if you weren't zooming in and out all the time. And dollying around using the Panaglide camera when it came in . . . the director wanted you to know he was there and on the job: 'Look, Ma, I know how to move the camera.' "

Essentially, what a director must know about cameras is how to determine when they have captured the images he needs. That requires an ability to concentrate on the performance. A director can't be "influenced by all the nonsense that goes on at a set, because it's a circus," says Jonathan Kaplan. "I've learned to sit and watch a take and then click off in my head . . . [what] I've got to fix. . . . You get lost when you get distracted. Like right after a take if six people are there asking you questions and you forget why you want to do it again. . . . Nobody wants to stick around and shoot useless coverage or useless takes if you've already got it. And I think the more you work, the more you realize that most time is spent shooting protection and doing things that it turns out you don't need."

Likewise, a director need not be an actor himself in order to know how to draw good performances from them. What he must know is how to communicate in their language. "One of the most important things they [young directors] can do is learn how to talk to actors," says Badham. "If a writer becomes a director he may talk to the actor in terms of writing. He wants his dialogue said exactly the way he wrote it. He's thinking in terms of story structure—things that the actor doesn't know about. Things he can't play. If an editor becomes a director he starts talking to the actor in terms of 'This next shot is your big close-up. I'm cutting to you after this line of dialogue.' Things again that the actor can't play.

"The actor needs to know how to approach not only his role in the more general sense, but in the more specific sense. . . . You tell him what the story is about. Now it might

seem obvious. . . . Well, little do you know how unobvious it
is until you start talking to the actor and find out he thinks
it is about something totally different. He is playing some
completely different drama than the one you are directing."

Indeed, the ability to communicate with each of his collaborators is a fundamental skill for directors, and one that
is rarely taught in film school. Allan Arkush recalls that when
he started working on film crews "my biggest impression was
how social filmmaking was . . . in the sense of how you have
to deal with so many people . . . you have to articulate what
you're doing and you have to be able to express yourself
clearly. It was a major shock that I couldn't just be a retiring
kind of shy person. I had to be someone who was out-front
and aggressive and had to become the center of attention in
a lot of working situations. That took some changing in my
personality to accomplish."

"If you don't have the ability to deal with people, or you
don't want to deal with people, then you have no business
being a director," says Badham. "George Lucas discovered
this and ultimately decided that he didn't want to be a director
anymore. He's a very nice man but a painfully shy person
who hates dealing with people. It's just very hard for him.
And he said after the first *Star Wars,* 'I'm not doing this
anymore. I'll hire directors and get the picture done through
them.' "

"Directing is eighty percent communication and twenty
percent knowhow," says Steven Spielberg. "Because if you
can communicate to the people who know how to edit, know
how to light, and know how to act—if you can communicate
what you want so that what they're doing is giving you . . .
[your vision], and what you feel, that's my definition of a
good director.

"And I think all the good directors of the past had that.
If you ever gave John Ford a camera, and you said, 'Light
that set, and take the meter readings, and show me where
to put the lights,' I'll bet Ford couldn't do it—not that well.
But with a guy like [cinematographer] Gregg Toland, you
would go to Toland and you would say to him, 'This is late
day, this is dusk, and everybody's come home hungry and

sullen, and I would love to see this scene in partial silhouette or in backlight.' Well maybe that's as much as Ford ever said. . . . And what Toland gave him were some of the greatest images ever put on black-and-white celluloid, in *Grapes of Wrath.*

"I just think a director has to communicate what he thinks because a director can't get on the camera all the time, he can't move the lights around, and . . . he usually doesn't sit down and physically cut the film."

A director must also be able to make decisions quickly. "The most important skill I have on a moment-to-moment basis is being decisive," says Jonathan Kaplan. "Just right away deciding even if it's arbitrary. . . . Don't leave people up in the air. Make a decision and push them in that direction. That makes them feel good. They feel like there's a captain of this ship. They know where the hell they're going."

Moreover, a director must be a good collaborator. "You have to be able to work with people," says Kaplan. "If you go in there with some kind of attitude like 'This is my personal vision and it can only be done this way,' you're lost. . . . You have to be able to have an idea of what you want and do whatever you can to get it without inhibiting the creativity of the people you're hiring.

"If that kind of environment can be created, you're going to get the best out of everybody. There's another way to do it, which is to scare everybody to death and beat the shit out of them and make them think they're going to lose their job every two minutes . . . but I've found that the way that works best for me is to encourage collaboration because it's a collaborative medium." Says Badham: "The days of the tyrannical directors are pretty much long gone."

The function of the director, says Michael Wadleigh, is "making sure that everybody contributes and feels that they're contributing . . . it's trying to make sure everyone knows what their job is and making them feel it was their idea to do whatever it is that they're doing. That seems like a technique that works very well.

"I'm a great believer that the actors and technicians have an enormous amount to contribute. And it only makes sense.

How much experience have I had in my life? If you open it up so that everyone's experience can come to bear it's amazing how good their ideas can be."

But many novice directors are afraid to appear anything less than omniscient, for fear of losing the respect of their cast and crew. "They won't listen to anyone," says Badham. "They don't want to appear ignorant . . . and will go ahead with what they're going to do, partially out of being stubborn, partially out of being afraid to look like they're not in charge. A smarter beginner will throw himself a little more on the mercy of the court, the mercy of the cameraman. . . . I don't say do that one hundred percent . . . but certainly it's a good idea to open yourself up and listen to them and see if you can make heads or tails out of what they're recommending."

A good director is like a sponge, soaking up suggestions and advice. "When I went to New York to direct *Saturday Night Fever,* says Badham, "I had never been in a discotheque in my life. I had never been in Brooklyn in my life. I went in and opened up every antenna on me and started listening and learning real fast and real hard. . . . And people [who saw the movie] were convinced that I had grown up in Brooklyn and that I understood it tremendously. I was lucky I had a lot of nice people around me. People who just lived nearby and would come in and comment.

"It's important to stay as fresh and current with what is going on as you can. I don't think you can stay in your own insular little box, which, as a person gets older, is easier and easier to do. It's easy to spend your money and get a big house and be insulated from the outside world.

"I've been working on a bicycle film, *American Flyers.* As we started to train the actors how to ride and get them in shape for the racing, I thought it would be a good idea for me to go out and ride with them every morning. . . . Well, sure enough, as we rode every morning for several weeks, we would bring along guys who rode the race circuit and learned a tremendous amount from them. . . . They would show me some trick ride or a technique and all kinds of things that I wouldn't have known about if I had been sitting in my office."

In addition to understanding their craft and being good collaborators, the best directors have something to say. "What makes a director an artist as opposed to a craftsman," says Nicholas Meyer, "involves not a knowledge of film but a vision of life. Most directors are craftsmen and not artists because they have no central vision, no moral relationship to the world. They like to make movies. They like to ride in the limo. They like to order sixty people around at midnight. They must be in love with the film regardless of the content of the film. . . . It's a very nice way to make a living. . . . But I think an artist is someone who has something to say."

"Goddamn, a director should be an artist," says Gilbert Cates. "Now an artist has to know his craft. . . . That's true. . . . But to assume that the principal ingredient is learning the craft and to forget that the purpose of the craft is to express ideas is a failing. [Mastery of] craft gives you the freedom to dream. . . . What is so disturbing is that so many people deal with craft as the end product. They assume that if you have the craft that you're a filmmaker. That's not it at all."

ACTORS AND STARS

Actors can be classified into three groups. The largest group, "fledgling actors," are those struggling to earn a living in the profession. They are occasionally employed to perform, but spend most of their time engaged in other activities, such as auditioning, taking acting classes and waiting on tables.

"Working actors" have advanced to the point where they work regularly and can financially support themselves from acting. They may be well-known "character" actors, like Ned Beatty, who are frequently cast in secondary roles, or perhaps they have a recurring role in a television series.

"Stars" are the elite group. They are powerful because pictures are marketed on their looks and names. Their strong public followings make studios eager to obtain their services. A star's participation in a project can induce otherwise ambivalent executives to green-light it. With a superstar in tow, they are willing to tackle risky projects, feeling invincible in their company. Until that illusion crumbles under repeated flops, the superstar remains a highly desired commodity.

While it's difficult for actors to climb from fledgling to star status, it's easy to slide down. Consequently, fledgling actors worry about whether they will ever achieve more, and stars worry about sustaining what they have. Working actors can worry about both.

And most actors have plenty of time to worry. One of the most unusual aspects of the profession is that its practitioners generally devote more time to seeking roles than performing them. "I think what it would be like for a lawyer to go to law school or a doctor to go to medical school and never be able to practice what they learned to do," says director John Badham. "Once every few years they could go in and do a minor procedure on somebody. Every three or four months they could go in and sew up a cut knee, or give somebody some pills for a headache. And that's it. Well that's what an actor's life is like.

"It's a life you wouldn't wish on anybody. . . . There are thousands and thousands of actors out here who are teaching in schools, driving taxicabs, selling real estate and doing everything but acting—the thing they trained for."

"The greatest problem is not knowing when you're going to work next," says Catherine Hicks (*Garbo Talks*). "Until you're at a point when you can book three pictures a year, the hardest part is having days go by and not being busy enough. I envy people who on Fridays are really exhausted from the normal workaday world. They have a reason to rest. [As an actor] there is too much rest. You can say you live at Jane Fonda's [exercise class], and learn French, and take cooking lessons, and plant your garden, but it's not a profession. . . . I mean it's fun, but to me they are just hobbies. I don't know how actors pretend to be into that because I think it's a kind of pathetic substitute for working."

Acting careers generally don't advance in a steady upward direction, but rather, they spurt, stall and fall without reason, as though the actor were on a roller-coaster ride. Sometimes he is hot and is offered every important role in town. At other times he can go for months or years without working. A slump can be particularly depressing after one has had a taste of success.

A cycle recurs. The industry becomes infatuated with an actor, turns him into a celebrity and then loses interest in him. Women's careers tend to be especially fleeting. "They have an extremely insecure life," says Badham. "If you're a talented woman and very beautiful . . . you will be kind of burned out within four or five years when the next beautiful talented girl comes along who is kinda fresh. You know, 'Ho, hum. We're tired of Teri Garr now, let's move on to Kathleen Turner.' And then four or five years later Kathleen Turner will be down the tubes." It's the rare actress, like Jane Fonda, who is able to sustain a career for more than a decade.

Talent becomes a less important prerequisite for acting success as the quality of movies declines. Films that rely on sex or violence or are aimed at a teenage audience don't demand a great deal of acting ability. Moviegoers don't go to see *Hot Dog* because of its fine performances. Consequently, many stars are screen personalities rather than actors. They either don't have the ability to perform varied roles or are not given the opportunity to do so.

"There are two types of stars," says Peter Coyote (*E.T.*). "There are transformers and there are icons or archetypes. Jack Nicholson, Dustin Hoffman, Robert De Niro and Jon Voight are transformers, and there is no limit to their range. Bob Redford, Burt Reynolds and Clint Eastwood are archetypes. The audience wants to see them be themselves. Burt Reynolds is actually a really good actor but the audience will not give him permission [to do something else]. When Burt Reynolds stops doing car-wreck movies, nobody goes to see him." The top women stars, such as Meryl Streep, Jane Fonda and Sissy Spacek, often appear to have greater ability than their male counterparts because audiences allow actresses to express a wider range of emotions than they do actors—just as women in general are allowed more freedom to express emotions.

More so than in most professions, an actor's fate is in the hands of others—whether it be producers, directors, studio executives or agents. An actor does not even know whether accepting a role will help or hurt him. A job well done may result in his being typecast. Explained Bert Lahr: "After *The Wizard of Oz* I was typecast as a lion, and there aren't all that many parts for lions."

Success is not apportioned justly. While those who work hard and have talent are more likely to succeed, there is no assurance that if you expend the time and effort you will be rewarded.

"You can be in this business for years and years and years and never work and then all of a sudden it just happens," says Steve Railsback (*The Stunt Man*). "I was watching an old television show called *Hawk* with Burt Reynolds. Who would have thought that would have happened with Burt Reynolds? And I saw a guest shot, a little hour show in 1968, and the killer in it was Gene Hackman. Here is a guy, I don't know how old he was when he became successful, but he was older. I mean he probably wanted to quit a thousand times and didn't. You just never know. It's the weirdest, strangest business in the world. And then there are other people who started out with me who are still hanging out in New York, still working at their craft and still don't have any money. And you go, 'Why? They're so talented.' "

"I have some friends who lately I don't call anymore," confesses Teri Garr. "I feel badly that I'm working and they just never are. There's no difference [in ability] in my mind between us. But I went to another level and they're working in a bank. And they were just as tenacious, just as competitive as I was."

Even actors who have received Oscars, Emmys and other critical acclaim are not assured of continued employment. "There are periods when you're in demand, but that won't last," says agent Martha Luttrell. "No matter how high up you are, there is someone else who is higher up who wants the role. There's always competition. And as good as you may be, they may not think you're right for the role."

The haphazard nature of an acting career makes actors apprehensive. "You feel like once you finish a job you are never going to work again," says Railsback. "You are always anxious. You are down most of the time. You are on your back most of the time. . . . So there is insecurity, there is fear, a lot of fear."

"You have to have a high tolerance for anxiety," says Peter Coyote. "It's a feast or famine existence. . . . You go from having a great deal of money to having absolutely none." Considering the drawbacks of the profession, it's amazing that anyone would want to be an actor. "We do it because we cannot not do it," says Martin Sheen. "If you have creativity you must explore it for your own personal salvation, your own happiness, your own joy. You will never be happy if you don't pursue it.

"It sounds awful, but you almost have to love the pain of it. You have to love the hard times as much as you do the good times. . . . I think a fellow actor would understand what I am saying. The public might think I'm psychotic—it is, almost."

Certainly the vicissitudes of an acting career discourage all but the most determined. "Being stubborn is important," says Kay Lenz (*White Line Fever*). "I said to myself, 'Nobody can tell me that I can't do it.' "

Only the most tenacious can overcome the rejection an actor regularly receives, a rejection that is particularly difficult to handle because it's so personal—the commodity an actor sells is himself. "A lot of people think they want to be actors," says Railsback. "And they're told in their hometowns that they look terrific. [But] it's the kind of business that if you can't stand rejection you shouldn't be in it. Because it's mostly rejection."

"Everybody who wants to be in this business has to have this enormous dream," says Teri Garr, "and I might say, live in a fantasy life. You have to be propelled by that because there are doors slammed in your face all the time."

Many successful actors say that they always had an unswerving belief in themselves. "I knew I was going to be a professional actor and I had no doubt about success, not even once in my life," says Martin Sheen. "I never doubted it. I've never met an actor who did doubt success.

"We lived in a rat-infested tenement on the Lower East Side for several years . . . and ate spaghetti, and I loved every minute of it. I loved it when it was happening [because] . . . I knew success would be coming.

"I remember getting evicted from a place in the Bronx, thrown out into the street with my wife and child—baby, seventeen months old. And I bummed a ride to Ohio to see my father, who had never met my wife or seen my baby, and to visit my brother, who was in jail, and try to help him out of jail. It was one of the worst times and the best times. "And I remember one of my brothers saying, 'You're a burden to our family.' And I got angry and I said, 'There is going to come a day, as surely as the sun rises tomorrow, when I will make more money in an hour than you'll make in a year. And I knew it was true. Despair, yes, but I always believed in myself. Absolutely."

Because of their strong egos and single-minded pursuit of their careers, actors are frequently accused of being narcissistic. Marlon Brando once said: "An actor's a guy who, if you ain't talking about him, [he] ain't listening."

Apparently there is some truth to the charge. Says Los Angeles psychiatrist Dr. Hyla Cass, "Many people go into the performing arts because of an inordinate need for the attention and approval of others. As children they were rewarded for what they did, not for who they were. Many had lonely, emotionally deprived childhoods and suffer from deep feelings of personal inadequacy. Performing makes them feel worthwhile, even for a moment superior."

The demands of the profession may be such that healthy, well-adjusted people are not suited for it. That's fine with actor-turned-producer Robert Evans, who says healthy people don't make good actors anyway: "The more normal one is the more boring the actor. Normalcy in acting breeds dullness. The imperfection in one . . . the more bent one is, the more brilliant one can be. The more schizophrenic one can be, the better the actor. . . . It's the imperfections, the neuroses that make actors interesting. Marilyn Monroe was as sick a person as there ever was. . . . You have to be neurotic to be really good. People don't want to see normalcy on the screen. They want to see something different.

"We are a strange breed. . . . Sometimes the most explosive actors on the screen are the most introverted people in life because they lead two lives. They're only happy when they're working . . . and outside of their work . . . they can't even converse with people . . . very few actors are entertaining people.

"You ever sit in a room and listen to a bunch of actors talk? They're the most boring people in the world. Not on the set. There they are wonderful. And with women the same way. The easiest women to meet are the girlfriends and wives of the movie stars. They are bored with their husbands or boyfriends because they have become their mothers. There is a line that is very true: 'An actress is more than a woman, an actor is less than a man.' Because it's the same thing, only on a woman it's attractive, and on a man it's not. They both need protection. When a man needs protection, a woman to protect him, it isn't manly. When a woman needs it, it's feminine."

Stardom is not all it is cracked up to be.

The glamour is mostly in magazines and the minds of fans, not in the lives of stars.

As Teri Garr prepared for her first publicity tour, she thought: "Now comes the good part. Now comes the glamour, the fur coats, the champagne. . . . [The studio asked:] 'Do you want to go on this publicity tour? It's ten cities in ten days.' I thought it sounded good. [But] ten cities in ten days is unbelievably hard. Everyplace I would arrive would be the best hotel in town, a suite, flowers, champagne. But did I have time to look at them? No. Because you have to have dinner with this one, a seven-thirty A.M. radio interview, then a TV spot. . . . There was no glamour. Plus I was all alone."

Back in Los Angeles she quickly tired of life in the fast lane. "Eventually all these parties where famous people are turn out to be work," she says. "It's just work. . . . You dress up and you go there and . . . you might as well punch in the time clock 'cause you have to say 'Hi' and be nice to everyone. . . . [It] is all about business and scoring points and everybody knows it and everybody does it. . . . But that's not how I choose to spend my time. I want to be with friends that I can relate to and say, 'Hey, let's go to the movies, or let's talk about this.' "

Jane Fonda says that the most surprising aspect of stardom is how little it matters: "You are still a human being, and you're lonely, and you have ups and downs, and you have a family to deal with, and kids to bring up, and being a star doesn't help."

Shooting a film is certainly not glamorous. "It's very hard . . . exhausting work," says Steve Railsback. Actors spend hours having their hair done and makeup applied, and may have to perform in uncomfortable costumes and in adverse weather. They often must leave their homes and families for extended periods of time. Winnebagos and hotel rooms, no matter how luxurious, soon lose their appeal. Moreover, actors are under a lot of pressure to hit their marks and say their lines correctly so as to avoid delays.

The shooting schedule is not arranged according to what is best for the actor but what is most expeditious for the production. "In the making of the movie the actor is one of the least significant parts," says Peter Coyote. "Just imagine that you are doing a peak emotional scene. It's highly emotional. And you just got your motors running, and you've done two rehearsals, and you're absolutely confident and you're ready to go. Everything is perfect for you, and the first AD [assistant director] yells, 'Lunch,' and they take off for an hour. And they feed you roast beef and Brussels sprouts, and chocolate ice cream and chocolate cake and Jell-O salad. And they call you back at one o'clock to get your makeup touched up and then they throw you into your high scene and ask you to find that same emotional peak again."

Actors are often required to perform in embarrassing circumstances, such as nude scenes. "I just did a picture for Orion called *Clay Pigeons,*" says Lisa Eichhorn, "and there were two scenes in it that were very difficult. One was a rape scene and the other was a scene where there are eleven of us, air force pilots . . . and there was a delousing, a shower scene. And emotionally it was very hard for me because I'm the only pilot who is female. It was also very hard for the . . . men."

Other scenes are downright frightening. Railsback recalls that while filming *The Stunt Man* he and Peter O'Toole had to go aloft in a small crane. "It scared the hell out of me. I'm not kidding. We wanted out of this thing . . . we did this three or four times and we were scared to death. And as we get off the thing, Peter says, 'Ah, the glamour of it all.' "

While many roles are offered to stars, few are desirable. Jane Fonda says her greatest frustration is "the lack of good parts, and the lack of good writing." Paul Newman says, "There are hardly any good scripts around. Redford has done two pictures in five years. I think Dustin has done one picture in three or four years . . . I've done two pictures in four years. The scripts just aren't very good or about anything. . . . I used to spend about fifteen percent of my time reading scripts, and eighty-five percent of my time reading whatever I wanted to read. [Now] I probably spent eighty-five percent of my time reading bad scripts."

Stars are most concerned that their participation in a movie not jeopardize their professional standing. They have an investment to protect. Unlike fledgling actors, who will take anything in the hope that it will gain them greater visibility, stars select roles carefully to ensure they don't end up in a flop. But it's difficult to determine which scripts will make good movies.

James Caan turned down the starring role in *One Flew Over the Cuckoo's Nest* ("all those white walls"), *Superman* (he didn't want to wear that funny suit), and *Kramer vs. Kramer* ("middle-class bourgeois bullshit"). Instead, he accepted parts in pictures that flopped and his career went into eclipse. "I made a couple of bad pictures," he told *Esquire*, "and suddenly I'm not a smart move to go with. Bob De Niro, Robert Duvall, I don't care how big they are now, a couple of bad pictures and they'll be back on their asses again, too."

Stars also have psychological problems. Becoming a star does not necessarily make one self-confident or erase one's fears. Despite all his accomplishments, Eddie Murphy admits he is insecure about everything: "I wonder if I'm good-looking, if I'm talented, if I can sing. I wonder how funny people really think I am, or if it's a fluke."

"Actors are people that have been shit on most of their life by everybody else," says producer Martin Bregman (*Serpico*). "All of a sudden they become rich. And it usually is overnight, not in terms of a body of work. You can be in theater ten years and all of a sudden you are very visible.

You've been beaten up for so long that you have some wounds. . . . You don't suddenly lose your paranoia, or get rid of all your pain, or forget the abuses you've taken."

But a star is not allowed the frailties of other human beings. Misconduct will be widely reported by the media. A star is always expected to be charming, willing to discuss intimate details of his or her life, and tolerant of photographers snapping pictures whenever they please.

Unlike lawyers and doctors, who become revered as they grow older, stars become obsolete. They might better be called meteors, considering how short their careers are.

Nowadays there are few roles for older stars. When asked why she accepted a part in the film *Burnt Offerings,* Bette Davis replied: "Well, you see, at my age, to get any kind of good leading character—it just doesn't come along. I like to work about once a year. It's healthy not to sit at home. This script came along, and at least she was kind of a nice, normal woman who didn't kill anybody, and she didn't go crazy and all that. I have never seen the film and probably never will, because I know instinctively that I would hate it. It turned out to be a much bloodier film than I thought it would be. I never saw so much ketchup floating around a set in my life. It wasn't ideal, but there just wasn't anything else for me to do, so I did it."

Davis was once so frustrated by the lack of parts being offered her that she took out an ad in the trade papers. It read: "Wanted—employment. Mother of three. Divorced. Thirty years experience. Reasonably mobile. More affable than rumored."

Stars also fear their fans. As the object of millions of people's fantasies, they must always face the possibility that some deranged individual may decide to make them a target. A distraught Jodie Foster fan shot President Reagan, and another fan killed John Lennon. Many stars receive crank letters and phone calls. While most threats prove harmless, one can never be sure.

Perhaps the biggest drawback of stardom is the loss of privacy. Although most stars enjoy their fame, at times they just would like to be left alone. But fans expect them to indulge incessant requests for autographs, no matter how intrusive the interruption. A trip to a park or other public place can quickly turn into an autograph session. "A couple of weeks ago I went to Disneyland with my family," says Teri Garr, "and I couldn't stand in one place for too long . . . [or] a bunch of people would say, 'There she is. Can I have your autograph?' "

"When it [fame] started to happen to me," says Lisa Eichhorn, "I ran away from it. I moved out of town to Connecticut. I wasn't ready for people to know who I was when I went into a restaurant. I wasn't ready to be walking down the street in New York and have people say, 'Hey, Lisa.' I would say, 'God, who is that?' Of course it's someone, but it's no one you know."

Fame is "embarrassing," says Martin Sheen. "To most people . . . you could just as easily be Rin Tin Tin or Lassie. They've seen you on television or in the movies and it has nothing to do with you personally. It's just the image, they don't know you. One thing they say very often is 'God, you look so much younger.' Or 'God, you look tired.' "

But one need not feel unduly sorry for stars. The job does have its compensations. Eddie Murphy reportedly receives $4 million a picture, while Barbra Streisand gets $5 million. Dustin Hoffman, Warren Beatty and Robert Redford are each $6 million men. Sylvester Stallone gets an astronomical $12 million a picture. Such fees are paid up front, and do not include participation in a film's profits. Hoffman is reported to have earned a total of $25 million for his work in *Tootsie*.

"Let's face it, actors are paid more than they're worth," says James Garner. "Producers are idiots for paying what we ask."

PRODUCERS

"Making a film is like going to war," says producer Martin Bregman. As the producer, "you're the Eisenhower of D Day. It's up to you to see that all of your elements drive in the same direction. . . . The director is responsible for one phase, the writer is responsible for another phase, actors are responsible for what they contribute. . . . And there is somebody who has to be on top with an overview."

A less grandiose view of producing is offered by producer Walter Coblenz, who describes it as "something between being a coach and a dictator and sometimes a baby-sitter."

Writer Ben Hecht said the producer's chief task was turning good writers into hacks.

But for most people, says producer Jon Avnet, "being a producer is like being a whore."

Such diverse views reflect the amorphous nature of the profession. It's a job that varies with the skill and training of each producer. Those with backgrounds as filmmakers function differently from those who have been deal-makers. Moreover, a producer's role varies with the circumstances of each project. A producer working with a novice director will play a greater role than one working with a veteran. Sometimes producers exercise great authority. At other times studios treat them as messenger boys to their directors and stars. Defining a producer is difficult because he changes like a chameleon.

Ideally, the producer supervises every aspect of a picture's making. But since he dabbles in everything and specializes in nothing, his contribution is not always apparent. Producer William Bowers (*Support Your Local Sheriff*) pointed to his cast and crew and noted: "I'm the only one who could be hit by lightning right now and the only thing that would happen is that two weeks from now somebody would ask what happened to that guy who used to come down to the set."

But while the producer's contribution may not be obvious, he often plays an integral part in the making of a film. He is a sounding board for the ideas of the writer and director, supplying another opinion on such matters as story and casting. He is the liaison with the studio—protecting his director from undue interference. He is the mediator of disputes between cast and crew members, soothing ruffled feathers. And he is an all-around problem solver, ensuring that the logistical, legal and financial aspects of production run smoothly. "He is a vaudeville plate-twirler," says Martin Bregman, "who is twirling fifteen plates in the air . . . [and making] sure nothing breaks."

Many producers feel they don't receive adequate recognition for their work. Like writers, they complain that directors get all the credit. Often critics won't even mention the producer in their reviews. When producers are acknowledged, they're frequently portrayed as mere moneymen and deal-makers. "The producer is usually the one who starts the project," says Bregman. "Most of the media doesn't understand that. They think producers are . . . [just] businessmen who bring money in. I don't bring money in. . . . I'm the one who brings the writer in, brings the director in. I people my projects."

"The collaboration between the producer and director is not talked about much anymore," says director Irvin Kershner. Nevertheless, "the producer is very very necessary and

I wish there were more creative producers," he adds. "The really great producer gives support, encouragement and judgment to the director. And I think it makes your life absolutely a bed of roses compared to what you have when you either don't have a producer or you have someone who is destructive."

The profession has been tarnished by the many inexperienced people who gain their position by virtue of money or connections. Consequently, many writers and directors try to protect themselves by producing their own projects. This way they can avoid interference from a meddlesome producer who knows little about filmmaking.

"My primary role of being a producer is that there is one less nose sticking in my pie," says director Billy Wilder. "In the old days, and there are still some, there were what you would call creative producers—Selznick, Goldwyn, Thalberg. . . . But usually nowadays a producer is a man who knew a second cousin of a reader who had gotten hold of an unfinished script at Random House about a big fish off Long Island, and for some reason or another his brother-in-law gave him ten thousand dollars and suddenly he has the rights to *Jaws,* and owning that, he becomes a producer. But that is not producing.

"Most producers make you feel that if they weren't quite that busy and not involved in six enormous projects which were going to revolutionize the cinema, they could write it better, they could direct it better, they could compose, they could possibly act in it. The truth is that if they can't write it, they can't direct it, they don't know how to write a note of music, they can't act, if they can't do anything, then they become the head of the whole thing."

There are some notable exceptions, of course, such as Steven Spielberg and George Lucas, talented filmmakers in their own right. They can offer valuable advice to directors and writers who work for them. And because of their stature they receive a great deal of media attention, so much so that they overshadow their writers, directors and stars. Which demonstrates again how difficult it is to generalize about producers.

The profession has also been tarnished by dishonest producers. Producer Tom Greene recalls a producer with Universal Pictures who not only paid himself a $1 million fee, but also stole another $1.5 million using phantom crew members. Salary checks were drawn in the name of his children, his third-grade teacher and other people whose names he made up. His dog was listed as associate producer for $50,000.

Interestingly, this man was not a struggling newcomer but a successful producer who had made a fortune in television. But he was terrified that he would wake up one day and people would discover the truth about him—that he didn't have any talent and had no taste—and he would never work again. "When the movie came out it bombed miserably," says Greene. The producer has subsequently "gone back to television and continues to make zillions with his trash-pit shows."

The producer's job begins with the selection of a story he wants to produce. He may conceive the story himself, or it could originate from any number of sources. He could read something in a newspaper or magazine that sparks his interest, or discover a book, poem, song, play or screenplay he likes. It could be a story a writer pitches him, or a remake or sequel of an existing film.

Since story selection is a task a producer usually handles without collaborators, he alone must be able to recognize a good story. "The producer has got to know how to read and be aware of the potential of material," says agent Martin Baum. "It doesn't come from an agent wrapped in a pink ribbon and is exactly what he wants to make."

It's a difficult task for many producers because they have little training or background in storytelling. "I feel sorry for these guys," says writing instructor Robert McKee. "If I had a master's in business administration from Harvard, and all the ego and vanity that comes from being successful in that regard . . . and I had two screenplays in front of me, one for a movie that's going to be a wonderful success . . . and the other is a piece of shit, and I read them both and can't tell the difference . . . I would get the chills. 'My God, I'm in a business where the product is these scripts here . . . [and] I don't know good from bad.' "

Not only must a producer be able to recognize good material, but he must also be able to snare the rights to it. Competition is intense for the best stories. Top producers usually get first crack at upcoming books. The material may be sold long before lesser producers even learn of it. Some producers bribe employees of publishing houses with cash or movie tickets in order to get an early look at material.

Robert Evans began his producing career by paying an employee of *Publishers Weekly* to alert him to upcoming books that looked like good candidates for movies. As a result he learned of *The Detective*, by Roderick Thorp, which he was able to option for only $5,000. The book became a best seller and Evans got his first studio deal.

Producers without the financial wherewithal to compete for books from major publishers may look for material among screenplays circulating around town. Choice material is difficult to find because most of what is available is the poorly written work of novices. Experienced writers are kept busy working for the studios. Finding good material is "like being a gold prospector in the wilds of Alaska," says producer Edgar Scherick.

When a story is secured that needs to be made into a screenplay, the producer develops the script with a writer, giving him advice and guidance on his work as it progresses. Story conferences are held, often with the participation of a studio executive. Reaching a consensus on a script can be difficult, however, particularly when a director or star is brought in who has his own ideas about the material.

After the script is complete, the producer must select his director, actors, cinematographer, art designer and other crew members. "The most important skill for a producer is being able to organize a creative team of artists," says Martin Bregman. "This is difficult because you're dealing with a lot of egos, a lot of points of view. It's your job to make sure that this boat filled with people who could kill each other somehow manages to get from one shore to the other."

In addition to working well together, the creative team

must comprise a package attractive to the studios. "Producers compete for top talent as if it were a matter of life or death," says producer Larry Turman (*The Graduate*). "It's like you are on the *Q.E. II* and it springs a leak and is sinking. A thousand people are on board and there's only one lifeboat that can hold twenty people." Rarely does a producer get his first choice of a director or star.

If a producer is lucky enough to get his project into production, he has the responsibility for keeping it on its schedule and within its budget. "There are a lot of forces working on a picture to push it out of proportion, to make it larger than it is or to distort it in one direction or another," says Edgar Scherick. "A producer is like the cowboy at the roundup. One of his jobs is to keep all the cattle together and moving in the same direction."

But producers don't always have sufficient authority. "I was making a deal with a studio once," says Leonard Goldberg, "where they said to me, 'We want an eat-in clause—if you go over budget we will start taking away your fee and points.' And I said, 'OK, fine with me, as long as I . . . have control over the firing of the director or the star.' And they said, 'Oh no. You can't have that.' I said, 'Well if you think that once the picture starts I have no authority to do anything about the star or director, why are you taking away my money . . . take away their money.' "

After a picture has been completed, the producer works with the studio on its marketing and distribution. Usually the distributor has the final say in this area, but a good producer will offer suggestions and try to ensure that his picture doesn't get lost in the studio shuffle.

Because producing is so difficult, careers tend to be short. "There are not more than twenty professional producers who are regularly turning movies out," says Al Ruddy. "Most producers who get a movie made are not around ten years later. . . . If you look down a list of a thousand guys who have produced pictures and then see how many have done five, it drops off to forty percent. Those who have done ten, it drops to ten percent."

With the demise of the studio system, producers constantly shift from one studio to the next. "Today a producer is scrambling from picture to picture to find a berth," says Martin Baum. "There is no security. No permanence."

Moreover, a producer's ability and the quality of his stories are often secondary to the strength of his relationships with powerful directors, stars and executives. "To be a producer is such a shaky job," says one insider. "If you're not always entertaining at Spago's [restaurant], when your term is up you're out. If you don't hang out with the players you're out of the club."

13

MARKETING

Studios are marketing their movies with increasing vigor. Outside experts have been brought in to adapt modern marketing techniques to the film business. The wild publicity stunts and hucksterism hitherto used to promote films are being replaced with a more sophisticated approach that stresses market research, merchandising promotions, press kits, television advertising and finely calibrated release patterns.

As the array of film-marketing tools has expanded, marketing executives have become more influential. Before a project is green-lighted, the resident marketing wizard will carefully consider how it will be advertised and promoted. Without his sanction, a project is unlikely to be made. Many studios have elevated their head of marketing and distribution to a position equal to their head of production.

Marketing became a vital concern after studios were divested of their theater operations. Without control over exhibition, studios could no longer keep second-rate pictures in release. Exhibitors, unshackled from their studio masters, were intent on maximizing their own profits. They would dump slow-moving films for something new. Studios had to

learn how to attract audiences for their pictures if they hoped
to keep them in release.

The competition intensified as television spread and movie
attendance dropped. Moviegoers became more selective in
what they would go to the theater to see once mediocre entertainment was available at home for free.

The latest surge of marketing fervor has arisen from the
realization that movies, cassettes, books and merchandise can
effectively cross-promote one another in an orchestrated
marketing campaign. Such campaigns require the expenditure of millions of dollars in advertising, sometimes more
than what is spent to produce the film.

Hollywood's emphasis on marketing has not met with wide
acclaim. Many filmmakers believe marketing executives have
become too influential and that they reject innovative and
offbeat projects on the grounds they will be difficult to sell.
Says producer Gene Kirkwood: "I hate marketing research.
It's all bullshit."

Market research has been criticized for being an unreli-
able predictor of audience taste. Twentieth Century-Fox's
research indicated that *Star Wars* would not appeal to women
because the word "war" was a turnoff and because neither
its robots nor its science fiction subject matter tested well.
Columbia's research on *E.T.* indicated that only eight-year-
olds would be interested in the film.

Joseph Farrell, head of The National Research Group, says
market research has polarized the industry. The believers tend
to have backgrounds in business, and think Hollywood should
be run in a more businesslike and "scientific" fashion. The
critics tend to be writers, directors and other creative types
who rely on gut instinct for what makes a good picture.

The type of market research most severely criticized is
concept testing. Here the public is asked whether it would
be interested in seeing a movie about a particular topic. Sometimes possible titles and stars are mentioned. The flaw is that
the public can only respond to suggested movies on the basis
of what they surmise the picture will be like. Movies that are
uniquely different from those made before are difficult for
people to envision. If, for example, the public had been polled

beforehand on *Star Wars* it would have thought in terms of earlier science fiction films with which it was familiar, and could not possibly have imagined the original characters and state-of-the-art special effects utilized in the film.

Concept testing is also flawed because it isn't the picture that is tested, it is only a brief description of the picture. As a result, the public's response to an inquiry will vary with its wording. If *Terms of Endearment* was described as a movie about a young mother dying of cancer, not many people would have said they wanted to see it. If it was described as a comedy about a daughter's relationship with her mother, it would probably have scored better. Yet no one would have predicted a box-office smash, because no one would have known that here was a great story that had excellent dialogue and was blessed with great acting.

Furthermore, concept testing is an imperfect measure because respondents tend to say what sounds impressive and what they think the interviewer wants to hear, rather than what they really think. People may say they can't wait to see the next Bergman film but when it comes time to purchase a ticket they are on line for the next *Rocky* sequel.

Even the promoters of concept testing admit its shortcomings. Joseph Farrell says it should be just one factor in deciding whether or not to make a movie. Concept testing can determine how well a movie's description interests the public, and films with strong concepts obviously have a competitive advantage in attracting an audience. But a well-made film based on a weak concept can nevertheless become a hit through word-of-mouth. Conversely, a picture based on a strong concept will not necessarily live up to expectations.

Market research is more reliable and valuable after a picture has been made. Screenings of the first cut can be used to measure the film's audience appeal. Aspects of the film that do not test well can be changed. Scenes can be reedited or excised, and confusion can be remedied by adding new material. On the basis of screenings, such films as *Absence of Malice* and *The Big Chill* have been reedited. After screening the latter, director Lawrence Kasdan decided to drop a flashback scene of the characters having dinner with their friend

Alex (whose funeral opens the picture). Audiences found the scene disconcerting and enjoyed the film more without it.

Market research is also useful in determining how best to advertise and promote a movie. Audience screenings are used to learn which demographic groups are most attracted to a film. A campaign is then devised to appeal specifically to these people. If research indicates teenagers like the film most, ads would be designed with them in mind and placed in media most likely to reach them.

The word of mouth a film will receive can be measured by market research as well. A picture likely to receive strong word of mouth might be opened slowly to give recommendations time to spread. On the other hand, a movie expected to generate poor word of mouth may be opened quickly in many locations in an attempt to grab as much business as possible before word gets out.

Advertising materials can also be tested. Shopping-center surveys are used to determine the effectiveness of various ad campaigns. Columbia spent nearly a year testing its campaign for *Starman.*

As a movie's release date approaches, surveys measuring public awareness of the film can be used to check the impact of advertising. An industry rule of thumb states that at least 60 percent of the moviegoing public should be aware of a movie before it opens.

Immediately after a film is released, audiences are polled to determine which demographic groups are seeing the film and what they are saying about it. If the demographics differ from expectations, it may indicate that the advertising campaign is not reaching its intended audience and a back-up campaign may be substituted.

The most reliable way to check both advertising and audience appeal is to test-market a film. From the results, a studio can project box-office performance nationwide. But studios are reluctant to test-market because they fear that a poor showing in one market will poison others. Word of an impending flop spreads quickly, making it difficult to get exhibitors to book the picture and deterring moviegoers from seeing it.

Instead of test marketing, studios often prefer to preview their pictures in a few theaters. Here audience reaction is more easily concealed, especially with sneak previews. However, sneak previews can be misleading because the effectiveness of a movie's advertising campaign is not tested. And since the preview audience has not been drawn into the theater by the film's advertising, it may not be representative of the audience that will ultimately want to see the film.

Moreover, even sneak previews can be risky. When *Close Encounters of the Third Kind* was previewed in Dallas, a critic sneaked in and gave it a bad review, panicking exhibitors and causing a drop in the price of Columbia's stock. Conversely, previews can be used to spread good word of mouth in advance of a picture's opening.

"I used to think that previews were vital," says producer Richard Zanuck (*Jaws*), "but now I think previews are vital for certain kinds of pictures and not for others. I think it's dangerous to release a drama without a preview; there might be a bad laugh of some kind. . . . I used to believe in [audience rating] cards, but I don't anymore. I can tell a great deal by seeing if people are fidgety and moving around, getting up to get a Coke or something. I don't think cards are sophisticated enough, and I think we are asking too much. The average viewer suddenly becomes Judith Crist. To be too influenced by cards can be dangerous."

Preview data can be easily manipulated. Filmmakers have been known to pack previews with friends in order to persuade a studio it had a hot picture. Director George Roy Hill (*Butch Cassidy and the Sundance Kid*) used a preview to settle a difference of opinion with his producer over the editing of *Period of Adjustment*.

"I had a big fight with my producer, Lawrence Weingarten," says Hill, "over a sequence I thought I had botched up and was embarrassed about and wanted out. He thought it was all right and necessary and he wanted it in. We went to the preview. I got up halfway through the movie to stretch my back. They were putting out tables in the lobby with preview cards, and I was seized by an inspiration. I went across the street to a drugstore and bought six different types of pencils and pens. I grabbed a handful of preview cards, went into the manager's office, and in different phrasing, criticized that scene and stuffed the cards into the box. Larry called me a couple of days later and said, 'You know, you were right about that scene.' Since that time I never allowed preview cards at any of my movies, because I think someone is going to try to pull the same thing on me sometime."

Studio marketing divisions include advertising and publicity departments. The former designs the ad campaign and allocates expenditures among television, radio and newspaper media. The latter encourages news coverage of a picture by preparing press kits, arranging interviews with the director and cast and screening the film for critics.

Advertising strategies have changed as the studios have increasingly promoted their movies through television. Because television can communicate aurally and visually, it can better evoke the drama, excitement and spectacle of a film than can radio or print ads. (For the same reason, coming-attraction trailers are effective, especially since they are targeted at moviegoers and, unlike commercials, they are something viewers enjoy.)

Newspapers remain an essential advertising medium because moviegoers habitually consult theater listings when choosing a film. While television is considered the more powerful sales tool, more money is spent on newspaper ads (72 percent of the $846.9 million spent on film advertising annually) because newspaper ads must continue for the entire run of a film's release, while television ads typically appear for just two weeks to open a campaign.

Although some marketers contend full-page print ads are unnecessary, the studios often purchase them, if only to please filmmakers and stars. Similarly, billboards on Sunset Boulevard in Los Angeles or in Times Square in New York may be bought as much for the ego gratification of talent as for their promotional value.

Radio is often the overlooked medium, which some marketing consultants think unfortunate since ads are inexpensive and many stations have large teenage followings.

The allocation of advertising is primarily a function of which medium can most efficiently reach the people most inclined to see a film. But it is not always apparent who would like a movie. Marketing consultant Jeff Dowd found that the audience for *The Black Stallion* was comprised of kids, horse lovers, fans of the *Black Stallion* books, admirers of director Francis Ford Coppola, people who appreciated fine cinematography, and parents looking for something to do with their kids.

To appeal to the diverse interests of the public, studios may run several different ads. Columbia promoted *Starman* with an ad emphasizing romance that it broadcast during the daytime soaps, and one displaying space hardware that was inserted in a prime-time science fiction program.

Studios may alternate ads in order to try to build on the primary audience for a film. *Porky's* opened with a campaign aimed at twelve- to twenty-four-year-olds that stressed the film's risqué nature. When Fox discovered that females who saw the film liked it more than expected, ads were changed in order to attract more women. During the fourth week of release the studio went after older moviegoers with the theme: "You don't have to be under thirty to like *Porky's*." The film was a huge success, grossing more than $120 million domestically.

While there is nothing improper about tailoring ads to appeal to the different interests of the public, studios sometimes get carried away, deceiving the public about the nature of a film. Misleading ads can be counterproductive because persons lured in under false pretenses, disappointed when their expectations are not met, spread bad word of mouth.

"The studios come up with these incredible ways of advertising a film that has nothing to do with it and that doesn't give the public a chance to even select correctly," says director Michael Wadleigh, who complains that his movie *Wolfen* was portrayed as a werewolf movie even though it was not. "Therefore it didn't reach the proper market . . . [we didn't get] the people in who would give it the right word of mouth and magnify its virtues. Trickery like that always backfires."

Sometimes deception is unintentional. The trailer for *The*

Stunt Man showed a bloody decapitation scene that deterred moviegoers who thought the film too violent. In fact, the decapitation was a gag.

Studios tend to hype their pictures because they are under pressure to fill theater seats fast. Unlike other products, movies don't have much of a shelf life. Says Jeff Dowd: "We constantly try to . . . create a sense of urgency . . . why they have to see this movie now. Why it's really special."

The amount of advertising needed to support a picture is often a subject of dispute. Filmmakers frequently complain that studios do not buy enough advertising to promote their pictures. But when it comes time to account for profits, filmmakers tend to protest that advertising expenditures were excessive.

Because studios take their distribution fee out of gross revenues while filmmakers share in net profits, additional advertising expenditures may sometimes be remunerative to the studio but not the filmmaker. "Buying the gross" is the practice of boosting attendance with greater ad expenditures, but net profits may not increase because they have been offset by greater advertising costs.

In addition to advertising costs, studios incur expenses obtaining news coverage. The publicity budget for an average film is about $100,000, and if the studio wants to make a big splash with a premiere party and all the hoopla, it can spend more than $1 million, which can be a worthwhile expenditure if it generates millions of dollars' worth of free publicity.

Studio publicity departments today have a multitude of tools at their disposal. Press kits with photos and background material are routinely sent to hundreds of magazines, newspapers and radio stations. Electronic press kits comprised of film clips and the latest innovation, canned interviews, are sent to television stations. Local stations may integrate these pseudointerviews into their newcasts so it appears they interviewed a star. Studios like these interviews because they can control their content and the need for expensive publicity tours is reduced.

Another newfound promotional device is the behind-the-scenes documentary. This film about the making of a movie is given to PBS or commercial stations and is often nothing more than a thinly disguised commercial.

Of course, there remain the traditional press junkets in which journalists are taken on location or brought to Hollywood to be wined and dined, and to rub shoulders with the stars. The trips are usually taken by reporters of smaller magazines and newspapers that could not otherwise afford firsthand coverage. More affluent and prestigious publications like the *The New York Times* prohibit their writers from accepting such gratuities and usually avoid such events anyway since they have the clout to obtain exclusive interviews.

Studio publicity departments are smaller today than in the days of the moguls. Much of their work has been contracted out to independent publicists. It became more economical to hire free-lancers and reduce permanent staffs as movie production and the studio's role in promoting stars declined. Why bother making someone a star if they can then go off and work for your competitors?

Not only has the size of publicity departments been cut but their influence has been reduced as well. "There has been a general attempt at demeaning the role of the publicist," says Mac St. Johns, president of the Publicists Guild. "The current group of executives in motion pictures today simply do not understand how to use publicity. . . . The amount of money spent today on advertising compared to what is spent on publicity is far greater than it has ever been. . . . They buy the space. It costs more but it's easier. It takes less creative effort.

"There was a time when it wasn't beneath the dignity of the studios to have a little fun with publicity," says St. Johns. For example, in 1937, when David O. Selznick opened *The Prisoner of Zenda* at Radio City Music Hall, he flew in the Canadian town of Zenda—twelve of its thirteen residents—for the premiere. The story was front-page news in New York City. Another stunt involved staging a casting call for three thousand dogs at a famous deli and feeding them hot dogs. But as the studios have grown into large public corporations they have become more image-conscious and more cautious about engaging in anything remotely controversial. Today they might question the wisdom of such stunts. Would animal-rights activists object to a dog casting call? What if the hot dogs contained harmful additives?

The wild publicity stunts of yesteryear have also fallen victim to a more skeptical press. Today the news media is suspicious of staged publicity events and is reluctant to conspire with publicists and report a story it suspects is false. When the 1939 picture *Juarez* was released, a New York City visitor hailed a cab in New York and asked to be taken to *Juarez*. Several hours later the cab driver stopped for gas and the passenger asked where they were. When told they were in Philadelphia, the passenger got upset, told the driver that he didn't want to go to Juárez, Mexico, but wanted to go to the movie house on Broadway. An argument ensued, the passenger refused to pay the fare and was arrested and brought before a judge. The story was given prominent coverage in New York City newspapers. Apparently no reporter bothered to investigate and discover that the entire incident had been staged by the Warner Brothers publicity department.

Today publicity stunts still work well in certain circumstances. Stunts that demonstrate ingenuity and panache are newsworthy, and those that have a good visual component —especially important for television coverage—are likely to be covered. For instance, when the Mel Brooks comedy *Blazing Saddles* was released in 1974, Warner Brothers arranged a special screening for horses. A drive-in theater was rented, a "horsepitality bar" built, and "horse d'oeuvres" (oats in popcorn containers) were served. At the appointed hour 250 horses and their owners arrived and the movie was shown. "The press got a good laugh out of the whole thing," recalls Warner Brothers publicist Marty Weiser, and the story made the network news.

Publicity remains an important marketing tool because it can reach people that ads miss. "Certain people read only the sports pages," says St. Johns, "or letters to the editor. Now if you're a good publicist you will get your stories into those other sections to draw people who normally don't read drama sections and normally don't go to pictures."

As the public has come to rely more on television for its

news, the studios have increasingly concentrated their publicity efforts on that medium. A mention on *60 Minutes, Good Morning America* or *Entertainment Tonight* reaches more people than any newspaper. Television reviewers such as Gene Siskel and Roger Ebert have become more important to the studios than print critics.

Even so, *The New York Times, Time,* and *Newsweek* are important because other media often follow their lead when deciding what to cover. *Playboy, People* and *US* magazines are valued for their large circulations. A mention in the *National Enquirer* is a good break, although many publicists are wary of dealing with it because of its sensationalistic approach. *Rolling Stone* is valued because of its young readership.

As a courtesy, and to ensure that reviews are ready by the time a film is released, studios arrange advance screenings for critics. However, if negative reviews are expected, the studio may decide not to screen a picture, hoping to delay the bad news. This annoys critics and may produce particularly harsh reviews when the movies ultimately appear.

Publicists often find themselves in a quandary when they are asked to promote dreadful pictures. They are expected to stress the positive and avoid or hide the negative. Many don't deal candidly with the press. Says one reporter: "They constantly lie. That's their job—to wreak havoc with the truth. They do a lot of misrepresentation. [Consequently] they're not held in high regard by any reporter, even the few [publicists] that are good."

Perhaps conflict is inevitable because journalists want the sensational stories that embarrass studios and stars the most. In the struggle over the molding of the news, publicists use access to celebrities as their club while the media threatens to withhold news coverage.

Over the past decade there has been a revolution in film marketing. When the 1973 novelization of *The Omen* sold three million copies, it made Hollywood sit up and take notice of the power of books to promote movies (and vice versa) and generate ancillary revenues. The book's success incited fierce competition among publishers for novelization rights, raising payments to studios to astronomical heights. Only after several books flopped did prices abate.

The industry awoke to the potential of movie spin-off products when *Star Wars* posters, T-shirts, toys, watches, candy and other merchandise reportedly grossed more than $1 billion retail—more money than the film took in at the box office. While spin-off products are nothing new—Walt Disney built a fortune from them—since *Star Wars* Hollywood has embraced merchandising with renewed vigor.

Product tie-ins are a no-lose proposition for a studio. The right to market products is licensed to outside companies, which incur all manufacturing and distribution expenses. The studio receives an advance, sometimes as much as $100,000 per product, and royalty payments, typically 7 percent of the revenues that the licensing company receives from retailers. Even if the products are not profitable, the studio benefits from free publicity for its movie. Only certain movies, however, can support extensive merchandising efforts. Action/adventure and fantasy films have the greatest potential because they can spin off toys and children's products, the mainstay of movie merchandising.

Existing products can also be used effectively to promote movies. The Coca-Cola Company put its marketing muscle behind Columbia Pictures, imprinting fifty-five million cans of its soda with the *Ghostbusters* logo—advertising worth $15 million—as well as displaying the movie's ghost logo in Diet Coke television commercials.

Not only can products sell movies, but movies can sell products. The rush to place products in films began in 1982, when the news media reported that sales of Reese's Pieces candy rose 65 percent after the friendly alien in *E.T.* enjoyed some on-screen. The product's success embarrassed the makers of M&M's, who had previously denied director Steven Spielberg's request to use their candy.

Examples abound of movies creating consumer demand for a product. When Eddie Murphy wore a Mumford High shirt in *Beverly Hills Cop,* the high school was deluged with requests for it. Recognizing its good fortune, the school began selling the shirt to the public. Similarly, the sunglasses Arnold Schwarzenegger wore in *The Terminator* became a hot-selling item after that picture became a hit.

Today many firms expend considerable effort to get their products in the movies. The manufacturer of the Care Bears funded the movie of the same name, undoubtedly realizing it would be a feature-length commercial for the toy (the $3 million picture went on to gross nearly $25 million domestically). Other toy companies have announced their own filmmaking plans, hoping to move into filmmaking as they have already invaded children's television programming.

Products not able to star in a movie of their own may be eligible for supporting roles. New Balance was able to get its running shoes worn in *The Big Chill*. Budweiser got Clint Eastwood to drink its beer in *Sudden Impact* while the rapist was served a competitor's brand. McDonald's maintains a full-scale facsimile restaurant near Hollywood that is available for use as a set. It features interchangeable interiors and exteriors, dressing rooms, ample parking and electrical power and other conveniences of a sound stage—plus McDonald's will provide staff, wardrobe and food.

There are about twenty-five product-placement firms that specialize in getting products into movies. The two largest each represent about sixty companies and hundreds of products. One charges anywhere from $10,000 to more than $100,000 a year in return for a guarantee to get a product in six pictures—and always have it portrayed in a positive light.

In just a few years product placement has become standard industry practice. Producers give scripts to product agents to review and suggest where their client's products can be inserted. Says one product agent: "These days . . . more times than not when you see a product in a film, a deal has been done with someone."

Many product agents claim they do not pay producers to place products in film. They say they merely provide merchandise without charge, accompanied by all necessary releases. Coors beer, for example, was supplied to the productions of *E.T.*, *Invasion U.S.A*, *Iron Eagle*, *Krush Groove*, *National Lampoon's Vacation* and *Pee-Wee's Big Adventure* for use in the movie and for the enjoyment of the cast and crew.

But many times inducements in addition to free samples

are given. Most often, a company will agree to engage in promotional activities on behalf of a movie in return for having its product in it. *The Wall Street Journal* reported that *Omni* magazine agreed to publish a major article on *2010* in return for being shown in the film. Similarly, *Newsweek on Campus* ran a full-page ad for the film *Back to School* in return for exposure in the film.

For the James Bond movie *A View to a Kill*, The Sharper Image company included artwork and photos from the film in three million of its catalogs. As part of the deal, the producers designed a credit-card-size calculator with the Sharper Image logo on it for James Bond to use in the movie—and to be sold in the catalog. The promotion was enormously successful for the Sharper Image, generating more sales than any prior catalog.

Some companies will pay to get their product in a movie. Nabisco paid $100,000 to have its Baby Ruth candy bar in *The Goonies*. The product was prominently displayed in a crucial scene in which a young boy earns the friendship of a monsterlike character by sharing a piece of candy. As part of the deal Nabisco also agreed to promote the movie with $1.5 million worth of network advertising and to offer free movie posters with the purchase of its candy in thirty-seven thousand stores nationwide.

Producers have welcomed the money and promotional benefits derived from product placements. Many actively solicit products for inclusion in their films. For *The Goonies*, a Steven Spielberg presentation, the producers entered into deals with six other product manufacturers besides Baby Ruth. The makers of Hi-C fruit drink, Budweiser beer, Peter Pan peanut butter, Baskin-Robbins ice cream, Jiffy Pop popcorn and Nature Valley granola bars each paid from $50,000 to more than $100,000 either to be in the film or to share in its promotion.

Movie marketing has also changed as music has become a powerful tool for promoting films. The film and music industries are able to promote the other's products effectively since the primary customers of each are young people.

The industries cooperate in several ways. Studios make a

special effort to produce a movie sound track with one or more potential hit songs, knowing that a song receiving national airplay provides invaluable free publicity for a film. Musical artists, in turn, are anxious to work in film because a hit movie gives them extensive exposure. And both stand to profit handsomely: the artist through his royalties, and the studio through sales of its sound-track album. Such movies as *Flashdance, Footloose* and *Purple Rain* sell a lot of albums, and even nonmusicals and box-office flops can derive substantial revenues from sound-track sales.

Both the movie and the record industries have benefited from the introduction of music videos and MTV. *Flashdance* was the first picture to exploit the new medium effectively. By excerpting segments of the film and running them as music videos, the studio benefited from extensive free promotion on MTV, and thus established the cable channel as an important marketing tool for movies. Today it has become almost obligatory to release a music video to promote a major motion picture—even if the picture is not especially well suited for one.

The growth of the videocassette industry has provided another promotional vehicle. Paramount included a trailer for *Indiana Jones and the Temple of Doom* on its cassette for *Raiders of the Lost Ark.*

The increasing importance of videocassette sales has affected film marketing in other ways. It has encouraged the studios to move up the release of home videos nearer a picture's theatrical run in order to capitalize on the large amount of advertising bought during exhibition. Studios now typically release cassettes within six months of the end of exhibition.

Besides the changes wrought by merchandising, music and new technologies, movie marketing has been affected by changing distribution patterns. Increasingly studios are releasing their pictures widely, placing them in as many theaters as possible. In the past, studios staggered their releases. The largest and most prestigious houses, usually in downtown urban areas, received a picture first for an exclusive run. Then the best suburban theaters would get the picture, followed by subsequent runs in towns and villages. Between each run there was a fallow period of several weeks during which the picture was not exhibited.

A staggered release requires that advertising be bought for several runs, an expensive proposition, while a wide release concentrates exhibition over a shorter period of time. By simultaneously exhibiting the picture in more theaters, the studios reduce the advertising cost per theater.

Wide releases are also favored because during the early weeks of a picture's release a studio may be entitled to as much as 90 percent of each theater's box-office receipts (after deduction of exhibitor house expenses), while in subsequent weeks the percentage drops. A picture opened widely collects more revenue early.

The widest release is a nationwide break. Here network television advertising becomes cost-effective. A national release also eliminates the risk inherent in rolling out a picture region by region, which allows a bad opening in one region an opportunity to contaminate other regions.

Nowadays a limited (or slow) release pattern is reserved for pictures that do not lend themselves easily to mass marketing. These films, typically low-budget and without strong concepts, focus on topics not thought to be especially commercial. They are frequently prestige pictures expected to get good word of mouth and reviews; they need such recommendations to succeed because the studio is reluctant to spend money advertising a picture it believes has limited audience appeal.

Nevertheless, a picture that is opened slowly sometimes catches the public's fancy and becomes a surprise hit. *Star Wars* opened on a mere thirty-two screens—the expectation was that it would only interest children and science fiction aficionados. When the movie opened the public deluged theaters, causing massive traffic jams. Soon exhibitors nationwide were clamoring for the film.

In the case of a limited release, studios will frequently open a picture in New York and Los Angeles, hoping that if it is liked by the nation's most important critics their reviews can be used to promote the picture elsewhere. Reviews can affect the box-office success of specialty films, although they have minimal impact on more exploitative fare like *Rambo*. Limited releases, however, are becoming increasingly rare for major studios. They prefer potential blockbusters they can mass-market. Consequently, smaller companies like Cinecom and Island Alive have arisen to market more specialized fare. Island Alive (subsequently split into Alive Films and Island Pictures) has distributed such films as *El Norte, Koyaanisqatsi, Choose Me, Stop Making Sense* and *Kiss of the Spider Woman.*

Specialized distributors have prospered by marketing pictures with maximum care and attention and minimum overhead and expense. Alive Films, for example, distributes films out of one office in Los Angeles with a staff of fifteen to twenty. The company saves on film-duplication costs by never releasing more than two hundred prints of any picture, rotating the prints from one region of the country to another. Grass-roots publicity campaigns and promotional screenings are used instead of television ads. Without a large distribution apparatus to feed, they are not under the same pressure as a major studio to keep up a constant flow of product. This enables them to pick and choose their products more carefully and spend more time planning their releases.

Specialized distributors have found a niche for themselves, says director Robert Altman (*Nashville*) because if a film doesn't fit into the majors' formula, they are not able to sell it. "Hollywood is Montgomery Ward's and Sears. Everything is the same and it's all sold the same way and it all fits the same pattern. . . . But a lot of people don't do all their shopping at Sears. They go to boutiques and specialized shops and they are finding things they want, not what is shoved down their throats."

"The audience for specialized films seems to be growing," says Lawrence Jackson, vice-president of the Samuel Goldwyn Company. "The average age of the audience is getting a little older as the baby boomers, who are more predisposed to going to the movies than any previous generation . . . get older. [They are] less interested in teenage comedy films and sophomoric horror films. . . . They are looking for something like *Choose Me,* which is a more appealing eccentric piece of comedic entertainment." Island Alive defined its primary audience as people "twenty to forty years of age, urban, highly educated and devoted to theatrical filmgoing"—in other words, yuppies.

Not only do specialized distributors often market pictures with greater care but they may also generate more profits. Majors spend so much on producing and marketing a picture that profits may be eroded. Although Columbia distributed *Gandhi* successfully, it spent so much money on television ads that it lost money on its domestic release.

"The majors offered me a lot of front money and a very nice opening," says filmmaker Henry Jaglom (*Always*), "but a picture's performance has a lot to do with how it's handled after it's opened. I know the studio mentality, and if the picture doesn't open the way they want it to, they just drop it. They've got so many other pictures they don't need it. [But] an independent who puts out two hundred and fifty thousand dollars up front has got to get that back and works very hard to open in every city, and he cares. It's a very big part of his life."

The major studios lack the entrepreneurial zeal of their smaller brethren, says marketing consultant Jeff Dowd. Executives at the majors are often so bogged down in internecine warfare that their marketing campaigns suffer. Furthermore, they often lack the incentive to try new marketing approaches.

"I used to be able to appeal to these guys by saying we will make money," says Dowd. "But that doesn't work anymore. They're more concerned with their careers than they are with making money for the company. The fact of the matter is that if *The Stunt Man* grosses thirty million dollars the guys who are working for Fox don't care. They are not going to see any of that money. It's not worth taking a chance . . . so the atmosphere is not conducive to be entrepreneurial. . . . And the irony is that I'm like a leftist who's teaching these guys how to make money. . . . It's incredible. . . . It's very funny what is going on. These guys can't even be good capitalists anymore."

In the case of *The Black Stallion,* says Dowd, "the people

at United Artists fought us all the way because several vice-presidents had gone on record saying the picture wasn't going to work. . . . I was fighting people the whole time . . . to deposit thirty million dollars in . . . [their] bank account." On *The Stunt Man*, says Dowd, Fox executives simply had no confidence in the picture. "I do a test run in Seattle and it plays for forty-six weeks. . . . That's *Star Wars* [kind of business]. . . . For it to play forty-six weeks in Seattle and only one week everywhere else in the country, there is something wrong."

Filmmakers may also be hesitant to hand over their film to a major studio lest it fare poorly competing against the studio's bigger movies. A small film may not be released at its optimum time but may be rushed out to fill a gap in the studio's schedule if a big studio release flops.

Observing the growing popularity of specialized films, several major studios decided to distribute such films themselves. They established semiautonomous classics divisions, which operated with moderate success for several years, but with the exception of Orion Classics and MGM/UA Classics, all of these divisions are now more or less defunct.

The classic divisions failed, says Larry Jackson, because their presence "created tremendous internal tensions . . . they would say they were there to provide an alternative to certain incapabilities of the large, labyrinthine, leviathan distribution divisions. So the pot is calling the kettle black in very close quarters. It tended to create situations where main divisions were constantly tolerating classics divisions at best and undermining them at worst."

Moreover, the profits derived from the classics divisions were an inconsequential addition to the studios' bottom lines. Says director Alan Rudolph (*Choose Me*): "If Island Alive could net a couple of million dollars off any film they would be ecstatic. And yet if Universal only netted two million dollars off a film they would be pissed because it wasn't worth the effort."

Notwithstanding its newfound marketing sophistication, Hollywood has limited influence with moviegoers. Most of marketing's impact occurs during the initial weeks of a picture's release, when it encourages people to sample a film. After that, word of mouth takes over. "We open movies," says MGM/UA marketing chief Irving Ivers. "Then they take on a life of their own, depending on how good or bad they are."

The ability of ads to lure people into theaters appears to be declining. "For a couple of years it was easy to get yourself a big gross with advertising," says MGM president Alan Ladd, Jr. "But then the market got saturated and people said, 'Hey, wait a minute. Let me find out how good it is before I spend my money.'"

For truly terrible films it is difficult to even get anyone to sample them. "It is always a mysterious thing as to why or how the public knows that something isn't very good," says Ladd. "But they certainly seem to know. They just don't go out even on the first day." Says distribution executive Ross Merrin: "The public has an amazing ability to smell a stinker." Likewise, the public often seems to know when a hit is about to open. Long lines inexplicably form at the box office on the first day.

While awful films cannot be sold no matter how brilliantly they are marketed and hit films will sell themselves despite inept handling, the commercial success of the remaining films—the vast majority—can be significantly affected by marketing. But it is difficult to gauge the impact of marketing because there are no controlled studies measuring the box-office success of a film under varying marketing campaigns. Moreover, a film's box-office performance is affected by many nonmarketing considerations, such as critics' reviews, publicity, and competition with other movies and entertainment.

The haphazard nature of marketing campaigns makes them like political campaigns, says marketing consultant Pacy Markman: "Two years before you get into a race you don't know who you are going to run against, you can't control what happens . . . there's publicity . . . other candidates . . . and it all leads up to one day when either the people buy you or they don't."

If there is no empirical data measuring the impact of marketing on film performance, there is anecdotal evidence.

When the movie *The Flim Flam Man* was released, for example, it fared poorly everywhere except when it was exhibited by a Midwest theater chain. There the exhibitor discarded the studio's advertising campaign, substituted his own and enjoyed blockbuster business.

When the Warner Brothers film *It's Alive!* was originally released in 1974, it bombed. "It was not a good movie," says Pacy Markman. "It was a pretty silly, awful horror movie that wasn't scary. It was about a baby that is a monster and the baby looks like a rubber pig." Yet three years after its initial release, when it was rereleased with a new ad campaign, it performed well at the box office, ultimately earning the studio $7.1 million in domestic rentals.

"I came up with an advertising idea that drove people into the theaters," says Markman. "I didn't use anything from the movie. The [television ad] pitch was a baby carriage with the music "Rock-a-bye-baby" playing. And as it comes into view you see this clawlike thing, this horrible thing coming out of the baby carriage and a voice says, 'There is just one thing wrong with the Davis baby. It's alive.' "

Markman says the movie's success is entirely due to the ad campaign. There was no publicity for the rerelease, and all the word of mouth had been awful. Of course, the picture may have done well because it was so bad that it had become camp.

Market research seems to have made a difference in the success of *Up in Smoke*. Since it was Cheech and Chong's first movie, the studio wanted its initial audiences to be filled with their hard-core fans. Research disclosed that for some strange reason the greatest concentration of their fans was in Canada and Texas.

"We opened in Texas to huge business," says marketer Gordon Weaver, "and then we opened it in Canada to huge business and terrific word of mouth—which signaled not only to exhibitors but to the media as well that here was a picture that had enormous potential because it had done so well in two such diverse places." The picture was a success and spawned several sequels.

But research seldom so clearly suggests a marketing campaign. More typically, data can be interpreted any number of ways. When Jeff Dowd was first presented with *The Grey Fox* he was at a loss as to how to sell it. "On the surface," he says, "it was a Western starring a sixty-two-year-old man nobody's ever heard of. Women don't like Westerns . . . it may change, but right now women aren't going. When we were all in college the boys used to go down and see Clint. . . . Now most people . . . are on dates and either side of the date has veto power. That's the critical thing to recognize.

"So I said, 'If we can't make this thing work for women we're going to be in trouble.' So I immediately got twenty women together and showed them the picture. I just wanted to see what they thought. I don't know if they're going to like it or hate it. [After the screening] I get about a dozen calls from women, saying things like 'You know I really like that picture,' and 'Is that actor Richard Farnsworth going to come to Seattle? Could I meet him?' And these are these women in their twenties and thirties. I'm saying, 'Holy shit, I got Paul Newman on my hands.'

"So then I had to figure out how to sell it. We had a woman's voice on the radio, and the trailer is very lyrical with romantic music saying that the movie is about 'the Grey Fox, the gentleman bandit.' I called it the *Officer and a Gentleman* approach, selling it to both sides of the date . . . the guys get to see the army thing and the women get to see the romance."

While the film marketers have had their successes, they usually do not play the role of savior. More often they are the object of criticism by filmmakers who feel their pictures have been sabotaged by inept marketing. Many times there is little cooperation between the filmmaker and the marketers.

"Usually distribution is where the headaches with the studio really start," says producer Carolyn Pfeiffer. "I find an extraordinary arrogance toward the filmmaker. . . . I find that they pay lip service [to you about participating in the creation of the advertising campaign] . . . and in the end if you despise what they are doing it is still the image they insist on. . . . People in these jobs are not in my opinion qualified. . . . They certainly didn't nurture any of my pictures."

"When a picture fails, the producer, director and stars

say the ad stunk and they put us in bad theaters," says distribution veteran Leo Greenfield. "The marketing and distribution people say we did a wonderful job, the picture just wasn't there."

One reason filmmakers may be suspicious of marketing is that they understand little about it. "One of the biggest problems is there's a wall between the creative community and the distribution community," says Jeff Dowd. "The guys in the creative community think the people doing distribution should be selling used cars, and the guys in distribution think the people in the creative community should be working in art galleries." The result is that often there is little or no communication between the marketers of a film and its makers—people who know a film best.

DISTRIBUTION AND EXHIBITION

Distributors and exhibitors often behave like Siamese fighting fish. They argue so vociferously it appears they are out to kill each other. Yet neither side can afford to destroy the other without committing suicide.

The battle began in earnest in 1948, when the studios were ordered to divest themselves of their theaters. Until then it mattered little how box-office revenue was split between exhibition and distribution since all moneys eventually ended up on the studio's bottom line. (When studios distributed films through each other's theater chains, gentlemen's agreements provided for reciprocal terms.) But after exhibitors began to operate as independent, profit-making enterprises, the allocation of revenues became an issue, with each side intent on increasing its share of box-office receipts.

In battle, the power of each side has shifted with the supply of and demand for product. "Distributors charge what the market will bear and exhibitors try to pay as little as they can," explains Bill Quigley, vice-president of the exhibitor the Walter Reade Organization. "Historically it has been a pendulum that swings back and forth. When studios . . . reduced their supply of product, then the terms, from the exhibitor's point of view, became exorbitant."

Fortunately, natural market forces come into play. The cycle begins when distributors become prosperous and start to produce more films, eventually glutting the marketplace. In such a buyer's market, exhibitors can obtain better terms, increasing their share of box-office revenues at the expense of the distributors. Production cutbacks follow, creating a seller's market, in which exhibitor clout wanes. Distributors can then get better terms, eventually becoming prosperous and beginning the cycle anew.

At times each side has resorted to anticompetitive practices. Distributors engaged in block booking in order to force a group of pictures on an exhibitor. Exhibitors, on the other hand, would conspire to split product among themselves, so as not to drive up prices through competitive bidding. Courts have found both practices illegal.

In their place has grown a system of allocating product based on relationships between distributors and operators of large theater chains. These "marriages" tie a studio to a particular theater chain for the release of their pictures. Terms are set by mutual agreement rather than by competitive bid. If a film performs poorly, the studio often adjusts the split to protect the exhibitor and maintain its goodwill.

While marriages have ushered in a new era of cooperation between distributors and exhibitors, such harmony may be short-lived. Independent exhibitors object to the practice, claiming it freezes them out of the marketplace. Seattle exhibitor Randy Finley has sued the major distributors on the grounds marriages are an illegal restraint of trade. He is asking that distributors license pictures on a film-by-film, theater-by-theater basis, determining placement solely on the basis of such factors as theater size, location and terms.

"We are trying to get it so that movies are not just sold to what we call a 'comfort station,' " says Finley, who claims distributors book their pictures on the basis of what is most administratively convenient rather than on what is best for a picture. "For instance, every film sold in the state of Washington by Fox has been sold to General Cinema for the last six or seven years. . . . It is easier to sell General Cinema and fill eighteen hundred theaters than it is to go out and shop your film market by market."

One studio vice-president concedes marriages are probably illegal: "When you pick and choose your customers at the expense of others, some exhibitors are not getting a fair shake at product."

Marriages grew in popularity as the market became glutted with product and studios grew increasingly anxious about getting their pictures exhibited. Moreover, studios like to have regular customers who will take their bad pictures along with their good ones. "The film companies have found such a policy is better for them overall," says Robert Selig, President of the Theatre Association of California. "They may get less basic film rental on a giant picture but they [are assured] . . . a play-off on all pictures . . . rather than bidding or jumping from here to there."

Notwithstanding the increase in marriages, competition continues to flourish in some areas of the country. Markets remain where exhibitors fight over product, and there are other areas where distributors compete against each other to fill the lone theater in town.

Distributors and exhibitors have a long list of grievances against each other. Distributors' foremost complaint is that exhibitors are slow to remit rentals because they want to earn interest on it and use it as leverage to reduce their payments.

"They just don't pay the money in many cases until the distributor calls up and says, 'You owe us money,' " explains Goldwyn vice-president Jeff Lipsky. "And then they will say . . . 'What do you want us to pay you?' . . . This is the only industry where when you make a deal, the deal is open to renegotiation no matter what." To accelerate payment, distributors often accept less than what they are owed.

Collections are a special problem for smaller distributors. While the majors can threaten to withhold the next blockbuster until past accounts are settled, smaller distributors lack such a club. "The independent film is told to wait four months or take twenty-five percent," says producer Martin Ransohoff. "The ability to collect is all based on clout."

Another distributor complaint is that exhibitors steal. Box-office revenues are siphoned in a variety of ways: Tickets are not torn and then later resold, ticket rolls are switched midstream, free passes are given in exchange for goods and services. Or the theater operator may simply underreport ticket sales. While less-than-expected revenues may raise suspicions, without an audit distributors have no way of knowing how many tickets were sold.

Distribution executives believe independent exhibitors are the worst culprits because they are under the most pressure to make ends meet. While some cheating takes place within chains, such abuses are thought to be isolated instances of dishonest employees rather than a concerted plan by management.

The threat of being cut off from product restrains exhibitor theft. Theaters jeopardize an enormous investment if they underreport box-office receipts. "Any rip-off will be detected if the theater is checked and audited conscientiously," says distribution executive Cary Brokaw. "A little rip-off is just as bad as a big rip-off as far as the reaction from the distributor. It is immediate grounds not to sell the exhibitor film. If they can't buy film, they are out of business. You can't very easily convert theaters into gas stations."

Exhibitors also cheat by overstating their expenses, which are reimbursable out of box-office receipts. The overhead, or "house nut," allowed exhibitors may be an arbitrary figure set through negotiation with the distributor, who may knowingly allow the exhibitor some "air," or profit, in its overhead. But when the nut is based on actual costs, exhibitors have an incentive to inflate their expense reports. They may deceive distributors, for example, by submitting phony receipts.

For their part, exhibitors recite their own litany of grievances against distributors. They most strenuously object to blind bidding, a practice that does not let exhibitors view a picture before bidding on it. Distributors respond that they don't always have time for advance screenings; furthermore, such screenings are expensive and are futile gestures since exhibitors have not demonstrated any better ability than studio executives to pick hits. (After *Amadeus* was screened, one theater-chain owner is reputed to have said: "It's a nice art film but nobody knows Mozart, and it won't sell a nickel's worth of tickets.")

Exhibitors appear to be winning the battle against blind bidding. To date they have persuaded twenty-four states to outlaw the practice. Studios have retaliated with veiled threats that they will not shoot movies in states with anti–blind bidding statutes. Nevertheless, the issue is becoming moot as marriages proliferate and fewer pictures are put out to bid.

Exhibitors also express dissatisfaction with the manner in which studios market their films. Studios usually insist on controlling advertising expenditures since they are footing most of the bill (exhibitors contribute to local ad costs). Some exhibitors think they could spend the money better themselves. "When we go in and buy our media we shop around and can buy it for fifty percent of what it is bought for nationally," says Seattle exhibitor Randy Finley. "The local . . . [media] know that they can put the screws to the New York and Los Angeles ad agencies, who are only interested in getting their commission."

Advertising money is often poorly allocated, says Finley, because distribution executives do not understand exhibition. "Universal came to me with *Under the Volcano*. They insisted on booking it into a two-hundred-and-twenty-one-seat theater and bought a full-page ad for it. They had to turn away people. Two thousand people showed up.

"There is very little understanding at any level. . . . The good people get out of distribution and go into production. They can't wait to get out of distribution. Only the people who are not bright and have no future in production stay in distribution. It is pretty bleak and is getting worse."

Marketing also suffers because exhibitors are not given time to arrange for local promotional activities. "Most film in the United States is sold Tuesday for a Friday opening," says Finley. "There is absolutely nothing being done by exhibitors to promote the film."

Another exhibitor gripe is that distributors release movies to cable and home video prematurely. Exhibitors are afraid that ancillary markets will reduce box-office revenues and might someday make theaters obsolete. Indeed, industry analyst Paul Kagan predicts that the studios will receive 1986 domestic home-video rentals of $2.3 billion, more than the $1.68 billion he predicts studios will receive from domestic exhibition rentals.

Nevertheless, there is little evidence so far that these new markets have hurt theater attendance. Indeed, exhibition revenues over the past decade have grown at a robust pace (at least up to the summer of 1985, when there was a slight downturn—which some observers say is merely the result of a poor crop of movies). In 1984 the nation's largest theater chain, General Cinema, reported its eleventh consecutive year of record earnings.

Robert Selig admits exhibitors are puzzled by the apparent health of exhibition in the face of expanding ancillary markets. One of the big surprises occurred when Paramount, in an unannounced test, released a videocassette of *Flashdance* during its theatrical run. "The moment they cut it loose," says Selig, "the gross in those theaters playing *Flashdance* went up. What happened nobody knows. . . . It was a shocking surprise to everyone. We thought that the whole bottom would fall out . . . but it didn't, for whatever reason."

Nevertheless, exhibitors object to the ever-shortening interval between a movie's exhibition and its release on videocassette. Most distributors now abide by an unwritten rule not to release videocassettes until six months after exhibition ends. But the increased public awareness of a film, derived from advertising bought during its theatrical run, is incentive for the distributor to release the videocassettes earlier.

The exhibitors hurting most from the growth of ancillary markets are those who show old films or X-rated movies. Fans of *Casablanca* need no longer wait for its annual appearance in the local revival house but can now build their own libraries of classic films to see whenever they want. Similarly, those who want to view X-rated movies need no longer be embarrassed by walking into seedy theaters. As a result, revival houses are changing their programming, relying more on current foreign, art and specialized films, and X-rated theaters are going out of business—at the rate of fifteen a month since 1983, according to *USA Today*. The videocassette has done what repeated protests against porn failed to do.

The number of X-rated theaters in the United States has declined from a peak of 780 to 500.

Exhibitors are also concerned about the prospect of pay-per-view television, a form of cable programming that allows viewers to buy movies piecemeal, in the same way some subscription television stations have sold boxing matches. If, as some industry observers predict, pay-per-view films are offered simultaneously with their theatrical run, many moviegoers may elect to view the pictures at home. Why pay for parking, a baby-sitter and $3 to $6 per person at the box office, when for $5 or so the whole family can sit in front of the television set and watch the latest release in the comfort of home?

For the studios, pay-per-view offers many advantages. If the public prefers to view movies at home, exhibition can be reduced or eliminated, and with it the expense of duplicating hundreds of prints and buying millions of dollars' worth of advertising. A pay-per-view showing requires only one print to be delivered to the cable company. No paid advertising is necessary because the cable system can promote the film itself through its monthly program guide and by showing trailers. Moreover, the studios like pay-per-view because it eliminates the administrative headache of collecting film rentals from hundreds of exhibitors.

But pay-per-view, like cable and home video, may ultimately have little effect on exhibition. Young people will always want to get out of the house and will always need someplace to go on a date. Home viewing is most appreciated by older viewers and families, groups who are not big moviegoers anyway. Moreover, some people prefer viewing movies on a large screen with a theater full of people. To make the theater-going experience more enjoyable, exhibitors have begun to upgrade their sound and projection systems and install more comfortable seating.

Some industry observers predict exhibitors will embrace new technologies that will enable them to offer moviegoers a visual experience far superior to what is currently available today. The Showscan system, for example, utilizes 70mm film stock shot at sixty frames per second, compared to the current industry standard of 35mm film shot at twenty-four frames per second. The larger stock and increased speed produce a sharper and more lifelike image.

A few theater owners believe ancillary markets actually benefit exhibition. They reason that the additional revenues studios derive from it will stimulate production and create a buyer's market. Indeed, as the new ancillary markets have grown, exhibitor profits have increased while studio profits have remained steady. Ancillary revenues have only offset the studios' rising production and exploitation costs, says Merrill Lynch analyst Harold Vogel.

Cable and home video may also help exhibition by keeping the interest of new movies high in the minds and desires of the twenty-five-year-old-plus crowd, says Paramount executive Robert Klingensmith. "The people in these demographics have traditionally fallen away from moviegoing due to family formations and career involvement. But with home video, pay TV and the rest of the chances to see movies, the movie-watching experience is extended to the point that when a bona fide hit occurs . . . many twenty-five-plusers say, 'That's a film I really want to see, let's go to the theater tonight.' "

Additionally, Klingensmith believes that movies shown in ancillary markets expose new talent to viewers, building their public following and increasing interest in the actor's subsequent work. "Michael Keaton's first film was *Night Shift*. It did modestly at the box office and was widely viewed in the ancillaries. His second film was *Mr. Mom* and consumers said, 'Oh, yeah, that was that really funny guy in *Night Shift*.' [There was] instant awareness through the ancillaries."

Moreover, exhibitors can directly benefit from the home-video revolution by participating in it. Exhibitors in small towns have done well selling videocassettes. In Knoxville, Iowa, for example, the lone exhibitor was operating at a loss and in danger of going out of business until he borrowed $30,000 and set up a videocassette-rental-and-sale facility in his theater lobby. He soon found business so brisk that he had difficulty filling all his customers' orders. He was generating more than $2,000 a week from the video mart—and experienced an increase in theater admissions! Business did not even abate when a competing video retail store opened nearby.

Indeed, exhibitors have some inherent advantages marketing videocassettes. They have access to a continuing flow of movie lovers, and setting up a home-video kiosk in their lobby requires less capital than establishing a separate store. Moreover, much of their overhead costs have already been paid for by the theater operation.

While the final verdict is pending, it appears that the new ancillary markets will not destroy exhibition. The threat is no different from past scares, says Selig. "I remember when radio came along and that was going to end the movie industry. They were all going to stay home and listen to *Amos 'n' Andy* or something. And then TV came along and that for sure was going to wipe us out."

Economic forces are reshaping the face of exhibition. The most fundamental change has been the spread of theater complexes, some with more than a dozen screens under one roof.

A multiplex theater has many financial advantages over its single-screen cousin. Flops have a less disastrous impact on an exhibitor because he never relies on just one picture to fill his house. Moreover, because the size of his theaters tends to be small, fewer seats need to be sold to fill them. As a result, the exhibitor can profitably exhibit pictures longer, giving the public more time to see them and more time for good word of mouth to spread. Smaller theater size also enables the exhibitor to profitably show a wider variety of pictures, including less-commercial fare. Alongside the latest blockbuster the theater owner can offer art films, foreign films and children's films.

Staggered show times allow the multiplex exhibitor to use his employees more efficiently and offer better service to patrons. The box office and concession stand operate on a steadier basis, without fluctuating wildly between idleness and being swamped with more business than can be handled. Patrons who arrive to find their film sold out are not simply turned away, but given the opportunity of seeing another movie.

The advantages of multiplexes have encouraged their rapid proliferation. Old theaters have been converted and new complexes built. The number of movie screens in the United States has increased from twelve thousand in 1963 to nearly twenty thousand in 1985.

At the same time that multiplex theaters have been popping up across the country—typically in suburban shopping centers—older theaters have been closing. The big theaters in many downtown areas are no longer economically viable because of their large overhead costs and the exodus of their patrons to the suburbs. Individual proprietors who operate local neighborhood houses are threatened because in many instances they lack the financial wherewithal to convert to multiplexes.

"It is a very, very expensive proposition today to go into the movie-theater business," says Joel Resnick, former president of the National Association of Theatre Owners (NATO). "In the old days you built a single screen, you took four thousand square feet and you put up a theater. Today you are talking . . . twenty-five thousand or thirty thousand square feet. The land and real estate is so expensive that it is not a business any guy off the street can get into."

Indeed, the business is increasingly dominated by theater chains. "Exhibition is getting very, very competitive," says exhibition executive Bill Quigley. "The trend seems to be toward consolidation, the bigger guys are getting bigger, and the independents are getting squeezed. . . . If you have one single screen with high fixed-operating costs, it is very hard to compete. . . . If you are a mom-and-pop operation in downtown Peoria and a major circuit drops a ten-plex down the street from you, for all intents and purposes you are going to be out of business."

Drive-in theaters have been particularly hard hit. "Drive-ins are a passing breed," says Resnick. "The value of the drive-in land in many instances has surpassed the value that they can take out of the movie business. It is better to convert that land to other purposes." In fact some drive-ins have been torn down to build shopping centers with multiplex theaters.

Only in sun-belt states have drive-ins continued to prosper. Here they operate year-round and can do well by appealing to young families. Seventy-two percent of drive-in audiences are young married couples with two or more children, according to a Pacific Theatres survey. For them, the drive-in offers a bargain night on the town. They get a double feature, can bring children under twelve in for free, and don't need to hire a baby-sitter.

Theater chains are also prospering at the expense of independents because the chains have greater financial resources to fall back on in the event of a run of bad pictures. Independent exhibitors are often operating on such thin profit margins that they gamble their existence on consistently booking the right films.

Exhibitors operate on modest profit margins. "I don't think if one were to be strictly honest that there is a theater in this country that could operate at a profit without the snack bar," says Selig. "You can't pay anywhere from forty-four cents up to fifty-two cents of every box-office dollar for film, and then have some thirty-plus expenses ranging from electricity, water, payroll, advertising and taxes and have anything left, without the snack bar."

Unlike box-office receipts, which must be split with the studio, exhibitors keep all revenues derived from refreshment sales. And the products are very profitable. A large popcorn sold for $2 costs the exhibitor about 25 cents. For drinks, the cost of the paper cup is greater than the penny or so it costs to fill it with soda. One insider estimates that only 30 percent of concession sales are needed to cover their cost of labor and inventory—the remaining 70 percent is profit.

To increase concession profits, exhibitors encourage the sale of larger sizes of their products, and limit selection—they reason that the more choices available to the consumer the longer it will take him to decide what he wants, which will result in fewer patrons being served. "We are not only in the fast-food business," says Resnick, "but in the fast-time-to-serve-the-fast-food business. We can't start serving hamburgers and other things and have people standing on line. By the time we have served one customer, we have lost all of the other customers coming into the theater." Currently, one out of every six moviegoers buys something at the refreshment stand.

Interestingly, refreshment sales vary depending on the

movie shown. "It's a funny thing psychologically or emotionally why people eat more at one picture than at another," says Resnick. Nobody has determined why some pictures are great popcorn movies and others are not. The films that appeal to kids do not necessarily have the greatest refreshment sales.

Changes in exhibition have affected distribution. The spread of multiplex theaters has increased the supply of screens, encouraging distributors to release pictures broadly—some say too broadly.

"What is happening in my opinion is that it is going beyond the point of diminishing returns," says Goldwyn's Jeff Lipsky. "I think that when a company . . . opens a film with more than thirteen or fourteen hundred prints . . . there is a negative cash flow taking place."

"I think we are going after too many theaters on national breaks," says De Laurentiis Entertainment vice-president Gary Persell. He believes the attention the news media pays to the number of theaters a picture opens in has encouraged the studios to put their pictures in as many theaters as possible. "We end up making a fifteen- or sixteen-hundred-dollar print for a theater whose earnings can't justify it, but we do it anyway because we are in a numbers game within the industry and on Wall Street."

Studios are also encouraged to distribute pictures widely so they can play them off quickly and release them sooner to home video. Furthermore, while a wide release may not earn maximum box-office rentals because of its large advertising expense, by buying itself a big gross the studio enhances the value of the movie in ancillary markets.

The studios' embrace of the wide release has in turn influenced the type of movies made. To fill all those theaters, the studios must appeal to the broadest possible audience of moviegoers. Consequently, only the most commercial projects are chosen. Today movies increasingly fall into one of two categories. They are either specialty films given a limited release or potential blockbusters.

INDEPENDENT FILMMAKING

Producing a studio movie is a major enterprise. An army of craftsmen is employed, a caravan of trucks is rented and elaborate sets are constructed. In terms of visual sophistication, state-of-the-art technology and expensive production values, no one makes films better than Hollywood.

But another kind of film is made away from the studios. Here crews are small, equipment basic and budgets minimal. Ingenuity and hard work compensate for the lack of resources. The results are often impressive. Such films are frequently described as refreshing, off-beat, innovative and daring.

These two types of films are the products of vastly different approaches. "Hollywood makes films like the United States fought the war in Vietnam," says French filmmaker Elio Zarmati. "There is tremendous firepower, tremendous technology and tremendous comfort. There is no other place in the world where you can get the money, talent and facilities to make a *Star Wars*." On the other hand, Zarmati likens independent filmmaking to guerrilla warfare. Small bands of individuals with limited resources struggle against overwhelming odds to make a film.

The films also differ in the motivations behind them. The majors make movies to make money, says director Alan Rudolph (*Choose Me*), while independents make movies because they have something to say. Indeed, "the goal of Hollywood movies is not just to make a profit," says Zarmati, "but to make a shitload of money. In talking to agents and investors I get the same feeling as walking into a gambling casino in Las Vegas." On the other hand, independent filmmakers often see their work as a labor of love. They spend years on projects knowing full well that they are unlikely to receive much money for their efforts.

The principal attraction of independent filmmaking is freedom from outside interference. "The studios want to talk to you endlessly about the script," says director Jim Jarmusch (*Stranger Than Paradise*). "They want a say in casting and want to talk to you about how you cut the film and what music to use—[all of] which for me is basically just a big waste of my time and energy because I know what [I want] to do. . . . I don't want people interfering with my ideas or trying to convince me to shoot color when it should be black and white, or put a sex scene in here because it is dragging, or put some violence in there."

"Studio filmmaking is a highly political and very expensive process that involves a tremendous number of compromises," says director Gregory Nava (*El Norte*). "Very often you . . . [begin] with a vision and by the time it is all over you have made so many compromises that you are really left with nothing of your own. Then it fails and your career is ruined and that's it."

Studio filmmakers "have to overcome a corrupt system from beginning to end," says director Henry Jaglom. "I want to have fun. I want to create. You can't create with committees overseeing you. All my friends [working for studios] are having nervous breakdowns. They're all fighting people, they're all saying, 'Shit, I didn't get the movie I wanted. . . . They wouldn't let me use the actors [I wanted]. They recut my movie. They released it badly.' Well, I've got control over these things."

That is not to say that the independent filmmaker does

not have to make compromises—it is just that the nature of the compromises are different. He must compromise his vision to suit his budget.

Nor does the independent filmmaker work in a state of creative bliss without concern for business matters. He is burdened with accounting, legal and administrative chores —tasks that studios often handle for their filmmakers. "You find yourself spending an inordinate amount of your time dealing with noncreative things when you are making independent films," says Gregory Nava. "All kinds of nagging little problems are constantly popping up that you have to deal with . . . it is very frustrating but that is the price you pay for your freedom."

Moreover, the independent filmmaker has the burden of fund-raising. The time saved not meeting with studio executives is spent soliciting potential investors. It took more than a year's full-time work for Joel and Ethan Coen to raise their $1.5 million budget before they could start shooting *Blood Simple,* their suspenseful murder tale set in Texas. Gregory Nava and Anna Thomas spent two years fund-raising for *El Norte,* a film about a Guatemalan brother and sister immigrating to the United States.

"It is extremely hard to find money," says Nava. "When we started . . . we said we would listen to one hundred nos and then stop. [But] we reached one hundred and kept going. I don't know how many times we heard no." Eventually, Nava and Thomas patched together a complex deal involving investors, presales and deferments of certain expenses.

Yet despite the hardships of making films on one's own, increasing numbers of filmmakers are trying it. "The lure of being in your own boat is so attractive," says Nava, "that you find people in the official industry are attracted to it. . . . People in the studio world envy . . . the romance of the independent world."

As the studios increasingly produce a more homogenized product designed for mass consumption, they have unwittingly encouraged filmmakers to go independent. Directors like Robert Altman, who have no interest in making formula films, are leaving Hollywood for the creative freedom to make films on their own. And independent filmmakers like Jim Jarmusch are no longer so quick to accept studio offers. "I don't trust people's aesthetics in Hollywood at all," says Jarmusch. "The films that are produced bear me out. They are always interested in remaking things, or if something is a hit then they want to make something just like that. They want to market the film and have it made for a specific audience. . . . I think this rash of teenage sex comedies and movies with endless virginity jokes has kind of indicated that their computers must have told them that was a viable marketplace.

"A script was sent to me that was a teenage sex comedy that sort of summed up Hollywood attitudes for me. There was a cover letter which said, 'We realize this story reads a little like *Risky Business,* but when our rewrite is done it will read much more like *The Graduate.*' Which I thought was pretty hilarious. Everything had to be related [to some other film]. The idea of being original is probably terrifying to them."

While independent filmmaking is as old as the movie industry, many of today's independent films are different from their predecessors. The independent films made during the fifties and sixties were frequently cheap exploitation pictures, such as Roger Corman's *Slumber Party Massacre* or Sam Arkoff's *I Was a Teenage Werewolf.* These were B pictures, without artistic pretensions, designed solely to make money by selling sex and violence. Their chief contribution to the medium has been as a training vehicle for young filmmakers who eventually went on to make better films.

The market for low-budget exploitation pictures has declined as the networks and studios have shown increasing willingness to make equally exploitative movies themselves. It is difficult for independents to compete in sex and violence when the studios release *Porky's* and *Scarface.* Consequently, low-budget exploitation films are being crowded out of the market by a higher-budget variety, which are now made by both studios and independents.

Today independent filmmakers increasingly compete in a market the studios have been deserting—the market for intelligent and unique films made for the more discerning moviegoer. Such specialty films as *El Norte, Eating Raoul, Return of the Secaucus 7* and *My Dinner with Andre* appeal to people interested in something other than ordinary studio fare. (Some independents like Cannon produce an eclectic mix of exploitation pictures like *Death Wish II* alongside such prestige films as *That Championship Season.*)

The production of specialty films has been encouraged by the growth of ancillary markets, which provide new sources of financing for the independent filmmaker. Yet few specialty films earn large profits. While there is nothing inherent in a low-budget format that precludes attracting a mass audience, most do not. "You take a film like *Repo Man* or *Blood Simple,* says marketing consultant Jeff Dowd, "and they are pretty much for a hip audience. So if you start playing them off in suburbia they don't last more than a week or so."

A successful specialty film today can expect to gross $3 million to $5 million at the domestic box office. After the cost of prints and advertising is deducted, and the exhibitor and distributor deduct their share of revenues, the filmmaker is left with about $500,000. He can expect another $600,000 or so from home-video and cable sales, and an additional $500,000 from foreign sales. While these figures are rough approximations, as a general rule one can say the revenue that can be derived from specialty films can support production budgets of up to $1.6 million.

Of course, independent films that appeal to a broader audience can earn more. *The Amityville Horror, The Trial of Billy Jack* and *Grizzly Adams* are examples of three particularly successful independent films. They garnered studio rentals of $35 million, $24 million and $22 million, respectively.

As independent filmmaking has grown, several organizations have arisen to nurture it. In 1979 independent filmmakers banded together and formed the Independent Feature Project (IFP). The IFP sponsors seminars, workshops and an annual film market to showcase independent films. It has 1,500 members.

In 1980 Robert Redford established the Sundance Institute to help independent filmmakers. The Institute arranges for independents to hone their scripts and improve their filmmaking skills under the tutelage of industry veterans, and then to rehearse with professional actors and technical crews.

The major studios have mixed feelings about the growth of independent films. On the one hand, they like to be able to pick up inexpensive independent movies to distribute themselves. But, on the other hand, "the mounting success of independent films frightens executives," says producer Leonard Goldberg. "There are certain companies that won't make pickup deals because someone in management might say, 'Hey, our pickups are doing better than the movies we develop ourselves. Why don't we just pick up all of them? Why do we need any of these [development] people here?' That makes executives nervous."

Moreover, independent films make independent distributors prosperous. Such companies as Cannon, Atlantic, Alive Films and Samuel Goldwyn are challenging the majors' hegemony over the marketplace. These upstarts pick up stories that the majors have passed on—projects that the studios lack the vision and courage to take a chance on, says Cannon chairman Menahem Golan—and then produce them for a fraction of what a studio would spend. Golan claims he can make a $20 million studio film for $5 million.

Fox chairman Barry Diller believes that independents are flourishing because the entire industry has been in a prosperous phase. But when the industry goes into an economic slump, which it inevitably does, many independents will fold. Eventually only those companies that have larger resources to fall back will be able to survive.

"I doubt that any independent in business today will be in business ten years from now," says Diller. "They have their time during the uptick of the business and then when it goes down they fall by the wayside."

Meanwhile, Cannon has announced its plans to produce between twenty-two and twenty-four films in 1986, more movies than any major studio. The company continues to earn record profits and recently purchased large theater chains in Italy and England.

* * *

The accomplishments of independent filmmakers are an affront to the major studios. These mavericks have demonstrated that they can make high-quality films on low budgets, and have often done so by violating the rules the industry lives by. Many of them disdain script conferences and marketing considerations, refuse to pander to the public and make films out of the courage of their convictions.

Moreover, independents are outspoken in their contempt for studio moviemaking. They believe the studios' emphasis on deal-making is antithetical to making good films. "I do not like the way the majors are run," says Golan. "I don't think creative people are at the heads of the companies . . . in most cases they were agents. . . . It is all my friend, your friend, who they know, what is our relationship. I'm a friend of this lawyer who is connected with this star and so all of a sudden the package is there. Sometimes the package is without the movie, without an idea, without a script. And in most cases that makes a fiasco."

Independents assert that good deals do not necessarily make good movies. "There are a lot of people [in the industry] who are not creative people," says Henry Jaglom. "They are sycophants of creative people, or they are users of talent, or they are ten percenters, who at least are honest about what they are—which is that they want their ten percent. They're deal-makers and they're interested in the deal, not the film."

Consequently, Jaglom says, such people don't care as much about the quality of the movie as the amount of money they can make from the deal. "The contracts are made so that half the money on these huge budgets goes to individuals. And the lawyers who put the deals together, who package them, are the main beneficiaries along with the producers, who get five hundred thousand dollars apiece, seven hundred and fifty thousand dollars apiece. The agents get tremendous fees for delivering people in addition to their ten percent. They have all kinds of side deals and they're suddenly partners [because] they brought their star into a piece of shit."

Independents also criticize the studios for being wasteful.

Independent budgets are minuscule compared to the $12 million to $15 million studios typically spend on a movie. Independent filmmakers made *Last Night at the Alamo* for $22,000, *The Brother from Another Planet* for $340,000, and *Hester Street* for less than $400,000.

Upon being offered a $28 million budget for a film, Henry Jaglom tried to convince the producers to let him make a series of low-budget pictures instead. "I said, 'Look, this is a stupid mistake.' And I told them how I could turn in ten films for that same twenty-eight million dollars at an average cost of two-point-eight million dollars, which is more than any other budget of my films. . . . Then I showed them what the down side is on that and the up side, which is that you are multiplying your chance of winning [tenfold]."

But the producers rebuffed Jaglom's suggestion because, he says, they stood to make hefty fees from the deal. "And who's going to stop them? It is good for every single person in the company except the stockholders."

Independents economize in a variety of ways. They rely on small casts and crews, select scripts carefully (avoiding stories that require large crowds or special effects), and may shoot on inexpensive 16mm stock instead of the finer-image 35mm film. Most of all they are ingenious in making do with less. They devise ways to make cheap effects look expensive.

"The less money you have the more you are forced to figure out ways to make things happen which are creative," says Jaglom. "What they [the studios] have done is take away the economic limitations. . . . They say, 'Kid, what do you want? You want to blow up a city? Well, we'll build a city for you to blow up.'

"A close friend of mine recently [duplicated for a movie] . . . the sixteenth floor of the Fairmont Hotel in San Francisco. I said, 'How much did this thing cost you?' He said, 'Four hundred and eighty thousand dollars.' I said, 'How much would it have cost to shoot it at the Fairmont?' He said, 'Twenty thousand dollars.' I said, 'That's a four-hundred-and-sixty-thousand-dollar [difference]. Why did you build this thing?' He replied: 'They let me.' "

Independent filmmakers and distributors have successfully recruited top writers, directors and stars to work for them for minimal wages. "It's easy to do," says Jaglom. "Jack Nicholson worked for me for a color television . . . my budget was one million and at that point he was getting one and a half million dollars to do a picture. . . . Karen Black gets two hundred thousand, two hundred and fifty thousand dollars a picture. She worked for me for seventeen hundred." (Although her share of the film's profits ultimately earned her more than $300,000, he says.)

"The powerful actors want to work in more-quality films," explains Alan Rudolph. "They want to do their best work and they see that a lot of the real good and interesting work is being done outside the [studio] system."

"All the stars are rich people," says Menahem Golan. "They're making a fortune but they only make one or two pictures a year. . . . What does a star do the rest of the year when he doesn't make movies? He gets frustrated, he divorces his wife, he goes to psychoanalysis and he plays tennis. . . . [But] what they really want is to make films. They want to work. So if you bring them challenging material, or if they have an idea [for a film] you can get them to work." Golan has already recruited such stars as Katharine Hepburn, Bo Derek, Faye Dunaway, Brooke Shields, Charles Bronson, Nick Nolte, Robert Mitchum, John Gielgud and Sylvester Stallone to make films for him (although he sometimes pays hefty fees to get them).

Independents also economize by hiring nonunion crews. Sometimes the crew is comprised of union members working under aliases. "There is a lot of waste on the studio lots because of union regulations," admits producer Don Simpson. "[There is] major featherbedding. . . . We have figured that a picture like *Beverly Hills Cop* . . . that cost over ten million dollars, we could have made for six and a half or seven million dollars if we didn't have to worry about the unions. We don't need all those people. I mean a movie set is ridiculous. They just load 'em up. Load 'em up."

"What you need on a set," says Jaglom, "is a cameraman, camera crew of two, one to focus and one to carry and reload, a sound crew of one or two, one or two grips and maybe one lighting specialist. Maybe someone to handle wardrobe and maybe someone to drive. Any way you cut it that's ten [people], certainly not more than a dozen . . . unless you want to support all the unions and their featherbedding . . . [but] you are not making the film any better. You're [just] supporting special-interest groups, which I think is insane."

Many filmmakers say nonunion crews are not only a financial boon but a creative one as well. "With jaded union crews you get people who are doing it just for the money," says director Jonathan Kaplan. "You get a lot of bored people who don't give a shit."

Union crews are set in their ways, says Jaglom, who recalls the difficulty he experienced with a 120-person union crew while making his first movie. "Everything I wanted to do, my cameraman and the whole crew said, 'You can't do that. It won't cut. It's not in the script.' I said, 'Let me worry, I'm the director.' They said, 'No, we won't shoot it. You can't put the light there, it won't look right.'

"Finally, I went to Orson [Welles], who was in the movie and I said, 'Look, they're driving me crazy. They're saying it won't cut, they're saying it is not lit right.' He said, 'Listen . . . just tell them it's a dream sequence.' I said, 'A dream sequence?' He said, 'Yeah.' I said, 'Why?' He said, 'They think dreams don't make sense. They still think life makes sense. . . . So if you tell them it's a dream sequence they will suspend all those rules about life.'

"I tried it after lunch," says Jaglom, "and it worked. The cameraman got on his back and he wanted to do all kinds of weird things. So I made the rest of the movie 'a dream sequence' and the crew was wonderful."

Besides ignoring union regulations, independent filmmakers sometimes economize by disregarding local and state laws as well. They may shoot without paying for required permits and licenses.

"If a rule gets in my way, I either circumvent it or ignore it," says Jaglom. On his film *Tracks* he was told that it would cost $6,500 a day for insurance and licenses if he wanted to shoot aboard an Amtrak train. Instead, he bought tickets for his cast and crew, sneaked his equipment aboard, posted lookouts and shot the film without permission.

When he needed to shoot a dinner scene, he paid the stewards to open the dining car. As extras, he used passengers on the train, asking anyone within camera range to either sign a release or switch seats. He says not a single passenger objected. "Everybody wants to be in the movies," he observes. "Nobody has ever turned me down."

Occasionally a conductor would intrude and ask to see his permit. "I would send him back twelve cars with a kid who was working with me who would go looking for an imaginary permit. The kid would keep looking while we finished up the shot and got off at the next stop."

Nor did the harried shooting schedule hurt his actors' performances. Says Jaglom, "Dennis Hopper was sure he was going to be arrested. . . . But that's great for the part because he looks like he is really paranoid and the character is paranoid."

But shooting on a shoestring is not always such an amusing, antic-filled experience. Independent filmmakers can experience serious problems. And, unlike their studio brethren, they do not have a rich benefactor in the background to bail them out.

Independents have been harassed by union representatives who resort to strong-arm tactics in an effort to get their members hired. Sometimes a shoot is disrupted by union men honking horns or making noise until their demands are met.

"That is why so many films are being shot in right-to-work states, where the law is on your side," says director Robert Altman. "You go to the governor of the state and say, 'I'm spending three million in your state, and I want protection against gangsters.' They take care of it the best that they can. . . . [But] you have to have a little courage yourself."

Even greater hazards may be encountered. During the filming of *El Norte*, Gregory Nava and Anna Thomas had their production manager and film stock seized by armed gunmen in Mexico. "It was just outrageous to encounter this sort of thing," says Thomas. "You expect problems but you don't believe your life is going to be threatened and that people are going to be coming in with guns.

"The people who came to the set identified themselves as part of the secret police, although this appeared to be an unofficial action. . . . But in Mexico that is the way things work. It is very corrupt.

"We started these telephone negotiations . . . [and] got our production manager released. Then we negotiated for the film stock that had been taken, which was a lot of our most expensive and important footage. It would have been extremely difficult if not impossible to reshoot.

"We had to pay . . . [$17,000] in bundles of cash in a parking lot in Mexico City at midnight. They wore dark glasses in the middle of the night. It was very scary."

After regaining their film, Thomas, Nava and the cast and crew fled Mexico. To complete their production, they had to build sets in Southern California that would match their Mexican footage. For several scenes that had to be shot in Mexico, they slipped back in and shot them with a hidden camera. "It was a very dangerous thing to do because of [the risk of] being caught," says Thomas.

Nava says their experience demonstrates why independent filmmaking is not for everyone. "What you want to say must be so important to you that you're willing to weather all the storms that you are going to encounter. . . . [If your attitude is] 'Oh, its fun, let's make a movie,' or . . . 'Wouldn't it be nice to be rich and famous and have beautiful lovers.' . . . If that is what you're interested in, you shouldn't get involved [in the first place]."

SEX, DRUGS AND CREATIVE ACCOUNTING

"It's better than being a pimp," said Harry Cohn of his job as head of Columbia Pictures. He built a reputation for never letting an aspiring actress out of his office with her underwear intact.

Cohn was not the only studio Casanova. Every afternoon at four o'clock a young, pretty girl would be let in to see Darryl Zanuck. His assistant Milton Sperling recalled: "The doors would be locked after she went in, no calls were taken, and for the next half hour nothing happened—headquarters shut down. Around the office work came to a halt for the sex siesta. It was an understood thing. While the girl was with Zanuck, everything stopped, and anyone who had the same proclivities as Zanuck, and had the girl to do it with, would go off somewhere and do what he was doing. I honestly think that from four to four-thirty every day at Fox, if you could have harnessed the power from all the fucking that was going on, you could have turned the tides at Malibu. It was an incredible thing, but a girl went in through that door every day."

According to Zanuck biographer Leonard Mosley, "a star-tlet . . . was [usually] chosen for this daily assignation, and it was rarely the same one twice. The only one who ever seems to have been called in more than once was a Fox contract feature player named Carole Landis. . . . . Otherwise, any pretty and willing extra was picked for the daily session, and after her erotic chore was completed, she departed by a side door. . . . Only then would Zanuck's door be unlocked again, the telephones would begin to ring, work would be resumed, and conferences would be called."

But as with other Hollywood traditions, the casting couch is an anachronism today. "It never occurs," says actress Catherine Hicks (*Garbo Talks*). "Not in any solid professional atmosphere. Not in any casting office or legitimate producer's office." Says journalist Jeff Silverman: "I think if people really learned about sex in Hollywood they would be shocked—at how little there is."

"There are some creeps around but mostly not," says personal manager Dolores Robinson. "On a low level there are men walking around town talking like they are producers. But [casting couches] are not found in major film and television offices. I have never had a client complain about someone ever putting the physical move on somebody . . . and they would tell me [if it happened]."

"I'm the kind of guy you would look at me and think I would fuck anything that walks," says producer Don Simpson. "And it is true, I will. But . . . [the casting couch] is such horseshit that my partner and I laugh about it all the time. I have never gotten laid less than while in the movie business. . . . There are a lot of fringe people in this business who claim to be producers or whatever, and it does go on there. They are taking advantage of people. And the people who are being taken advantage of aren't that bright. But anybody who thinks they can fuck their way into this business is an idiot."

Producer Tom Greene recalls only one instance in his thirteen years in the industry in which sex was offered him. "I was director of project development for [director] Robert Wise and an agent sent over a girl who was a hooker. She was tall, blond, had huge tits and looked like a Vegas showgirl. She was wearing a tight skirt, high heels and had that Jayne Mansfield kind of look.

"She came in the door and said, 'Hi, I'm from the so-and-so agency. Here is the script.' Then she said, 'Boy it is hot in here,' and sat down on the couch and took off her shoes. I said, 'Well, I have some work to do.' She replied, 'Why don't you read the script right now and I'll help you,' and started to unbutton her blouse and take off her bra.

"My first reaction was 'Boy, I must be sexy.' Then I realized, 'Hey, I'm not that sexy.' . . . I said, 'Whooah, stop. Time out.' She explained that if she didn't do anything she wouldn't get paid. So I told her, 'You can tell them anything you want. Just leave, I'm not interested in this.'

"The truth is the casting couch has never existed for me or for anyone else who is a reputable producer. Honestly. I have never had an actress do that. Never fuck anyone to give them anything, because you can't. If they aren't good, you're fucked."

As the stakes involved in moviemaking have increased, producers have been unwilling to risk millions of dollars casting an unqualified person in an important part. If a producer is disposed to pay for sex it is much cheaper to hire a prostitute than offer such an expensive quid pro quo. "If you were able to get somebody to give you ten million dollars [to make a movie], you are not going to spend it on a piece of ass," says producer Martin Bregman. "You would have to be crazy."

A producer's primary concern is getting his projects made. Consequently, he will package his project with actors who will make it viable, irrespective of his personal relationship with them. "I have cast people who I hate personally," says Simpson. "I mean I loathe them as individuals. But they are talented. So I use them. Not only would they not make it with me, they would not give me the time of day. It doesn't matter to me. It's business."

Changing mores have also played a part in the demise of the casting couch. "I think there is so much sexual freedom [today] that you don't have to go to those extents anymore," says producer Leonard Goldberg. "I mean it just is not a big deal anymore to have sex with someone. It used to be then."

With the rise of women's liberation, says agent Martin

Baum, "women will go to bed when they please and with whom they please. And the men are not as sexually starved as they were when there were such things as casting couches. Sex is too easily available to both sexes for the need for casting couches to exist anymore."

Moreover, the industry is no longer as male-dominated as it used to be. The presence of women in studio inner sanctums has changed the atmosphere in which studios conduct business.

That is not to say that sexual harassment doesn't exist in the industry—it does, although it's difficult to ascertain its frequency. Some women say they never experience any problems, while others complain they're repeatedly harassed. But the harassment that exists today is of a less blatant and onerous variety than before—no studio head today uses his office as a bedroom.

Sexual relationships are, however, frequently used by both men and women to advance their careers. Actresses use sex to get closer to men in positions of influence in the industry, according to Los Angeles psychiatrist Dr. Hyla Cass. "There is a trade-off. In exchange for sex the women get connections with people in power." Says Dolores Robinson, "I know actresses who date producers who frankly confess they are not in love but are doing it to advance their careers." Similarly, men make contacts and become producers by dating female stars.

"I think it happens in every business," says manager-producer Jay Bernstein. "We read all the time that someone is advancing their career by giving sexual favors to somebody. But I don't think it goes on a lot and I've never seen it work more than one time. I saw one actress who got ahead by selective intercourse. But I have only seen it that one time out of thousands of female stars. . . . [And] it is not something that really works well. It only works to get you from a one to maybe a two. It doesn't get you to a nine."

"Some women may have fucked themselves into the business," says agent Gary Salt, "but ultimately no matter how you got the opportunity, if you cannot do your job, you will be fired."

There is also plenty of sexual activity within the industry that is based on nothing more than mutual attraction. Hollywood is a town, after all, with more than its share of attractive men and women. But insiders say there is less sexual activity in the industry than the news media suggests.

"I have never in all the years I have been in Hollywood been involved in a real great orgy, much to my regret," says writer Stirling Silliphant. "I have friends who have been invited and some have participated and some chickened out. But by and large I would say there is more of that in the fashion business and a lot of other businesses. I always found Hollywood essentially monogamous among many people. . . . I'm talking about the really working people in town, not the people who are trying to break in. Because when you come in off the bus and are trying to break in you will do almost anything. You sleep around and do all kinds of numbers.

"We are talking about the guys who are vice-presidents of development at studios and networks. A lot of them are young people, very serious people. A lot of them have been detoxed and are no longer into drugs. I would say most . . . are very sincere, straight if not square people who, if anything, are into Perrier with lime, go to aerobics classes, who shop at Mrs. Gooch's [health-food store], who really care what they put into their bodies, including guys or girls, and tend to be anything but the old picture of Hollywood. I don't think we have the Fatty Arbuckle syndrome here very much. At least if so, a lot of us are not exposed to it."

Many insiders say there is no more promiscuity within the industry than anyplace else. "You have beautiful people who are very bright and very powerful," says one psychologist, "and they may sleep around, they may have multiple relationships. [But] you go into any small town and they are doing the same thing. Hollywood just seems to get all the attention."

"Those who talk most about the greater amount of sexual 'goings-on' in Hollywood," wrote anthropologist Hortense Powdermaker in 1950, "are either puritanical or ignorant of sex life in other places. Actually, a large number of Hollywood people live more or less 'normal' family lives. . . . The myth of Hollywood's greater sexuality, however, still prevails."

Today even those in the industry who are inclined to be promiscuous have been reducing their sexual activity, if for no other reason than fear of catching Herpes, AIDS and other sexually transmitted diseases. These ailments have had a "staggering effect on what people are doing," says one psychologist. "There is a real movement back toward monogamy."

While promiscuity is on the decline, drugs remain a serious problem. "There is no question that there are a lot of people in Hollywood who use drugs," says Stirling Silliphant. "It is not only accepted but considered chic in certain circles.

"If you go to any big party you will see the party instantly breaking up into oil and water. The druggy crowd usually finds itself very quickly and goes off in another room where you hear laughter start to rise louder than anywhere else. And by and large that crowd seems to enjoy the party a lot more than the rest of us who try to do it the slow way with martinis."

Drug use in the industry is not much different from that in society at large, says Steven Chatoff, director of the Chemical Dependency Center of Brotman Medical Center in Los Angeles. "We are talking maybe three percent more . . . and I don't think it is any more prevalent than in any other type of high-pressure industry . . . whether it be aerospace or Silicon Valley."

Chatoff estimates that 50 to 70 percent of the working public use drugs or alcohol socially, while another 25 to 35 percent are abusers who binge periodically, and 10 percent are addicted to alcohol or drugs. Tom Kenny, director of the substance-abuse program for the Motion Picture and Television Fund, estimates that 20 percent of the people in the industry are either alcoholics or addicts.

While alcohol remains the most abused drug in the industry, cocaine has quickly seized second place. It has become popular because it increases energy, produces euphoria and enhances self-confidence—effects that many users believe help them succeed at work. "There is a lot of pressure to perform well and there is a lot of money at stake," says Dr. Hyla Cass. "In order to face up to that kind of challenge some people need to get themselves up with drugs like cocaine which give an artificial sense of being able to handle situations. It gives you a false sense of security, even grandiosity, where you feel you can do anything.

"But while they have this illusion of being more powerful, more competent, in fact their performance really deteriorates. They think they are doing great but everyone around them notices that they are really messing up badly. Then they start having symptoms like runny noses and an inability to concentrate. . . . [Ultimately] they become irritable, intolerant, impatient, paranoid and aggressive."

Cocaine is particularly insidious because users do not recognize their growing dependence on it. Even occasional use tends to change one's character, says Los Angeles psychologist Dr. Jack Rosenberg. "It has a way of creeping up on people. They start doing it only on the weekends or at parties. [But gradually] they are losing their jobs, they can't function as well, their relationships are going downhill. Their whole life is kind of falling apart. It is not [an abrupt change] . . . but their sense of identity is [slowly] being undermined."

Widespread cocaine use has affected moviemaking. "A lot of deals have been made when people shared that in common," says Stirling Silliphant. Conversely, deals have fallen apart because of cocaine use. "We have had writers go into a meeting with a studio executive who was bouncing off the walls," says agent Bobbi Thompson. "The writers walked out thinking they had a deal and two days later the guy didn't remember what they had discussed."

As the number of poor decisions, bad performances and cost overruns caused by drugs has increased, the studios have begun to crack down. "Hollywood really understands money more than anything else," says one insider. "When a picture costs twenty million dollars to make, they don't want to risk it on people who are stoned and not going to perform their best."

"I think what's finally happened is that the people in management have finally said no," says writer-director Joan Tewkesbury. "I know that people have not been hired because of drug habits. I've heard it discussed in meetings, whereas I never heard it discussed before."

There has also been a change in attitude among many people who work in the industry. "Because of all the recent publicity about the problem," says Dr. Cass, "cocaine is not considered so fashionable, so hip anymore. There is a new emphasis on healthy living, on diet, nutrition and exercise. The focus is shifting away." Numerous rehabilitation programs have sprung up to help people with drug-dependency problems.

"Cocaine is no longer considered the innocuous drug it once was, and people are getting hep to it and smartening up," says Tom Kenny. "A woman told me that she was at a party recently and the host brought out the cocaine at the end of the dinner and said: 'Party time.' And all these people who at one time used cocaine refused it."

"The attitude has been changing a little bit because people see other people who have been hooked on it," says Dr. Rosenberg. "I think there is less of it than there used to be," says producer Leonard Goldberg. "I think it reached a peak five or six years ago. I think that every time someone is arrested, it makes . . . [others] shape up."

"There are a hell of a lot of people cleaning up in our industry," says Kenny. "Some crews are totally clean and sober. If you get a camera operator who is clean and sober . . . they usually hire only clean and sober guys. That is why you have some shows that have no drugs and alcohol on them."

While drug use remains a serious problem, many industry observers say there is a more prevalent addiction. "This is a workaholic's town," says journalist Jeff Silverman. "When you have to get up at five o'clock in the morning and be on the set at seven, and shoot until ten at night, there is just not time to fool around. That is partly why cocaine more than any other drug is so prevalent. It keeps you going, same as speed."

"I would say work came first, drugs came second and sex came third," says Leonard Goldberg. "I would say work would be a very strong number one. Strangely enough sex comes third. . . . In the days of the moguls there were no workaholics and there certainly was very, very little drug usage, so they had lots of energy left [for sex]."

"By other people's standards it is a glamorous [life-style]," says production executive Susan Merzbach, "but that doesn't mean it isn't exhausting . . . two nights a week you are at screenings and bumping elbows with the high and mighty, and the third night you have dinner with network vice-presidents or studio heads. It can be pretty heady and that is probably why people work so hard on the weekends. Because if they stop working . . . it is going to be a long fall."

The one function that most filmmakers agree studios perform with sufficient creativity is their accounting of profits. A favorite topic of conversation is how studios cheat filmmakers. There is a widespread feeling that since you are unlikely to ever see any profits from a film, it is wise to get your money up front.

"If you don't get your money up front you can forget about it," says director Martin Ritt, "unless you have an *Indiana Jones* or a *Star Wars,* because you can't steal beyond a certain point. I mean it's just too embarrassing. But on an ordinary successful film, it's very rare they go into the black."

"It is an enormous problem," says producer Harry Ufland. "It is a struggle on each film. It is absolutely intentional. In some cases worse than others. There was a former vice-president at a studio who really had no bones about telling people that his job was to see that they didn't get money."

Ufland says the modus operandi of studios is to delay payments as long as possible so they have the use of the money. "They have these huge legal departments so it is cheaper for them not to pay and get sued. And eventually they will settle."

Audits invariably pay for themselves, says Ben Newman of the accounting firm of Laventhol and Horwath, which charges $20,000 for an initial audit. Newman says that virtually all successful movies are audited. His largest recovery for a client has been $1 million.

Newman, who is too diplomatic to characterize studio behavior as theft, says "errors" are of two types. First there are clerical errors. "People make mistakes," he shrugs with a smile, "usually to the benefit of the studio." Such errors, he says, arise because studio accountants don't read the contracts made with filmmakers. They may be lazy or may find it advantageous to engage in "tacit neglect" and not bother to do anything that will cost them money. When clerical errors are brought to the attention of the studio, however, it will usually rectify them without a fuss.

The other type of error arises out of contract interpretation. Newman says the studios operate under the philosophy "When in doubt resolve it in our favor and we will fight it out later if it is contested." Despite the meticulous construction of studio contracts, new areas of ambiguity constantly arise.

For example, a recent dispute concerned how home-video revenues should be computed. Many studios have begun to market videocassettes through wholly owned subsidiary companies. The question arose as to whether a studio's revenues from videocassette sales should be considered the amount received by the subsidiary or the amount remitted to the studio. If the latter, how much is the subsidiary required to remit? Is the subsidiary entitled to make a profit and if so, how much? And what overhead costs can be deducted in computing that profit?

Lawyers representing filmmakers try to resolve such ambiguities beforehand. But different lawyers may settle these questions differently. Consequently, over the course of many dealings, each entertainment law firm has evolved its own version of a net-profits definition for each studio. Use of these definitions saves the parties from having to renegotiate the same issues for every client.

Creative-accounting problems first arose in the industry when stars began to share in the profits derived from their pictures. In the earliest days of the industry there was little room for quarrel since stars received a flat fee. But as competition for stars grew, studios agreed to share profits with them, thereby opening the floodgates to disputes about how the studios kept their books and calculated net profits.

Studio contracts provide that certain expenses, fees and allowances are deductible from their gross revenues (money received from exhibitors and ancillary sales) in computing net profits. These expenses include the cost of producing the film, the cost of prints and advertising, interest on these expenditures, a distribution fee and an overhead fee. Each of these deductions has provided fertile ground for dispute.

Print costs have been challenged as excessive in instances where duplication was made by a subsidiary of the studio. Advertising expenses have been contested when the studio failed to account for year-end rebates. Studio overhead charges are often thought excessive, especially when the film is not shot on the studio lot.

Interest charges are a frequent bone of contention. Studios consider the money used to finance a movie an expense. Irrespective of whether the studio actually has to borrow this money, the producer is assessed interest on it, usually at a rate higher than that which the studio borrows. A question often arises as to when this interest charge should start and stop running. Some studios, for instance, do not credit exhibitor advances against this charge. Thus the studio simultaneously collects interest on advances while refusing to credit them against the interest being charged the producer.

The methods a studio uses to allocate expenses among its films raise other issues. It is to the studio's benefit to allocate as many expenses as possible to a successful picture in order to reduce the amount of net profits that will have to be paid out. Consequently, all kinds of items—limousines, lunches, executive travel—may be tacked onto successful films even if these costs were incurred on a different movie.

The allocation of revenues is similarly subject to abuse. When studios license a group of films to television, the revenue they receive should be attributed to the films in accordance with their worth. Obviously, *Star Wars* deserves to get more revenue than a box-office flop. But it is advantageous for the studio to allocate as much of the money as possible to the flop because its losses are so great that it can soak up a great deal of revenues before any money has to be paid out to profit participants.

In fairness to the studios it must be noted that a lot of complaints about creative accounting have no legal merit. Many filmmakers knowingly consent to onerous terms and then in retrospect complain that they are being cheated. In fact, they are not being cheated because the studio is only taking what it is legally entitled to.

"The artists and the agents are dummies because they don't read their contracts," says Don Simpson. "It is not a question of cheating. It is all there in black and white."

"There is no creative accounting," says producer Martin Bregman. "What there is is shitty deals going in. But you have the choice. . . . I don't have to make that deal. . . . If they get fifteen to twenty-five percent overhead, which is unconscionable . . . it is done up front, it is all on the table."

An ICM agent says, "The whole question of creative accounting has been blown out of proportion. The accounting is for the most part honest. People are getting fucked legally because they don't have the leverage to get a better deal . . . a lot of agents are not good about explaining the terms of contracts to their clients."

"The time to complain was when they went into the deal," says attorney David Nochimson. "A lot of these companies do really account according to what's contracted. The fact is the studios have the leverage, they beat up on these net participants, and they pretty much dictate their terms. And when the picture is successful everyone cries."

Moreover, while the major studios are frequently criticized for their accounting practices, the bookkeeping of independent distributors is often worse. "The majors don't screw around all that much," says attorney Tom Hoberman. "But with independents it's terrible, because they can throw in the kitchen sink and try to justify it. Universal's up front. They give you the toughest fucking net-profit definition . . . and you accept it, and they account based on that. 'Cause they already fucked you."

Furthermore, it should be kept in mind that while the studios' share of revenues may be great, they are taking all the risks of failure. "They are making a lot of money," says Bregman, "but they are putting up the dollars. I have yet to see actors, directors and producers get together and put their own money into something."

"Any business that gives away fifty percent of its profits and incurs one hundred percent of its losses has to have creative accounting," says producer Robert Evans. "If a picture costs twenty million dollars and does three million, no one gives back the seventeen. Sure there is creative accounting, but it isn't unfair. It would be different if the person was a partner in the business and shared the losses as well as the profits."

Moreover, the studios absorb millions of dollars in losses each year from developing projects that are never made.

Essentially, the amount of profits a person is entitled to receive is a function of his clout in the industry. The highly desired artist can force the studios to give him a better definition of net profits. Those with the most clout are able to negotiate deals that permit them to share directly in the studio's gross revenues. Such deals largely eliminate disputes about creative accounting since few, if any, deductions are allowed.

But the controversy over creative accounting has hurt the industry. It has inflated production costs by encouraging filmmakers to demand large fees up front, and people who don't believe they will ever see profits have less incentive to restrain production costs. They figure they might as well live it up at the studio's expense while they can.

17

HOLLYWOOD JOURNALISM

The moviemaking community are a quarrelsome lot who rarely agree on anything. But they are united in their contempt for the press, which they accuse of spreading fallacious, biased and sensationalized stories. And Hollywood is good and angry about it. "Don't even ask me about the press," says Jane Fonda. "I think the press is abominable."

Says producer Martin Bregman: "I think the media in the entertainment industry sucks. I think they are ill-informed. I think they are pompous. And I think they are basically destructive."

"By and large I find that the press is . . . greedy, ambitious and they will do anything to succeed," says Stirling Silliphant. "The media press is strictly an exploitive bunch of people. . . . [S]ome of them are extremely prejudiced toward the Hollywood community and use their columns as platforms for doing some real clever smart-ass writing."

The most frequent complaint is that news reports are rife with errors. Barry Diller says the media is "generally inaccurate." Paul Newman says only 5 percent of what they report is accurate.

Moreover, there is widespread sentiment in the industry

that the press is more interested in selling news than in telling the truth. "They are selling a product," says agent Martin Baum. "They are selling newspapers and they are trying to entertain as against reporting facts."

"The media is more interested in the exploitative aspects of filmmaking than what really happens," says Martin Bregman. "If John is fucking Mary on the set, boy that is terrific [copy]. . . . I find most of the entertainment . . . [reporters] are an extension of being gossip columnists."

"*People* magazine is the metaphor for the type of coverage the media gives Hollywood," says Silliphant. "It is extremely superficial, basically star-oriented or personality-oriented. . . . It has very little intellectual or weighty content in terms of where Hollywood is going, the kinds of films it is making, and what the effect of those films is on society. That is all considered much too heavy. They are into the fact that Joan Collins has a new tit job, or someone has signed an eighty-two-million-dollar contract, or that someone is now keeping a racehorse in a Beverly Hills backyard. It's all very colorful but I don't think it does anything except titillate the reader."

"The press in general will tend to distort the truth in terms of looking for that banner headline that will get people's attention," says producer Leonard Goldberg. "It is sad, but Hollywood seems to provide . . . [many] magazines and newspapers with almost their total copy. And they have to keep manufacturing it. [Their attitude is:] 'It is great if it is true, but if it isn't true, that is not so important either. We will just make it up then.' "

The press also wreaks havoc with the truth, industry insiders say, simply because it does not understand the business. Many years ago veteran screenwriter Ben Hecht said: "Nobody ever goes to the trouble of getting anything straight about Hollywood. The ways of the town are, to the press, as dark as the practices of Tibet."

"They don't know how it works," says Bregman. "Nobody has ever been in the factory. Which is wild. Nobody has been there. They still don't understand the process, they really don't. It is like a film student just getting out [of school]. They have a totally misguided unrealistic view. . . . [*New York Times* correspondent] Aljean Harmetz knows nothing. I am stunned by her lack of knowledge. I am absolutely stunned. I mean she is a nice lady. She is a bright lady, but she lives in a cocoon."

"They don't have a clue as to what is going on," says producer Don Simpson. "It's an arcane business. It's not difficult to understand but you have to have participated in it. . . . They have never been part of it so they deal in the myth. . . . As an insider you read these articles and it is hysterical. You laugh, it is so ridiculous. . . . [Consequently] most people in this business don't like speaking to the press. . . . There is a lack of regard for them because the feeling is that they don't know what the hell they are talking about. Forget about being misquoted, they just don't get it."

For example, Simpson says, the press was fooled into believing that Sherry Lansing was the first woman to head a major studio. Simpson and others point out that she was merely the president of production, was accountable to several men above her, and did not control distribution, which was run by her co-equal, the president of distribution. "Senior vice-president of production is the classic title [for her job]," says Simpson. "When Sherry Lansing was given the title president of production it was to create publicity for Fox. . . . [She] had the power to do nothing. And everybody in Hollywood knew it and only the press was stupid enough to buy the [story]. . . .

"It was just funny to me to see the press react because she was a woman and was nice, bright and attractive. They saw that word 'president' and they actually thought she was president of the studio." Indeed, Fox insiders at the time confirm that Lansing did not have the authority to greenlight pictures—power considered the sine qua non of a studio head. They say Fox chairman Alan Hirschfield hired her because he thought he could easily control her. But the press either didn't uncover these facts or chose to ignore them.

Another example of media ignorance is offered by agent Martin Baum. He criticizes the press for reporting box-office grosses as the measure of a picture's success. Gross figures are misleading, he says, because they do not account for the cost of producing and marketing a picture. The only meaningful measure is how profitable a picture is.

But if the media is unenlightened about the inner workings of Hollywood, it is at least partially because the industry finds it useful to keep them in the dark. Calculations of a picture's profits cannot be made unless the studios disclose their expenses, which they are reluctant to do. Consequently, reporters often are left to trade in rumor, hearsay and conjecture.

Even the trade papers *Variety* and *The Hollywood Reporter*, with their concentrated coverage of the industry, are often unaware of important developments. "Half the time, anybody who is anybody in the town knows what is going on before the trades do," admits one of their reporters. "The trades are among the last to know. The [only] people who learn something from the trades are the fringe people."

Moreover, the pursuit of truth is obstructed by misinformation fed the press. Many in the industry will shamelessly use the media to hype their projects, influence public opinion and create visibility for themselves. They have little compunction about lying and are often quite adept at it. Says Barry Diller: "You are dealing in a business where manipulation is a true art form. . . . The media is very manipulable. . . . [Consequently] most of the informed written opinion is not informed."

There is great incentive to use the media because of the tremendous influence it has. "Heat is important in this business," says journalist Jeff Silverman. "If you're perceived as hot, if you're perceived as having power, you're hot. Somebody calls you up tomorrow and says . . . 'I just read you got this deal, I want to make a deal with you.' . . . [If] your name is in the paper they perceive you as being something. And that's real important in this town."

Similarly, community members are quite sensitive to criticism. "People in this town are very conscious of their image," says one trade reporter. "They're overly sensitive. They read every word of the trades every day. They know everything in the trades and they look to the trades as their Bible and as their image and identity."

Because the artistic worth of a movie is so subjective, reviews can be very influential within the industry. "There are people in high places in the industry who don't know anything about movies," says director Joe Dante (*Gremlins*). "They don't even know whether they like one or not. So reviews can influence these people." Says journalist Gregg Kilday: "There is often an exaggerated importance to what the press writes because we provide the most immediate feedback."

Furthermore, reviews and news stories can directly affect the industry's pocketbook. A scathing review can damage box-office prospects, while a positive cover story can be worth millions of dollars of publicity.

Because of the tremendous power of the press, the industry usually swallows its feelings of frustration, contempt and hostility and tries to ingratiate itself. The studios need the media to publicize its movies, and stars and filmmakers need it to gain visibility.

The media, in turn, needs to maintain good relations in order to ensure continuing access to information and celebrities. Besides, many media outlets benefit from studio advertising.

This mutual dependence forces the industry and press to work together. Theirs is a symbiotic relationship in which neither can function well without the other. Consequently, disputes, no matter how acrimonious, inevitably give way to rapprochement.

The public is generally unaware of how closely the industry and press collaborate. Stars are not exploited nearly so much as it may appear. Before granting interviews, their publicists will set ground rules determining which areas are open to inquiry. Other deals are made. A star may agree to reveal intimate details of his life in exchange for prominent news coverage. Sometimes he is able to win the right to approve the selection of the reporter and the use of photos.

For its part, the press is far more restrained in its coverage than one would think of a profession that fancies itself the torchbearer of truth. In fact, the press suppresses news regularly, ignoring or downplaying indiscretions and idiosyncracies of industry figures. Journalists are well aware of those in the industry who are gay, alcoholic, addicted to drugs, engaged in extramarital love affairs or dying of terminal diseases. Yet rarely will reporters write all they know. Rock Hudson's gay life-style was common knowledge among journalists, yet for years no one wrote about it.

The press censors itself out of compassion for its movie-industry friends. Journalists recognize that certain disclosures can ruin a career. If an actor is reported to have cancer, no one will employ him for fear of his dying during production. Insurance companies would refuse to issue coverage or would demand large premiums.

Moreover, such disclosures are avoided because they are difficult to document. Nobody will go on the record and say that a certain producer is sleeping with a starlet, even though everybody in town suspects it's true. If a publication prints such a rumor it may be vulnerable to a libel suit.

But most of all the press suppresses embarrassing disclosures because it does not want to imperil its information pipeline. "*People* magazine tries occasionally to apply hard news [standards] . . . to the industry," says its West Coast bureau chief Martha Smilgis. "[And] we have a lot of trouble when we do it and a lot of doors slam in our faces. . . .

"If we start to do something negative on George Lucas, and George tells Steven [Spielberg], and Steven tells everybody . . . that's it. . . . If something goes wrong with one it's like a chain reaction . . . the whole studio will blackball you. . . . They're not going to deliver their celebrities when you need them. And with *People* we traffic in so many celebrities—this is our bread and butter—that it's very hard to really nail them."

Reporters accustomed to covering other beats are often unaware of how much Hollywood expects them to censor themselves. When Bob Woodward researched his book *Wired,* about John Belushi and drug use in Hollywood, he palled around with Belushi's friends, some of whom spoke candidly about their own and others' drug use. Woodward printed what he was told, to the outrage of those who expected him to be more discreet. But Woodward either didn't know what was expected of him or did not care because he had no plans to make a career out of covering the industry.

For those who must continue to work in the industry it is difficult to be a crusader. "You run into your sources all

the time," says journalist Jean Vallely. "It's hard to do somebody in when you've just had dinner with them."

The journalist new to Hollywood quickly learns that information is obtained from friendships one has forged rather
than by attending the rare press conference. "Hollywood is
a schmooze town," says journalist Jeff Silverman. "It's all
done through schmooze. So as a journalist covering the town
you've got to be involved in the schmooze as well. You've got
to be part of what you cover, in a sense. . . . So you're constantly dealing through your friendships all the time . . . going
out with studio heads, playing tennis with this star or that.
And a lot of . . . [journalists] don't want to cross that line.
But in fact to do your job correctly you have to constantly
cross that line. [The tough part] is to remain objective enough
to call it as you see it."

"The successful journalist is the one who goes to the majority of the receptions that he or she is invited to," says one
trade journalist. "And that can be three a night. You go there
to schmooze. . . . [You] work hard at becoming a member of
the community. . . . [You] make friends with lots of people
who are vice-presidents and producers and so on who will
then call you up and say, 'Did you hear about so and so?' "

Industry members, for their part, assiduously court the
press, wining and dining reporters, trying to earn their favor.
"There are very few times that you get any news in this town
without a meal being attached to it," says one trade reporter.
"I've never seen any other industry where there is always
food. . . . You want to do an interview, they want to do it for
breakfast or lunch. . . . It's like they've got to stroke you, they've
got to give you something. And it's the way the whole industry
thinks. It's a sell. It is not like covering straight news where
when I did an interview nobody would even ask if you wanted
coffee. Here they will ask you ten times if you want coffee."

In addition to food and drink, gifts are bestowed. While
some publications prohibit their reporters from accepting
such rewards, others turn a blind eye on the practice. "I've
never seen this in any other industry," says a journalist for
The Hollywood Reporter. "You do a story and the next day
there's wine on your desk. This very day I came back and
found a huge box of Godiva chocolates for something I had

done. There's a lot of that. A lot of trunks are filled. In 1983 I got sixty-four gifts for Christmas from production companies, producers, publicists, everyone. And they ranged from cases of wine to vases to shirts. But mostly wine and liquor. Big tins of popcorn. In 1982 I got a VCR from Twentieth Century-Fox."

Some reporters claim that such gifts do not influence their coverage. Others see no harm since they do not consider themselves investigative reporters anyway. "The reason I don't have any problems taking these gifts is that I'm not a muckraker," says a writer for *The Hollywood Reporter*. He adds that his editors do not want exposés. "I have to interview [some] people who are the biggest jackasses [I've ever met] in my life and I want to push them over the balcony . . . [but] the fact of the matter is they're going to get a good story no matter what."

Underlying the "friendships" that develop between reporters and industry members is distrust. Both know that the relationship is predicated on need and not genuine affection. Reporters realize they are being lied to and used, and interviewees are wary of being burned.

One trade reporter likens Hollywood to a mansion: "It is a company town and everybody is in the mansion. The studio executives and producers have suites. Lower-level executives have small rooms. The publicists are the servants. . . . Reporters knock every day on the door of the mansion, are led in through the front door and . . . are wined and dined there. But at the end of the day you must leave, you cannot stay overnight. . . . You get invited to every party . . . but only as long as they need you. Then you are tossed aside."

At the same time that reporters are courted with meals and gifts, their employers are seduced with advertising revenues. Although studios will rarely retaliate and slash advertising because of one objectionable article, the possibility is felt, especially by the trade papers, which are heavily dependent on industry ads.

"The trades will take in two million dollars each, possibly more, from the [ad] campaigns for the Academy Awards," says one of its reporters. "Last year *The Hollywood Reporter* did an article . . . that Fox was pissed about. Fox canceled their entire campaign. It meant a revenue loss to *The Holly-*

wood Reporter estimated between two hundred fifty and three hundred thousand dollars. . . . Although the trades try to be objective, it's always in the back of your mind that you're dependent on the studios for your livelihood. . . .

"If I had to put into words how the trades cover the industry, [I would say] it is an independently published house organ. Like when you get on the airlines and you see the United Airlines magazine. . . . You are going to get some of the negative side of the industry. If a film flops it's going to be there in big headlines. If somebody goofs and gets fired it's going to be there. . . . [But] you don't burn bridges. . . . You don't go after people who do lousy jobs or say so-and-so is lousy even though everybody in the industry is talking about it. Because a year later that person is going to be in a bigger job and you're going to need their advertising and their articles.

"I think it's fair to say that it is a very odd relationship. I don't think there is any other industry that's covered by the press where there is such a 'You scratch my back, I'll scratch yours' [attitude]. . . . I don't think in the trades you'll ever find a story that's not complimentary."

While the trades avoid harsh criticism of the industry in their news columns, they do take greater liberties in reviewing movies, disparaging those they do not like on both cinematic and commercial grounds. *Variety* can be quite critical.

Reporters, by and large, do not object to the conciliatory tone of their employers. There is little for them to gain and much to lose by exposing wrongdoing. "There are no rewards for digging deep," says one ex-journalist. "So the negative uses basically benefit no one. They don't benefit the sources and they don't benefit the reporters." Even if a reporter wanted to muckrake he would find few Deep Throats. "In politics you get leaks from one side of an issue in order to embarrass the other side. . . . Here . . . people tend to see the press as a sales tool for the business."

Reporters have more to gain by maintaining good relations within the industry than from the momentary recognition derived from an exposé. A lot of journalists hope eventually to work for a studio or producer, as many of their predecessors have done. The money, glamour and life-style of an industry job can be seductive. Some do not even wait to leave journalism before they begin writing screenplays. "What happens to most journalists out here is that there is a terrible crossing over," says screenwriter-journalist Jean Vallely. "You become part of the industry you cover.

"What happened to me was that an article I wrote for *Esquire* was bought and made into a movie. I was then offered a script to write. It's kind of hard to turn that stuff down— the money. But also it's fun to try something else. . . . Journalists come out here and they go Hollywood, they're bought off. . . . [You] begin to wonder can I do this. You spend years [developing] this critical eye for movies . . . and then if somebody hands you the opportunity to do it and gives you all that money, it's very hard to turn down. I'm not sure there is an industry where there is quite so much [crossover]."

Says Jeff Silverman, "You look around and you see all these people making so much money with ideas that don't seem to be as good as your own, who don't seem to be as smart as you are, so you say, 'Well I can do it too.' "

The widespread impression that entertainment reporters cannot wait to join the business damages their credibility as journalists. Many in the industry assume that any talented writer would certainly rather make a bundle writing screenplays than continue to work as a journalist. That impression is fostered when, as sometimes happens, writers present screenplays to stars and directors while interviewing them.

The low point for Hollywood journalism occurred with the Begelman scandal. The embezzlement embarrassed the entertainment media—not so much because of the theft but because it was uncovered by out-of-towners like David Mc-Clintick of *The Wall Street Journal*. As a result, the *Los Angeles Times* has upgraded its coverage of the industry, hiring reporters with hard-news backgrounds to examine the business dealings behind the glitter of moviemaking. Other media outlets have also begun to pay increasing attention to the business of show business, occasionally doing investigative pieces.

Yet there are still no hard-hitting journalists who regularly investigate the industry, notes Martha Smilgis. Perhaps only an outsider like McClintick can parachute in and accomplish such a mission.

18

CONCLUSION

The moviemaking system in Hollywood is a complex and cumbersome machine. It operates at great cost and with little efficiency. It's subject to the vicissitudes of bureaucratic in-fighting within the studio and to pressure exerted from the outside by stars, directors and their agents. It's overseen by executives so worried about keeping their jobs that they're reluctant to risk trying new talent or ideas, preferring to make formula pictures with established stars. Considering its shortcomings, it is a wonder that anything worthwhile is ever produced.

It's not a system designed to foster the production of movies of artistic excellence or popular appeal. Decisions are not made on the basis of what will make a good film but rather on the basis of what will make a good deal. Writers, directors and actors are selected for their ability to get a studio to green-light a project, their talent and suitability for the project are of secondary importance.

It's a system rife with waste. Scripts are frivolously re-written, properties are bought and shelved, millions of dollars are spent producing and marketing pictures that the public rejects. It's also costly in human terms. Talented writers, directors, stars and executives are discarded, their expertise lost in favor of whoever is hot at the moment.

Good films are made in spite of the system, not because of it. They come from the conviction, courage and talent of individuals who are willing to fight the battles necessary to protect their work—individuals who refuse to make decisions based on what is artistically safe, politically expedient or personally remunerative. But unfortunately they are in the minority. Most of those who work in the industry are of modest ability and are only too willing to sell themselves for money, fame and an appealing life-style—besides, they don't have much to say anyway.

The system is the product of an industry whose executives, by and large, are unschooled in writing, drama, acting, cinematography and the other elements of filmmaking. Those at the top haven't achieved their position by working their way up the ranks of production, but by virtue of their deal-making prowess. Although they have a limited understanding of how movies are made, they supervise a multitude of artists and craftsmen in an enormously complex endeavor in which millions of dollars are at stake.

The industry's major companies operate in a fluid marketplace over which they have limited influence. In other businesses companies are able to maintain their market share because of their financial wherewithal and reputation for supplying a desirable product. But in the movie business bigger budgets do not necessarily produce better movies, and company reputation counts for little, if anything—there is no brand-name loyalty for the product of any studio. Moviegoers don't care how much a film costs or who is distributing it; their only concern is whether they like it.

Even massive advertising can have a limited impact. While millions spent promoting a new soap can create a demand for the product, no amount of money can convince moviegoers to see a movie their friends have told them is awful. Perhaps in no other business does word of mouth play such an influential role.

Unlike some other industries, the studios are unable to

dominate the business by monopolizing the raw materials of production. The commodity they are selling is essentially creativity, and unlike wheat, oil or gold, the supply cannot be cornered. Inspiration has the annoying habit of popping up where least expected. Studios hire renowned performers and directors and spend millions on state-of-the art technology, only to see their lavish productions die at the box office while an unknown filmmaker without stars produces the next hit on a shoestring.

In many ways the major studios are weaker than they used to be. With the breakup of the studio system, considerable power has shifted to stars, directors, producers and agents who take the initiative in developing and packaging projects, with the studios increasingly playing the role of specialized banks. Although the new ancillary markets bring in substantial revenues, the studios' share is modest. Because they were slow to recognize its potential, they let middlemen like HBO control cable and siphon off much of its revenues. In home video the studios established their own distribution companies, but they are unable to share in videocassette rentals, which represent 80 to 90 percent of retail transactions.

The major studios continue to dominate smaller distributors—who release more films yet only capture about 10 percent of domestic rentals—by virtue of the momentum they have built up over the years. Their standing in the industry gives them first crack at the most promising books, scripts and talent. Stars and directors like the prestige of working for them and the visibility that comes from participating in films that will be widely advertised and promoted. And, of course, the majors pay handsomely, supply generous perks, and their paychecks don't bounce.

Furthermore, the majors have a valuable asset in their film libraries, which generate a steady flow of revenue, giving them a financial cushion to fall back on in lean times. Because banks perceive the major studios as more stable and less risky than their smaller brethren, money can be borrowed on better terms.

The majors also benefit from their strong relationships with exhibitors. Small distributors who sporadically release films don't have the clout of a steady supplier of star-studded extravaganzas backed by big ad budgets. Consequently, exhibitors favor the majors, granting them the best theaters and playdates. More important, the majors have the clout to collect money due them.

While the studios have become parts of conglomerates in order to spread financial risks, in many ways moviemaking is not well suited to conglomerate ownership. Conglomerates are run by managers who seek to avoid risks. They like to chart steadily increasing earnings year after year. Consequently, they breed executives who favor making movies with proven commercial appeal rather than taking chances on something different. But the paradox of the movie business is that that which appears to be commercial usually is not. The public doesn't want imitations of past hits, they want something new and different—a frightening prospect for managers who find comfort in predictability.

It's very frustrating to these large companies that they are unable to quantify what makes a hit and therefore cannot manufacture them in a businesslike fashion. Instead, they are forever scrambling to imitate the latest blockbuster and wooing its creators into their fold. Rather than rely on their own taste and judgment in deciding which films to make, executives look for insurance in impressive-looking packages for whose failure they cannot be blamed.

The state of the industry today has been greatly influenced by technological advances. The rise of television reduced the demand for feature films, which, combined with the impact of divestment, led to the breakup of the studio system. Without long-term contracts the studios' control over talent was lost, and power shifted to stars, directors and their agents. As a result, salary and production costs have escalated, and at times gone out of control.

After seeing their business shrink as the demand for feature films fell, the studios decided to diversify and began producing for television themselves. Later, cable television and home video would change the industry by generating new revenues and stimulating production.

Television is largely responsible for the rise of the blockbuster film. First, it reduced the market for ordinary movies by providing similar entertainment at home for free. The market for movies today is for that which cannot be obtained at home—largely either specialized fare that can be distributed profitably in a limited release, or mass-appeal potential blockbusters released in a great many theaters simultaneously. Second, television has given rise to the blockbuster by providing the means to promote it through television advertising. Third, television has encouraged blockbusters by paying handsomely for the right to broadcast them.

Notwithstanding all that is wrong with Hollywood, one must concede that it produces some wonderful movies. Overall, its pictures are far more appealing than those produced by any other country. Indeed, Hollywood's pictures succeed in world markets to an extent unrivaled by other American products. In those countries that allow American films to be exhibited freely they dominate the box office—people preferring what Hollywood has to offer over locally produced fare.

The impact of these pictures on the world is difficult to measure, but no doubt great. Hollywood's movies can, literally overnight, affect the tastes, attitudes, beliefs and mores of millions of people. They can produce laughter and joy around the world, and can focus attention on contemporary problems and inspire people to solve them. On the other hand, movies can also feed prejudices and encourage violence and hatred.

While a single film rarely has a demonstrable impact on society, the cumulative effect of movies is pervasive. Movies have the ability to mold people's perception of the world they live in. They reach far more people than books and plays and can do so in a more compelling manner than any other mode of mass communication. They have greatly affected how the world views America and have effectively promoted American values, life-style and products.

America built an empire with motion pictures, says Cannon head Menahem Golan. Movies spread American culture and language the way Rome's legions did at the height of their empire.

"I was a child who grew up in a town called Tiberias [in Israel]," says Golan. "I grew up in the forties and fifties on Humphrey Bogart and Gary Cooper, on the American musical. If I didn't go twice a week to the cinema I was starving. That was my bread and butter. And I was not alone. Every Saturday night every kid in town was fighting for a ticket to the cinema. We had a municipality with two synagogues and two cinemas.

"American movies were always better, just as American products for years were always better than any other product in the world. . . . [American pictures] had a professional perfectionism to them. They were always slick, had beautiful colors. It was unreal, it was beyond reality.

"And people wanted two hours of entertainment to get away from reality. . . . With a dreary life one needs a fairy tale. And America knew how to do it. That's what America did in their motion pictures. It gave a better life. It was princesses, rich people, fairy tales and Westerns. Gangster movies and action. It was everything one couldn't, didn't exactly live . . . [and it] brought you fairy tales that you really believed existed . . . in America.

"I learned about jeans and hairstyle and music and the way to dress and the way to dance and the way to eat and about hamburgers, and you name it. I became Americanized like every child in the Western world. . . . This Hollywood dream . . . was actually what made America what it is today in the eyes of the world."

Unfortunately, many of the movies Hollywood produces today reflect poorly on America. Movies that have something intelligent to say, such as *Prizzi's Honor, Network* and *The China Syndrome,* are becoming increasingly rare. In their place moviegoers are served *Porky's, Scarface* and *Rambo*—movies that trade on sex and violence and have little redeeming social value. It is troubling to think of the image of America these movies project and what will be the impact on future generations that grow up watching such fare.

Filmmakers and studios make exploitation films when they can't think of anything meaningful to say. When the creative well has run dry they resort to gratuitous sex and violence, reasoning that such an approach is a surefire way to sell a lot of tickets.

Instead of reworking its tired formulas, Hollywood should be constantly exploring new terrain. There is a wealth of human experience the industry avoids because of its preconceptions of what the audience wants to see. There are few films made about the lives of poor and working-class people, for instance. It would be difficult to persuade a studio today to make *The Grapes of Wrath.* "It's too downbeat," they might say. Or "It won't play well on MTV."

"However tyrannical and stupid the moguls were," says I.A.L Diamond, "they did care about pictures. Because what you had was a bunch of poor kids who became rich in this business, and they were interested in quality. They wanted the prestige of awards. They wanted class.

"But the people who run the studios today come from Harvard Law School or the Wharton School of Business. They think they already have class. All they give a shit about is money. I mean they want the Rolls, the Mercedes and to be able to serve a better brand than the record producer that lives next door. They have no interest in and no knowledge of movies. They don't care. They care about the bottom line, the downside risk. That's what they learned at business school. If *Porky's* makes money, then *Porky's* is what we get. And *Porky's IV* and *Rocky IV* and all the rest."

"There are no people anymore who have their own pride in the product as far as the companies go," says director Irvin Kershner. "I mean corporations are not individuals. They do not have a common heart or a common head. . . . Coca-Cola owns Columbia . . . [a conglomerate owns] Paramount. . . . The pride isn't there.

"The pictures of the last few years that had any value were jammed down the throats of the distributing companies. Literally, they were brought to them and jammed down their throats. I mean Saul Zaentz put the money up for *One Flew Over the Cuckoo's Nest* after no company wanted to make it. And when it was finished no company wanted to distribute it, except United Artists said, 'OK, we will take it.' The same thing happened with *Amadeus.*"

"The moguls came out of other businesses entirely and they were entrepreneurs," says Leonard Goldberg. "They were people who had an entrepreneurial spirit, people who would have made it in any business. [But] what you have now are people who are the agents, the lawyers, the people who have utilized other people's talents to be involved in the process. . . . They are not people used to acting as principals. . . . They are second people, they act for principals. And suddenly you put them in a position that requires principal action and you don't get the appropriate action, in my opinion.

"A head of a studio said to me, 'Why don't you see if you can get Sean Connery or John Travolta for this picture?' I said, 'But you told me you didn't like the script.' He said, 'I don't, but if you get Sean Connery or John Travolta [we will make it].' I said, 'All you would have then is a more expensive movie that would not be successful if you are right about the script. Sean Connery and John Travolta are not going to make a bad script good. The only way to do that is to bring in another writer.' He just stared at me.

"I was recently at an industry luncheon where I was listening to the heads of various studios who actually said, 'It seems to us that the only thing the audience is interested in seeing is sequels.' A staggering thought.

"I said to them, 'Well, first of all, what about *Cocoon*? [They responded:] 'Well, *Cocoon* was a really original movie, but how many of those can you come up with?' Think about that, they actually said that.

"Then I said, 'Well what about *Back to the Future*?' [They said,] 'Well, *Back to the Future* is a sequel, because it is a Steven Spielberg presents.'

"OK, then there is the final one, guys. 'How about that in order for all these sequels to be made someone had to decide to make the original. Did that escape you? That originally they were made by someone who believed in the movie. . . . Someone made the original *Rocky*, the original *Indiana Jones* and the original *Superman*. Somebody made those decisions.'

"And they all looked at the floor, because it ain't gonna be them. If a law could be passed saying that only sequels

could be made, or pictures with major stars like Clint Eastwood, or Goldie Hawn, or Dustin Hoffman, in my opinion
these people would be the happiest people in the world. Then
they wouldn't have to exercise any judgment at all."

"From my point of view the film industry died in 1965,"
George Lucas told *New York Times* correspondent Aljean Harmetz. "It's taken this long for people to realize the body is
cold. The day I won my six-month internship and walked
onto the Warner Bros. lot was the day Jack Warner left and
the studio was taken over by 7 Arts. I walked through the
empty lot and thought, 'This is the end.' The industry had
been taken over by people who knew how to make deals and
operate offices but had no idea how to make movies. When
the six months was over, I never went back.

"Down there [Hollywood], for every honest true film maker
trying to get his film off the ground, there are a hundred
sleazy used-car dealers trying to con you out of your money.
Going down there is like visiting a foreign country.

"I've been saying for a long time that Hollywood is dead.
That doesn't mean the film industry is dead. But for one
region to dominate is dead, although it will take ten or fifteen
years to have that visible. The film maker hasn't figured out
he doesn't need the agents and the studio executives. What
is Hollywood? An antiquated, out-of-date distribution apparatus, a monopoly, a system designed to exploit the film
maker. The system is collapsing because of new technologies.
The movie companies are structured inefficiently. In good
times, it doesn't show. But they won't be able to survive the
bad times.

"The technology of making movies is getting more ac-
cessible. With a small, dedicated crew, you can make a movie
with a very small outlay of capital. You could make a profes-
sional-looking film for quite a bit less than a million dollars.
I think it is only a matter of time before one of the thousands
of film-school-trained guys goes back to Kansas City and makes
a *Rocky* or an *American Graffiti*. The distribution system will
be located in Los Angeles for quite a while before it breaks
up. But even that will break up eventually as cable TV and
cassettes and other markets open up. You can sell to cable

TV by making five phone calls out of your house."

Whether Lucas's prediction will prove true is uncertain. But there is no doubt that Hollywood faces an immense challenge if it is to continue its dominant role in moviemaking. The industry must not only be able to adopt to a changing marketplace and new technologies but must also recruit executives who understand and love movies, and encourage them to take risks. It must create an atmosphere at the studios where creativity flourishes and politics and internecine warfare are kept to a minimum. It must find a way to work with talented filmmakers without smothering them in a large bureaucracy and stifling their creativity. Otherwise, Hollywood will become a monument to past glory—and present folly.

NOTES

This book is based on interviews conducted with the more than 200 persons listed in the Acknowledgments, and the following sources:

CHAPTER ONE
"Welcome to Hollywood"

Page 27   Domestic rental figures for *Rhinestone*: "1980–84 Big Buck Scorecard," *Variety,* January 16, 1985, p. 58.

28   Stallone was reported to be licking his wounds: Michael London, "The Rocky Road to a Hollywood Flop," *Los Angeles Times,* July 20, 1984, Part VI, p. 12.

28   Stallone's reported $12 million fee: "Blood, Sweat and Cheers," *Newsweek,* June 3, 1985, p. 62.

30   Louis B. Mayer adage: *The Book of Hollywood Quotes,* compiler, Gary Herman (London/New York/Sydney/Tokyo/Cologne: Omnibus Press, 1979), p. 38.

31   Davis profits on sale of Fox: "Fox Officially Becomes Murdoch's," *Daily Variety,* December 5, 1985, p. 1.

CHAPTER TWO
The Rise of CAA

Page 38   CAA beginnings: Charles Schreger, "CAA: Packaging of an Agency," *Los Angeles Times,* April, 23, 1979, Part IV, p. 13.

38   William Morris has 150 agents: "Morris Office at 85," *Daily Variety,* June 8, 1983, p. 2.

38   William Morris earns $30 million and has more than 2,000 clients: Todd McCarthy and Joe Cohen, "Abe Lastfogel, WMA Guiding Force Dies," *Daily Variety,* August 27, 1984, p. 1.

42   SAG packaging report: Released April 24, 1985.

42   "Packaging was designed": Ellen Farley and William Knoedelseder, Jr., "TV Package Deal: Power for the Few," *Los Angeles Times,* April 6, 1983, Part I, p. 24.

43   "It's really a form of extortion": Ibid., p. 1.

48   Federal judge's description of MCA: Dan E. Moldea and Jeff Goldberg, "The Deal's the Thing," *Los Angeles Reader,* November 2, 1984, Vol. 7, No. 3, p. 8.

CHAPTER THREE
The New Power Brokers

Page 49   "Right now agents have more power": *Filmmakers on Filmmaking, The American Film Institute Seminars on Motion Pictures and Television,* ed. Joseph McBride (Los Angeles: J. P. Tarcher, Inc., dist. by Houghton Mifflin Company, Boston, 1983), Volume I, p. 174.

50   Studio profits on loan-outs: Hortense Powdermaker, *Hollywood, The Dream Factory* (Boston: Little, Brown and Company, 1950), p. 214.

50   Olivia de Havilland suit: *Anatomy of the Movies,* ed. David Pirie (New York: Macmillan Publishing Co., Inc., 1981), p. 18.

50   The Paramount decision: Michael F. Mayer, *The Film Industries* (New York: Hastings House, 1978), pp. 108–116.

50   Studio bosses could no longer bully talent: Leonard Mosley, *Zanuck, The Rise and Fall of Hollywood's Last Tycoon* (Boston: Little, Brown and Company, 1984), p. 380.

51   Multiple-picture contract figures for Pryor and Keaton: Richard Natale, "Studios Focus on Comedy," *The Hollywood Reporter,* May 22, 1984, p. 1.

52   $25 million pact for Murphy: Richard Grenier, "Eddie Murphy's Comic Touch," *The New York Times*, March 10, 1985, Sec. 2, p. 1.

CHAPTER FOUR
Inside the Studios

Page 67   "There was this obnoxious little character": Herman, p. 54.

70   "You know you are going to end up hating me": Aljean Harmetz, *Rolling Breaks, and Other Movie Business* (New York: Alfred A. Knopf, 1983), p. 120.

75   "If someone comes in": Maureen Orth, "High Noon in California," *California*, October 1981, p. 102.

78   "What happens after you do a script": McBride, Vol. I, p. 186.

CHAPTER FIVE
Studio Business

Page 83   Zanuck matching stars to projects: Leonard Mosley, *Zanuck, The Rise and Fall of Hollywood's Last Tycoon* (Boston: Little, Brown and Company, 1984), p. 393.

85   Hirschfield's speech: "1984: Year of Reckoning in the Entertainment Business OR Where'd You Hide the Profits?" April 19, 1984.

86   "I can't say to a star client": McBride, Vol. I, p. 169.

86   Fox lost $85 million: Dale Pollock and Al DeLugach, "Fox Moving to Raise Cash in Wake of Big Losses," *Los Angeles Times*, November 29, 1984, Part IV, p. 1.

86   Paramount made $110.5 million: Lawrence Cohn, "SEC Filing Shows Par A Frontline Contributor to G&W's '84 Net," *Daily Variety*, October 15, 1984, p. 1.

88   Studio revenues from videocassettes based in part on: "Consultant Sees Big Homevideo Profits for '84." *Daily Variety*, March 21, 1984. p. 7.

88   $4.55 billion retail market for videocassettes estimates by Fairfield Group Study: Tom Bierbaum, "Study Puts '85 Homevid Retail Biz at $4.55 Bil," *Daily Variety*, January 7, 1986, p. 1.

88   80 to 90 percent of video transactions are rentals: David Robb, "Counter's Grim Pic-Biz Picture," *Daily Variety*, October 24, 1985, p. 1.

89   Video piracy estimates: Tony Seideman, " '83 Vidpiracy Nears $1 Bil," *Daily Variety*, December 21, 1983, p. 1.

89   *E.T.* grossed $619 million worldwide: John M. Wilson, "E.T. Returns to Test His Midas Touch," *Los Angeles Times*, June 16, 1985, Calendar, p. 22.

89   "*Star Wars* and *The Empire Strikes Back* have grossed": Harmetz, p. 248.

89    $250 million of record sales from *Saturday Night Fever*: Calculated by using an average retail price for the double album of $8.50 (list price: $12.98) multiplied by sales of 30 million. Frank Meyer, "RSO Puts Label on Disk Biz via Blockbuster LP," *Variety*, January 3, 1979, p. 223.

89   CBS paid $25 million to license *Star Wars*: Lillian Ross, "Onward and Upward with the Arts," *The New Yorker*, November 8, 1982, p. 48.

90   "This business is like the commodities game": Thomas O'Hanlon, "Close Encounters at Columbia Pictures," *Fortune*, December 1, 1980, p. 71.

91   Producer Joseph E. Levine's $5 million profit from presales": "Inside Hollywood," *Newsweek*, February 13, 1978, p. 70.

92   Frank Price on pickups: O'Hanlon, p. 71.

92   Surge in production: Todd McCarthy, "Pic Prod'n Hits 10-year High," *Daily Variety*, January 3, 1985, p. 30.

93   Holdings of the Coca-Cola Company: The Coca-Cola Company 1983 annual report.

93   Holdings of Gulf & Western: Gulf & Western 1985 annual report.

93   How Coca-Cola advertising purchases help Columbia: Myron Magnet, "Coke Tries Selling Movies Like Soda Pop," *Fortune*, December 26, 1983, p. 122.

94   Coke bottles in *Murphy's Romance*: Jack Mathews, "Film Clips," *Los Angeles Times*, November 15, 1985, Part VI, p. 1.

94   Skyrocketing sales of Reese's Pieces: Karen MacNeil, "Celebrity Foods," *American Health*, January/February 1984, p. 56.

94   Alan Trustman on conglomerate benefits from studio ownership: *The Atlantic Monthly*, January 1978, p. 65.

95   Studio heads earn more than presidents of parent companies: Powdermaker, p. 87.

96   Nicholas Meyer quote: McBride, Vol. I, p. 189.

97   "There were giants in the industry": Herman, p. 119.

98   "[I]n the movie industry right now the middleman": Claire Townsend, "What's Wrong with Hollywood," *Princeton Alumni Weekly*, March 9, 1983, p. 20.

CHAPTER SIX
What's Commercial

Page 99   William Goldman quotes: William Goldman, *Adventures in the Screen Trade* (New York: Warner Books, 1983), p. 39.

100   Powdermaker quote: Powdermaker, p. 91.

100   "The great gamblers are dead": Michael Ventura, "Spielberg on Spielberg," *L.A. Weekly*, December 9–15, 1983, p. 12.

101   "Lucas was the most surprised": Ibid., p. 16.

102   Alfred Hitchcock quote: Herman, p. 25.

103   Sam Spiegel quote: Herman, p. 27.

106   Riots erupted when *Birth of a Nation* was shown: Benjamin B. Hampton, *A History of the Movies* (New York: Covici, Friede, 1931) reprinted *History of the American Film Industry* (New York: Dover Publications, Inc., 1970), p. 129.

106   *The Moon is Blue* controversy: "Hullabaloo over 'Moon is Blue,' " *Life*, July 13, 1953, p. 71.

108   Audiences rejected *A Woman of Paris*: Hampton, p. 233.

109   Public lost interest in war pictures: Ibid., pp. 201–2.

111   Statistics on trend toward more sexually explicit and violent films: Todd McCarthy, "Number of Films Rated by MPAA Off 8% for the Year," *Daily Variety*, December 27, 1984, p. 1.

111   X-rated films comprise 5 percent: Will Tusher, "Valenti: X Doesn't Equal Porn," *Daily Variety*, October 18, 1985, p. 1.

113   MPAA study: "Incidence of Motion Picture Attendance," August 1984. The study was conducted by Opinion Research Corporation, Princeton, New Jersey, based on a sample of 2,259 individuals.

115   H. L. Mencken quote: Herman, p. 27.

115   MPAA figures on frequency of attendance from its study "Incidence of Motion Picture Attendance," August 1984.

CHAPTER SEVEN
Breaking In, Moving Up, Holding On

Page 118   "You've got to be neurotic": McBride, Vol. I, pp. 198–99.

127   Data on DGA training program: *Application for Training*, Assistant Directors Training Program, 1985.

130   It took Kasdan six scripts and five years to get an agent: Harmetz, p. 78.

135   Robert Aldrich quote: McBride, Vol. I, p. 198.

136   *Kentucky Fried Movie* domestic rentals: "Champs Among Bantam Weights," *Daily Variety*, June 13, 1983, p. 18.

137   *Airplane!* rental figure: "All-Time Film Rental Champs," *Variety*, May, 1, 1985, p. 109.

138   SAG membership in 1953: "SAG Individual Earnings, 1983." SAG-Producers Pension and Health Plans, *Screen Actor*, August 1984, p. 109.

139   SAG earning figures: Ibid.

139   Joyce Selznick quote: McBride, Vol. II, pp. 187–88.

143   "Unless they're in a runaway hit": Ibid., p. 186.

143   Boris Karloff quote: Herman, p. 43.

CHAPTER EIGHT
Deal-Making

Page 155   Billy Wilder quote: Herman, p. 118.

158   "With *Villa Rides*": Brady, pp. 386–87.

158   "If Steve McQueen said he wanted to play": Ibid., p. 153.

160   Shirley MacLaine quote: Herman, p. 22.

163   Eric Weissmann quote: Direct interview and from tapes of a course he has taught at UCLA.

CHAPTER NINE
Writers

Page 173   Sam Goldwyn quote: Herman, p. 31.

174   "Almost everyone unconsciously feels he knows as much about writing": McBride, Vol. I, p. 185.

177   "Almost anyone can do what a director does": Ibid., p. 186.

177   "Unless you've worked on a film": John Brady, *The Craft of the Screenwriter* (New York: Simon and Schuster, 1981), p. 427.

177   "There is absolutely no way to individuate": Ibid., p. 290.

177   Ben Hecht quote: Herman, p. 63.

187   Schrader on screenwriting: Brady, p. 262.

195   Paddy Chayefsky quote: Ibid., p. 59.

195   Anonymous screenwriter quote: Herman, p. 60.

CHAPTER TEN
Directors

Page 197   Directors as servants of studio: Mosley, p. 145.

197   Gore Vidal quote: "Dialogue on Film," *American Film*, April 1977, reprinted *American Film*, June 1985, pp. 25–26.

200   Sydney Pollack quote: McBride, Vol. I, pp. 194–95.

201   Robert De Niro quote: "Dialogue on Film," *American Film*, March 1981, reprinted *American Film*, June 1985, pp. 27–28.

201   "Stars are a pain in the ass": Brady, p. 165.

201   "Very often big stars are barely trained": "Dialogue on Film," *American Film*, March 1976, reprinted *American Film*, June 1985, p. 100.

201   "A director is caught between the frying pan": "Dialogue on Film," *American Film*, June 1984, p. 15.

207   Spielberg quote: Ventura, p. 14.

CHAPTER ELEVEN
Actors and Stars

Page 213   Bert Lahr quote: Herman, p. 45.

216   Marlon Brando quote: Ibid., p. 44.

219   James Caan anecdote: Barbara Long, "The Wrath of Caan," *Esquire*, July 1984, p. 153.

219   "I wonder if I'm good-looking": Ben Fong-Torres, "Eddie Murphy," *Moviegoer* magazine, December 1984, p. 15.

220   Bette Davis quote: McBride, Vol. II, p. 112.

220   Davis takes out want ad: Ibid., p. 113.

221   Salary figures for stars: "Inside Moves," *Esquire*, April 1985, p. 212.

221   Dustin Hoffman reputed to have earned $25 million: Army Archerd, "Just for Variety," *Daily Variety*, December 20, 1985, p. 3.

221   James Garner quote: Herman, p. 95.

CHAPTER TWELVE
Producers

Page 223   Writer Ben Hecht said: Herman, p. 31.

224   William Bowers quote: McBride, Vol. II, p. 208.

225   "My primary role of being a producer": McBride, Vol. I, pp. 61–62.

CHAPTER THIRTEEN
Marketing

Page 232   Fox's market research on *Star Wars*: Dale Pollock, *Skywalking: The Life and Films of George Lucas* (New York: Harmony Books, 1983), p. 180.

232   Columbia's research on *E.T.*: John Koten, "How the Marketers Perform a Vital Role in a Movie's Success," *The Wall Street Journal*, December 14, 1984, p. 1.

233   *The Big Chill* and *Absence of Malice* reedited: Ibid.

234   Columbia spent year testing *Starman*: Ibid.

235   Impact of early review of *Close Encounters of the Third Kind*: Harmetz, p. 226.

235   "I used to think previews were vital": McBride, Vol. I, p. 38.

235   George Roy Hill quote: McBride, Vol. II, pp. 217–18.

236   72 percent of all ad expenditures are spent for newspaper ads: Per Newspaper Advertising Bureau, cited by Richard Gold, "Pic Print Ads Hold Own Despite Cost Hike," *Daily Variety*, September 25, 1985, p. 1.

237   Columbia ran two sets of *Starman* ads: Koten, pp. 1, 23.

239   *Prisoner of Zenda* stunt: Bob Thomas, *Selznick* (New York: Garlend Publishing), p. 130.

241   Impact of the novelization of *The Omen*: Roberta Kent, "Exploiting Book-Publishing Rights," *The Movie Business Book*, ed. Jason E. Squire (New Jersey: Prentice-Hall, Inc., 1983), p. 87.

242   *Star Wars* merchandise reportedly grossed $1 billion, which exceeds its box-office receipts: Bill Desowitz, "Marketing Has Impact on Films at Script Stage": *The Hollywood Reporter*, April 24, 1984, p. 33.

242   Merchandise license and royalty figures: Richard Gold, "Summer of '84's Pix Boost Status of Spinoff Licensing," *Daily Variety*, June 12, 1985, p. 1.

242   Coke's imprinting of 55 million cans: Will Tusher, "*Ghostbusters* Gets $15 Mil Free Promo O'Seas From Coke," *Daily Variety*, October 3, 1984, p. 1.

242   Use of Diet Coke commercial to promote *Ghostbusters*: Dale Pollock, "Outtakes," *Los Angeles Times*, September 30, 1984, Calendar, p. 18.

243 "Care Bear" figures: David Pecchia, "Outtakes: The Fur Flies Again," *Los Angeles Times*, November 10, 1985, Calendar, p. 15.

243 Product promotion: *Two on the Town*, KCBS-TV, January 16, 1985, and Michael Forman, "Madison Ave. Meets Hollywood," *American Way*, November 1984, p. 138.

243 McDonald's facility: Ad in *The Hollywood Reporter* 55th anniversary issue, 1985, p. 81.

244 *Omni* promise to publish article on 2010: Koten, p. 23.

246 *Star Wars* opened on 32 screens: Martin A. Grove, "Hollywood Report," *The Hollywood Reporter*, December 9, 1985, p. 3.

248 Columbia spent so much on advertising *Ghandhi* it lost money on domestic release: Koten, p. 23.

251 Original release of *It's Alive!* bombs: "*It's Alive* Should be Dead," *New York*, June 6, 1977, p. 8.

251 *It's Alive!* earns $7.1 million: "All-Time Rental Champs," *Variety*, May 1, 1985, p. 109.

CHAPTER FOURTEEN
Distribution and Exhibition

Page 255 It mattered little how box-office receipts were split: Lee Beaupre, "American Film Distribution," unpublished paper, p. 9.

255 Gentlemen's agreements between studios: Ibid.

260 Paul Kagan figures: "$6.7 billion to fill U.S. Exhib Coffers from Total Sources," *The Hollywood Reporter*, January 2, 1986, p. 1.

260 General Cinema record profits: Kirk Ellis, "General Cinema Increases 13% to $111 Million Record Earnings," *The Hollywood Reporter*, December 20, 1984, p. 1.

260 *USA Today* survey on decline of X-rated theaters: Dennis Hunt, "Home Video Executes Lure of X-rated Theatres," *Los Angeles Times*, May 10, 1985, Part VI, p. 15.

261 Showscan system: James Greenberg, "Showscan Developer Sees Changes in Viewing Habits," *Daily Variety*, December 12, 1985, p. 8.

262 Additional ancillary revenues stimulate production: Joel Resnick, *Encyclopedia of Exhibition*, National Association of Theatre Owners, 1983, p. 7.

262 Harold Vogel statement: Ibid., p. 58.

Klingensmith statements: Robert V. Klingensmith, "Hollywood Report," *The Hollywood Reporter*, August 29, 1985, p. 5.

262   Experience of Knoxville exhibitor selling videocassettes: Will Tusher, "Video Biz Pumps New Life Into Small Town Theater," *Daily Variety*, March 23, 1984, p. 8.

263   Economic advantages of multiplex: Stanley H. Durwood and Joel H. Resnick, "The Theatre Chain: American Multi-Cinema," Squire, pp. 331–32.

264   12,652 movie screens were in the United States in 1963: *Encyclopedia of Exhibition*, p. 22.

265   Exhibitors encourage sale of large sizes: Phillip M. Lowe, "Refreshment Sales and Theatre Profits," Squire, p. 347.

265   One out of six moviegoers buys refreshments: Ibid., citing study by the National Association of Concessionaires and Coca-Cola.

CHAPTER FIFTEEN
Independent Filmmaking

Page 271   Rental figures for *The Amityville Horror, The Trial of Billy Jack* and *Grizzly Adams*: "Champs Among Bantam Weights," *Daily Variety*, June 11, 1984, p. 53.

274   Cost of *Last Night at the Alamo*: George Wead, "Where Eagle Dares," *American Film*, September 1984, p. 55.

274   Cost of *The Brother from Another Planet*: Dale Pollock, "Brother Director Is an Alien to Hollywood, *Los Angeles Times*, October 20, 1984, Part V, p. 1.

274   Cost of *Hester Street*: Molly Haskell, "How an Independent Filmmaker Beat the System (With Her Husband's Help), *Village Voice*, September 22, 1975, p. 83.

CHAPTER SIXTEEN
Sex, Drugs and Creative Accounting

Page 279   Harry Cohn quote: Herman, p. 34.

279   Daryl Zanuck's sexual habits: Mosley, pp. 176–77.

282   Women complain of harassment: Marlaine Glicksman, "Ms. Treatment," *Film Comment*, December 1985, p. 20.

283   "Those who talk most about the greater sexual 'goings-on' ": Powdermaker, pp. 23–24.

CHAPTER SEVENTEEN
Hollywood Journalism

Page 294   Ben Hecht quote: Herman, p. 16.

    296   Joe Dante quote: Independent Feature Projects/West seminar, July 15, 1984, Beverly Hills Theatre.

    302   Upgrading of Hollywood coverage since Begelman scandal: Gary Diedrichs, "Beyond Indecent Exposure," *Los Angeles*, October 1984, p. 178.

CHAPTER EIGHTEEN
Conclusion

Page 311   George Lucas quotes: Harmetz, pp. 246, 260–61.

INDEX